1959

The Year That Inflamed the Caribbean

1959

The Year That Inflamed the Caribbean

by

BERNARD DIEDERICH

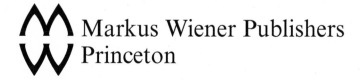 Markus Wiener Publishers
Princeton

Photos are courtesy of the Diederich collection.

For information, write to Markus Wiener Publishers
231 Nassau Street
Princeton, NJ 08542
www.markuswiener.com

Library of Congress Cataloging-in-Publication Data
Diederich, Bernard.
1959 : The Year That Inflamed the Caribbean / by Bernard Diederich.
    p. cm.
ISBN 978-1-55876-491-0 (hbk. : alk. paper)
ISBN 978-1-55876-492-7 (pbk.)
    1. Haiti—Politics and government—1934-1971. 2. Duvalier, François,
1907-1971. 3. Cuba—History—Revolution, 1959—Influence.
4. Haiti—Relations—Cuba. 5. Cuba—Relations—Haiti. I. Title.
F1928.D53 2008
972.94'06—dc22
                                        2008026364

Markus Wiener Publishers books are printed in the United States of
America on acid-free paper and meet the guidelines for permanence and
durability of the Committee on Production Guidelines for Book Longevity
of the Council on Library Resources.

Contents

INTRODUCTION

As the entire world was celebrating the first hours of Thursday, January 1, 1959, the Caribbean's largest island literally exploded onto front pages everywhere. 1959 was the year in which the young rebel Fidel Castro and his *barbudos*[1] toppled dictator Fulgencio Batista y Zaldivar in Cuba. Many newsworthy happenings occurred around the globe in that pivotal period, but it was the Cuban revolution that had the most important impact on our insular world of Haiti, the broader Caribbean and the entire world.

Not since the heyday of the Spanish Main freebooters and pirates, centuries earlier, had events in a single year so changed the face of our region's laid-back, sun-splashed, sand-ringed, and rum-sipping islands. As a publisher of Haiti's sole English-language weekly and independent newspaper in Port-au-Prince, I had the opportunity to report firsthand the tidal political effects that the Cuban upheaval had on Haiti and the formerly quiescent Caribbean.

In this third book of the series on my *Haiti Sun*, I relay these events as they happened, and describe their multiple impacts. I was indeed publisher, but also journalist and resident foreign correspondent, affiliated to several major media outlets in the U.S.

Nowhere did Castro's overthrow of Cuban dictator Fulgencio Batista exert more immediate effects than in Haiti, only forty miles from Cuba, across the waters of the Windward Passage. As I reported in my news dispatches, Castro's victory had the unintended consequence of actually strengthening Haiti's then-dictator, Dr. François Duvalier, by casting him as yet an additional bulwark against the spread of communism elsewhere in the Caribbean. Though the United States was by no means enamored with Duvalier, as the author witnessed and recounts, Washington nonetheless supplied him with weapons, military training, and additional diplomatic support that doubtlessly prolonged his grip on power.

1

The island of Hispaniola was shared by Haiti and the neighboring Dominican Republic; Dominican dictator Generalissimo Rafael Trujillo Molina sought Castro's head, deeming him a threat to his own autocracy. In Haiti, the up-and-coming tyrant Duvalier was caught in the middle. This Houdini of Haitian politics was forced by Castro's victory to switch back to his "quiet country doctor" persona, at least for a while.

*   *   *

There is a historic pattern within Haiti's political system, with but few exceptions: the chief of state has often taken the form of an all-powerful chieftain, in the full sense of the term. From the National Palace, this authoritarian ruler quickly set the rules for the Caribbean country's society, stifling political opponents and acting as the sole arbiter of life and death. Cynical to the extreme and long antedating George Orwell's "Big Brother;" he miraculously turned lies into truths. His blunders and crimes were glossed over as evils necessary to protect the fatherland. Unashamedly transparent and arrogant, he embroidered his rule with the rhetoric of deceit. He liked to be called "Papa," father of the nation and of all its citizens. Cored deep within the center of this incongruous order was the country's amoral political culture, like the metastasis of a perpetual cancer carried on from one "papa" to the next. In the modern era, the most notorious "papa" was Papa Doc, Francois Duvalier. Not long afterwards came a slew of military chiefs and then a real père, this time: a Roman Catholic priest named Father Jean-Bertrand Aristide; if anything, Titid was even more of a demagogic tyrant.

Haiti's "papas" dealt swiftly with rivals, marginalized intellectuals and smothered free expression, curtailing creativity while making a mockery of justice. Their only concern was that of enhancing their power. Whether they were ultimately overthrown and exiled, they managed to escape any culpability for their crimes, principally because the justice system that remained after them had been — as in the case of Papa Doc — appointed by them.

My last photos of Fidel were taken with my small Sure Shot camera near a government-built hotel not far from Siboney in Oriente. It was Jan. 3, 1984, after Fidel had delivered a long late-night speech in Santiago de Cuba. Fidel arrived unexpectedly and we greeted him. He had invited an Indian woman who worked for *Newsweek* to a barbecue in the nearby Sierras. When I insisted on tagging along, he said, "Next time." (Photo: Jean-Pierre Lafond)

Cubans referred to him as El Che. He was born in Argentina, traveled widely, and earned his credentials directing agrarian reform in Guatemala, met and plotted with Fidel Castro in the 1950s in an obscure little café near the monument to the Mexican Revolution in Mexico City. The rest is history. He was one of the dozen to survive their landing from Mexico and made a name for himself in the fight against Batista. He was a devoted chess player and wrote about chess in the party newspaper *Revolución*.

However, the roots of such a diseased political system lay not only in the megalomania of power-mad individual men; the system has perpetuated itself in large part because of a society that also has been sick. To protect their privileges, which the "haves" considered their birthright, they collaborated with nearly every regime. One must note that doing otherwise could have often proven suicidal. Sadly, the whole country was caught in a web of contradictions, as the lack of social concern between the various sectors of society, and insensitivity to the needs of the have-nots became the paradigm of the national logic.

The engine driving this out of hand, derailing train developed into a hefty mechanism of corruption, and as the vast gap between each regime's nouveaux riches and the poor grew wider, education and health suffered—and the only growth was in population, in spite of high child mortality.

At this writing in 2007, however, there are once again some positive signs that democratic checks and balances have finally entered Haiti's system, allowing the hope that the "papa" era is at an end.

*   *   *

By 1959, the *Haiti Sun*'s ninth year, the still young Duvalier regime was already moving in the same evident direction as that of its toughest nineteenth-century predecessors. The bloody and abortive 1958 mini-invasion of Haiti, led by Haitian ex-Capt. Alix Pasquet from his exile base in Miami had only helped President Duvalier in his conquest of total power. Papa Doc had maneuvered to make the incident's outcome symbolize some sort of patriotic victory. His supporters saw the quixotic incursion, in which four American mercenaries had participated, not only as an attempt to topple the self-styled Haitian liberator who had been elected only the year before, but also as an assault on Haitian sovereignty.

Moreover, the cold-blooded, execution-style killings of brothers Ducasse and Charles Jumelle was a clear signal to all citizens that their inscrutable, enigmatic leader, himself a physician, had only contempt for human life when it came to insure his power. Ducasse Jumelle had been a cabinet member in a former administration and also the head of Haiti's Freemasons. His brother Charles was a respected *vodouisant*. Both had been close friends of the Duvaliers. Their brother Clément was an illustrious political figure whom Duvalier had also befriended but later envied, hated and competed against in the last election. This, perhaps, had sealed the brothers' fate. To all, the two murders signified that no one was safe under Papa Doc's grim sky.

And so began a time of collective denial and frozen expressions, in this traditionally exuberant Caribbean land, as if Medusa had magically turned us all, foreigners and Haitians alike, into stone. No outcry or expressions of revulsion were heard. All that we could do was bury our heads in shame, rather than protest and have our heads — quite possibly literally — chopped off. Though in fact everyone was vulnerable to the bizarre twists and turns of the tightening autocracy, I knew that as a man of the media, I was particularly vulnerable. Usually, the first chronological casualty of dictatorship is a free press. I myself could become another of Papa Doc's victims or, conversely, be condemned by his opponents as guilty of collaborating with the regime, by the mere fact of continuing to exist. Notwithstanding all of this intricacy, I decided to stand firm in my quest for independence and objectivity, yet kept doing my best not to annoy Papa too much. I don't believe I failed as a foreign correspondent, but as a publisher under the growing controls of the media by the authorities, I could only do my best.

As for the Haitian press, it would become essentially irrelevant, as far as courageous political reporting was concerned. Conscientious Haitian journalists, most of whom were my friends, tasted the bitterness of revulsion. Yet many helplessly morphed into purveyors of the palace's propaganda pabulum. For my part, I foresaw that a nightmare of fear and bloodletting would be acted in full swing before President Duvalier was through, regardless of his initial portrayal as a humanitarian country doctor by the foreign media. I thus did my best within the new restrictive atmosphere to maintain my English-language newspaper as a serious, truly informative journal, but concessions had to be made in the interests of survival.

One of those concessions was an increasing emphasis on social news and gossip. This self-defense move was not too difficult to implement. Even before Papa Doc, the *Haiti Sun*'s columns were literally sprinkled with "society" items, which are a staple of weekly newspapers everywhere. This was especially the case in Haiti, for the country's own society is in many ways like that of a small town, where communications are basically conveyed via word-of-mouth grapevines.

I must share that during this period, the *Sun* published a social note, which turned out to have a very special meaning to me. The item reported a visit to Haiti by actress Anne Bancroft in the summer of 1958.* It was early in Papa Doc's regime, and tourists, including stage and screen celebrities, were still arriving in the Caribbean island republic.

In recounting this episode in my personal life, I hope to evoke the schizophrenic aura surrounding Papa Doc's early rule — on the one hand, welcoming tourists and the money they brought and on the other, initiating a creepy dictatorship in which, unbeknown to partying foreign visitors, people disappeared during the night.

Reporting news in such a climate presents major hurdles, one of which being that dictators not only write the rules, they also write their own history. Therefore, it is incumbent upon journalists to be even more rigorous in the pursuit of truth. My learning experience in Haiti served as a harsh reminder not to rely solely on the second-hand versions of others, but to search out the nooks and crannies for hard facts when humanly possible and to fundamentally do the *real* reporting. I did my best to rise to that challenge, and I believe the *Haiti Sun* archives confirm that in great measure I indeed succeeded.

*   *   *

Early in life, I had learned a lot about fascism; it was in fact a subject I studied well during and after World War II. The precursor story of my arrival in the Caribbean begins with yet other worldly turbulences, many years before. In 1936, apart from the three-year rise to power in Germany of a madman named Adolf Hitler, two other geopolitical tragedies were being played out in the movie newsreels, and they left a deep impression on my generation. One was the strutting Benito Mussolini in Rome sending his legions to bomb and shell the primitively armed Abyssinian tribesmen in Ethiopia. It was a shocking display of the use of brute force against weaker people, and it violated my youthful sense of values.

The other international calamity, the Spanish Civil War, had begun on my tenth birthday, July 18, 1936. On one side was Gen. Francisco "El Caudillo" Franco, who styled himself as savior of Spain's Roman Catholic Church and who, aided by fellow fascists Adolf Hitler and Mussolini, rose up against the existing government in Madrid, known as the Republicans. Our family's priests and nuns seemed to rationalize Franco's unlawful intervention by warning us that the Spanish government, up to that point, had consisted of anti-Christ Bolshevik-Leninist and Stalinist hordes that had misguided the working class into supporting their ideas. It was true that the Republicans enjoyed support from the Soviet Union, labor unions, and left-wing intellectuals everywhere. Franco, we were told, was fighting to halt the pillaging of churches, atrocities against priests and nuns, and the encroaching red tide of communism in Spain.

The far-away struggle divided our family in my homeland of New Zealand. My father sided with the Spanish Republicans, as did many of his friends. My Irish-Catholic mother, needless to say, followed the dictates of our mother Church and sided with Franco.

On September 1, 1939, the drama in Spain was overshadowed by Adolf Hitler's march into Poland, igniting World War II. Great Britain and its remaining empire (which included New Zealand) declared war on Nazi Germany. Mussolini's Italy later declared war on Britain, which in turn declared war on militaristic Japan. I was thirteen years old when it all began and was ready to fight the fascist Axis. A map of the European war theatre went up in our home, later to be coupled with a map of the Pacific theatre, after the Japanese bombed Pearl Harbor and even threatened New Zealand. At sixteen,

I followed in the footsteps of Joseph Conrad and went to sea on the Pamir, a great, tall, four-masted barque with thirty-four sails and no engines. Sailing across the Pacific four times from New Zealand to San Francisco proved to be the greatest experience and training for a youth. After two trips to American West Coast, I joined the crew of a U.S. oil tanker, which supplied the war machine as the troops moved from one bloody island to another.

*   *   *

In the beginning of January 1949, I had the occasion to spend several months visiting the totalitarian state created in Spain by Franco. A year earlier, he had declared the country's civil war officially over, and the Republicans vanquished. Though I found the Spanish to be a very simpatico people, they were still to a great extent a muted people. The ghosts of their bloody war were still close at hand. Prisons were still full and prisoners were still dying.

In Málaga during the Santa Misión, an annual religious Easter event, even I who was brought up a Catholic was shocked by the parade of followers hidden under flowing robes and hooded hats akin to those worn by Ku Klux Klan members in the U.S. The scene was a reminder that this was the country of the Spanish inquisition. Men staggered under the weight of statues of the Holy Virgin and Jesus.

Poverty in Málaga was not as obvious as in some smaller towns, but one incident remains in my memory. It happened at a downtown fountain. I was besieged by a group of small, barefoot children who were begging. With my primer Spanish greatly improving, I agreed to help them, but only if they washed away the dirt from their legs and face. I purchased soap from a nearby shop and witnessed a cruel sight, as the children climbed into the fountain and bathed. One little six-year-old scrubbed her younger brother so hard he cried out in pain. The fountain was soon filled with soapsuds. I gave them each a few pesetas and they scurried away laughing. It was an endearing, yet heartbreaking moment.

The dehumanizing effect of a people marginalized by dictatorship, civil war and economic deprivation was also still very much evident in Sevilla and other cities. While attending a bullfight in Valencia, I was reminded of stories I had been told in London by Spanish exiles, relating that Franco's forces had used this bullring as a prison for the defeated Republicans. One day, as I was walking down an avenue in Valencia, an elderly lady whispered behind me, "Please follow me." She had evidently recognized me as a foreign visitor. She stepped into the hall of an apartment building, and quickly begged me: "Take these letters to England for me.... My husband is in prison, he has committed no crime. He is a member of the Freemasons."

Startled, I responded with an instant reaction: "Sorry I am not going to England." I suspected that it could be a setup and that the woman could perhaps be an agent provocateur of the Franquist secret police. I knew that freemasons were deemed undesirable, as were Marxists and other leftists. Such are the fears that pervade any dictatorship. Nevertheless, the thought that I had perhaps failed to help this woman in distress bothered me for years.

George Orwell's book *Homage to Catalonia* gives a vivid and masterful firsthand account of his fighting in the trenches alongside the anarchists' militia, during which he was wounded in the neck. Orwell was a journalist who had joined the militia to battle Franco. His eyewitness reports from Barcelona particularly interested me. He had been a victim of the Spanish Republican government's crackdown on the anarchists' militia in 1937. Even though the latter were also fighting Franco, they were labeled anti-Stalinist Trotskyites by the former. The hunting down and imprisoning of leftists by fellow leftists was an important reminder that anti-fascist, self-styled revolutionary idealists are not without their own authoritarian methods.

Orwell finally managed to flee to France and journey back to England, where he became famous for his books. Among them: *1984*, which excoriated "Big Brother"-type government.

In Barcelona, while strolling along the Ramblas, that wide tree-lined street running from the quay into the heart of the city, the mother of a pretty young child in a party dress noticed my camera and asked me to take a picture of her child. We did not exchange more

Author in Barcelona in January 1949

than the briefest salutations before she rushed off. In 1949 Spain, one didn't take any chances.

I visited most points of interest in Barcelona that Orwell wrote about, and at night relaxed at my favorite small nightclub off the Ramblas in the Barrio Chino. La Bohème was a low-ceiled nightclub where one entered into its smoke laden interior through a delicatessen shop, ducking under a literal forest of cured hams. (Food was in short supply only for those who could not afford it.) Some of the best musical and dance artists in Barcelona would take to the stage, and the audience would decide whether or not they should be rewarded with a few pesetas for an outstanding performance. A beautiful young flamenco dancer captivated us all. She regularly moonlighted at La Bohème. Other cafes on the Ramblas near the quay were patronized by tall blond men who sometimes introduced themselves in English saying "Sir, as your former enemy, I invite you to accept a drink." I always pretended not to hear them and steered clear of their lairs after the first encounter. They were members of the *Wehrmacht* seeking passage to South America, I was told; Hitler and Franco had been pals, and Spain came very close to joining the Axis, during the War.

*   *   *

The contrast between postwar Spain and Great Britain was amazing. Both countries had food scarcities, but in England, no families were living in caves, a troubling sight which I had witnessed many times in the hills behind Tarragona. Nor were people sleeping in huge drainpipes, as I had beheld in Sevilla next to the Guadalquivir River. What a difference London was, on a Sunday at Hyde Park Corner. There, speakers thumped on rostrums and ranted their heads off, portraying themselves as true believers in whatever cause had moved them. The spectrum of orators ranged from anarchists, pacifists, Trotskyites, and freethinkers to Marxists-Leninists and religious zealots purporting to have a direct line to God. The cacophony filled the free air. The London police "bobbies" just stood around, amused by the spectacle. No one cared what was said, except those who foolishly tried to change the speaker's mind. It was a site enlivened by extreme idealistic fanaticism, yet no danger could be felt whatsoever; all was conducted within the safe boundaries of thorough civility.

Later on in a further chapter of my life, I was to realize that Papa Doc, by comparison, indulged in an empty rhetoric assembled from a verbal tapestry that he initially called democracy but then, after violently cracking down on the opposition and suffocating free speech, labeled "*my* revolution."

We, at the *Haiti Sun*, had the unenviable task of translating and publishing Papa Doc's speeches ad nauseam; we were not foolish enough to try to change the enigmatic tyrant's mindset.

CHAPTER 1

Pact with the Devil

B
y late 1958, the Caribbean had already been caught up in a
brewing regional war of political ideologies, mostly amount-
ing to threatening words. However, in Cuba, Fidel Castro's
rebels were waging a very real war against Dictator Fulgencio Batista.

In an August 13 speech, President François Duvalier had revealed
the extent of Batista's assistance in crushing the failed July 29, 1958
mini-invasion of Haiti. "The Cubans," Papa Doc declared, had
"spontaneously offered to expose their chests by coming to the aid of
the immense sacred band of Duvalierists." It so happened that
Duvalier's relationship with Cuba, at that point, was also determined
by the pro-Batista stance of his formidable neighbor, Dominican dictator Rafael Trujillo. Simple economics were for him another incen-
tive against the potential new Cuban rebel regime: Batista bankers
had scalped three million dollars from Cuba's Banco de Colones,
which they promised Duvalier's government. Those monies were from
a 7-million-dollar treasure in unclaimed deposits, which had belonged
to poor Haitian cane cutters.

Batista wanted to avoid the funneling of arms and men from Doc's
domain to Castro's in Cuba's Sierra Maestra; the promised funds
were intended as a guarantee against such a situation. Three Cubans
had already been arrested and jailed in Haiti on the suspicion that
they were headed for the hills to help their comrades.

Second to Batista, the foremost adversary of the Cuban 26th of
July Movement was the Dominican strongman Trujillo. From the
very outset, El Benefactor, as he liked to be called, had branded

Fidel Castro in the mountains during his war with Batista.

Castro and his guerrilla fighters communists. In this, Trujillo shared a habit common to many right-wing despots during the Cold War; these tyrants found it expedient to label their enemies communist, no matter what ideology the latter indeed espoused.

*   *   *

Leading up to Castro's ultimate triumph, Duvalier had had other priorities than the surveying of unrest in Cuba. He had not spent an inordinate amount of time listening to foreign radio broadcasts, and few of his aides who understood Spanish appeared to have been following the regular transmissions, from the Sierra Maestra's "Free Territory," of Castro's Radio Rebelde.[2] Among those in Haiti who did, besides myself, was a Cuban émigré, Antonio Rodríguez Echazábel. Owner of the Oso Blanco[3] butcher shop in downtown Port-au-Prince, Rodriguez was also a clandestine coordinator of the M-26-7.[4] He was deeply involved in helping anti-Batista exiles return to fight Batista in Cuba via Haiti. One of his relatives worked in the mountains with the rebel radio outlet. Celestino Fernández, a former union organizer in Havana, was another representative of the Cuban rebel movement in the Caribbean.

Meanwhile, Trujillo had decided it was time to sign a mutual-interest treaty with Duvalier. The Dominican caudillo was concerned about the guerrilla rebellion in Cuba, but he also feared that his own enemies might find in Haiti a safe haven and a hospitable political climate from which to attack him, across the relatively open, unmarked Haitian-Dominican border. In the past, fear of Trujillo's police state had been sufficient to keep even the most desperate Haitians — except poor sugarcane workers — from fleeing across the frontier. Dominicans, for their part, viewed Haiti as a land of *Vodou* and "black magic"; they thus largely kept their distance. Aside from the diplomats and numerous undaunted ladies of the night who dominated Port-au-Prince's prostitution market, many Dominicans avoided Haiti as a place to settle. More than any physical barrier, it was dread that sealed the border between the two countries.

Doc's secret police chief, Clément Barbot, had already established close working ties with his two Dominican counterparts, the feared Johnny Abbes Garcia and Lt. Col. Luis Trujillo Reynoso. The latter, son of the Dominican dictator's brother Arismendi Trujillo, had recently been appointed military attaché at the Dominican embassy in Port-au-Prince. The Coca-Cola shaped Garcia had developed the SIM[5] into the largest and most efficient secret service in the Caribbean, with agents spread throughout Central America and the U.S. During the signing, the three grim-faced men stood in the second row behind their respective leaders.

Despite the risks inherent in Trujillo's overture, Papa Doc had agreed to the goodwill pact. The meeting between the two leaders took place on December 22, 1958 — nine days before Castro's January 1, 1959 takeover of Cuba. It was arranged to be held in a humid no-man's-land situated near a border post between Jimani on the Dominican side and Malpasse in Haiti, on the edge of its Lac Saumâtre. Naturally, the rare meeting of the two suspicious, unfriendly strongmen neighbors was a big story for the *Haiti Sun* and for my international media clients. Uninvited, I nonetheless decided to drive from Port-au-Prince to the location; I got there at daybreak that morning.

The setting was not unlike that surrounding a medieval joust, with two separate stands facing each other, each for its respective dictator and retinue. Always punctual, Trujillo arrived at precisely 8 a.m. in a dust-covered Cadillac. He was wearing a light grey suit, but the airiness of its garment was no match to the suffocating humidity and scorching temperature being felt, which gradually rose to perspiration levels as he and his party waited for Duvalier.

While awaiting the tardy Haitian delegation, I attempted to take a close-up photograph of Trujillo. His pancake makeup[6] was running in rivulets down his jowly face. As I climbed the steps of his wooden pavilion and raised my camera, he jerked his right hand up as if pulling a gun. He then pointed his right forefinger directly at me. Startled, I took a step backward, lost my balance on the steps, and came close to falling down; Trujillo broke into laughter. His subordinates joined in, smiling and laughing appropriately, as if congratulating their *Jefe*. It was the only moment of merriment during the tense

President Duvalier, center, listening to the reading of the document he signed with the two Trujillos. To Papa Doc's right at the table is Generalissimo Rafael Trujillo; to his left is acting Dominican president Hector Bienvenido (Negro) Trujillo.

border session. I prudently didn't take another picture until the official signing.

Not until 9:30 a.m. did Duvalier and his entourage show up. Papa Doc was habitually late for meetings, but this time, it might well have been intentional. Trujillo was not a favorite of Haitian nationalists; they were pleased with Duvalier's letting Trujillo broil for an hour and a half in the oven that was Malpasse.

Cloaked in the usual anti-communist rhetoric, a joint statement was issued by the two dictators, in which they promised to prevent infiltration of communist subversion in their respective republics, especially that of political exiles, whose actions could prejudice good relations between the two states. The two leaders also promised ritually to consult each other as much as possible, in order to harmonize their countries' respective positions at the United Nations and the Organization of American States, in conformity to the principles of inter-American solidarity.

Earlier in the year, Trujillo had beamed *Kreyòl*-language radio blasts at Haitians, claiming that Reds were taking over their country. One target singled out had been Lucien Daumec, Duvalier's brother-in-law, principal aide, speechwriter, and executive secretary. The Dominicans noted that he was an ex-member of the Haitian Communist Party — no secret in Haiti. Daumec stood smiling throughout the border proceedings, commenting privately to the author about the hypocrisy of it all.

The only break with protocol was when, at the top of the red-carpeted stairway, Trujillo stood up and walked around the signing table to greet Aubelin Jolicoeur, who was there photographing the event. Trujillo had met Jolicoeur right after Duvalier's electoral victory, when the Haitian newsman had accompanied General Antonio Th. Kébreau on a state visit to the Dominican capital. At that encounter, Trujillo had even prodded the general, Haiti's then military junta president, to overthrow President-elect Duvalier before his investiture. One must wonder what El Jefe felt at the Malpasse summit, sitting there next to a fellow statesman who he had tried to *knock over* a few months before.

It's been said often: human history is mostly ironic; notwithstanding all those diplomatic niceties, it was by the hands of his own internal enemies that Trujillo would meet a brutal death, less than three years later. As for Papa Doc, he was to later struggle with repetitive guerilla incursions launched from the neighboring country.

CHAPTER 2

Hello Fidel

Then came January 1, 1959. Two hours into the New Year, while celebrants were still partying in Havana, Dictator Fulgencio Batista fled Cuba in the darkness of the night. Aboard a military plane bound for the Dominican Republic, his exile thus began. The shocking news broke on radio and television. Even Fidel Castro himself, who was preparing to attack Santiago de Cuba, was caught by surprise.

In the Dominican Republic, Dictator Rafael Trujillo was also attending a night-long party when he heard the news. El Jefe was reportedly furious and outraged that a fellow autocrat had fled instead of fighting to the end; and what was worse—he was headed for Ciudad Trujillo. Astoundingly, without any advance notice or request for permission, the Cuban dictator, his family and closest associates were about to join another dictator-in-residence in the Dominican Republic: Juan Domingo Perón of Argentina. Partly in retaliation, Trujillo is said to have mercilessly squeezed Batista out of every possible dollar, before the fallen Cuban strongman moved on to the Portuguese island of Madeira, then Gaudalmina, Spain, where he died in 1972.

*   *   *

In Port-au-Prince, Antonio Rodríguez Echazábel received the news from Cuba shortly after dawn. Alerted by the Oso Blanco butcher-

19

Batista in exile in Ciudad Trujillo, playing checkers with his former government aides at Hotel Jaragua. (Photo: John Hlavacek)

shop owner, I hurriedly dressed, forgot my *mal makak*[7] and drove to the Cuban embassy, which happened to be on the Port-au-Prince exposition grounds across the street from the *Haiti Sun*'s editorial offices.

Several excited young Cubans and their Haitian friends were already waiting in the little garden before the embassy chancellery building. The Cuban ambassador, Dr. Gabriel Breton and military attaché Colonel Valdivia were absent, having returned to Cuba for the Christmas holidays. Rodríguez simply took charge of the diplomatic mission and sent someone to fetch the embassy secretary; when she arrived, she gingerly produced the keys to the building, after having been told of the change of government in Havana during the night.

The scene outside the embassy was surreal. Given the early hour on New Year's morning, there were very few other Haitian onlookers. The streets of the exposition grounds were deserted. The adjacent International Casino, ironically enough, had featured the National

Dancers of Cuba a few hours earlier; its last patrons had departed. Watchmen at the nearby construction site of a planned U.S. embassy building showed scant interest.

Yet the young Cuban visitors — in Haiti en route to the Sierra Maestra — managed to turn the moment into a solemn, dignified act of victory over tyranny, of good over evil. A large red-and-black M-26-7 flag was produced and hoisted on the embassy flagpole, under the national colors of Cuba. The youths stood to attention and sang both the 26th of July hymn and Cuba's national anthem. Inside the embassy, the takeover was made with great restraint. A framed photograph of now-exiled President Batista was carefully removed from the wall and placed in a drawer. A far less formal portrait of Fidel Castro replaced it. To toast to the triumph, only two bottles were removed from a case of the liberated embassy's champagne.

Across the street at the *Haiti Sun,* we began laying out the weekly issue. Sunday's edition of the *Sun* headlined: "Cuban Embassy taken over by Fidel Castro officials Jan. 1." The story was illustrated with two photographs, one of the flag raising and the other of the takeover group posing inside the embassy before pictures of Cuba's revolutionary heroes throughout its history.[8]

*   *   *

François Duvalier and his government were stunned and dismayed. Papa Doc quickly pressed his aides for analyses that would explain what the events in Cuba would mean to Haiti in the near future. But if the triumph of the Cuban revolution proved a difficult moment for him, he secretly knew full well why: in an effort to politically destabilize and bring down the Magloire government, Papa Doc had accepted money and technical assistance for the manufacture of bombs from Dr. Carlos Prío Socarrás, the wealthy Cuban ex-president who was simultaneously helping finance Castro's guerrilla war. Prío's assistance to Duvalier in the form of terrorism expertise was granted on the condition that Papa Doc, once in power, would facilitate clandestine travel and logistical assistance to the Cuban rebels. But Duvalier had reneged on his promise to Prío, and then accepted money from Batista, with the understanding that the anti-Batista forces would find no safe haven in Haiti. In effect, Papa Doc had double-crossed the rebels, and they had now seized power, just a few miles away from Haiti's northwestern tip.

When he learned of the Cuban embassy takeover in his own capital, the Haitian president sent for Rodríguez Echazábel, who only two weeks earlier had been released from a three-week imprisonment for having openly supported the candidacy of Doc's political opponent Clément Jumelle. Rodríguez quickly suggested that Duvalier release the Cuban *fidelistas* being held in the National Penitentiary. It might, Rodríguez hinted, win Doc some points with the new Castro-dominated regime in Havana.

Duvalier promptly gave the order, readily obliging to anything that could get him on the right side of the new men coming to power in Cuba. The fact that four of the jailed Cubans were awaiting trial for having hijacked a boat and stabbed its Haitian captain to death didn't appear to bother Duvalier; a total of eight Cubans were freed from prison. Papa Doc ordered a Haitian Air Force C-47 to fly them to Santiago de Cuba, in the Oriente Province. Ever the solicitous physician, Papa Doc sent along a token gift of medicine.

"Get ready," Rodriguez told me when he came by my office on Saturday. "We are going to Cuba." He added that the *"Haiti Sun"* would have a historic scoop, as no other newsman would accompany us. On Monday, January 4, Rodríguez, Celestino Fernández, and I were flying to Santiago de Cuba with a group of freed fidelistas, courtesy provided by Papa Doc.

The mood aboard the Haitian plane was one of subdued excitement. Several of the group released from prison had recognized me as having taken photographs of them as they were being brought ashore under arrest by the Haitian Coast Guard, after having hijacked the *Barracuda*, the said Haitian tourist boat, in an effort to join the M-26-7 rebels in Cuba. At the time of the incident, there were no tourists aboard. The Cubans insisted that the death of the boat's captain, Joseph Bazile, had been an accident, resulting from his inability to

Fidelistas, captured after hijacking a Haitian tourist vessel, being led away by the Haitian coast guard.

understand Spanish and their inability to speak French or Kreyòl. Caught, the hijackers were then imprisoned and charged with murder. On the aircraft they thanked me for having documented their arrests with pictures, which they said allayed their fears of disappearing without a trace into Duvalier's dungeons. "Tell the Haitian people we are sorry," twenty-five-year-old Orlando Romero Alfonso begged the author. "Tell them that we are not killers, that we only wanted to return to our country and fight the real killers." Alfonso, who was returning to a wife and two children, said he had deserted the Cuban Navy to fight as part of the 26th of July Movement.

At least two of the returning Cubans were survivors of Castro's July 26, 1953 assault on the Moncada army barracks in Santiago, the date of which hence provided the name for the rebel movement. One of them was Orbein Damian Hernandez, who had survived to join the anti-Batista Havana underground. After numerous arrests and beatings by the Cuban police, he took refuge in the Venezuelan embassy. He had subsequently flown to Haiti, just six weeks prior to our air trip, preparing to rejoin the fight in Cuba — only to be jailed by Papa Doc, then released. Yenaro Hernández said that after having survived the abortive assault on the Moncada, he had worked in sabotage in Havana. With the police on his heels, he said that he'd had no alternative than to take asylum in the Ecuadorian embassy and eventually fly to Haiti.

Bearded and emaciated, Pedro Manuel Rodríguez Lili said he had been a law student who began opposing the Cuban dictatorship in 1952. Lili had also been subjected to numerous beatings and fifteen trips to jail, under Batista.

The oldest returning fidelista was Juan Lovaco Diaz, 42, who said he was a veteran of the Caribbean Legion. When asked why he carried such an enormous suitcase, he grinned and explained that it had allowed him to carry two rifles and 600 rounds of ammunition from Caracas to Port-au-Prince, and to make three trips with arms supplies from Mexico to Cuba. Only one of the trips from Mexico had failed, he said, when their boat sank.

Saturnino Morales, the driver to the embassy's military attaché, had been an agent of the M-26-7; the twenty-four-year-old Cuban army corporal was happily returning home.

*   *   *

Cleared to land at Santiago de Cuba's Antonio Maceo airport, we were met by Maj. Manuel "Barba Roja" Piñeiro, whose luxuriant red beard would have made a Scottish Highlander jealous. As a member of Raúl Castro's column, Piñeiro had been named guerilla commander of the city. Fidel, we learned, had already left for Havana on his extensive overland victory journey through the virtual length of the island. That day, he was in nearby Camagüey. The Haitian Army plane refueled and returned to Haiti.

The changes in Santiago were extraordinary; startling was the apparent ease and expertise with which the 26th of July Movement had taken over the running of Cuba's second city, which I had last visited in 1954. To stake out their victory, a general strike had been called by the *26 de Julio* in this cradle of Castro's revolution; the strike was now over.

During my visit, I noticed that Batista's heavily armed security forces had been replaced by guerrilla patrols in jeeps; its young and old fighters wore tropical green fatigues, shoulder-length hair and beards. Boy Scouts directed traffic. They friendlily waved to Haitian consul Lamy Camille, recognizing his DKW jeep. *Guayaberas* were no longer in fashion at the old Casa Grande hotel, on Cespedes Square. Raul Castro's column held the province, and the rebellion's 16th Column, named "Nicaragua," had also rolled into town. The latter were fighting on the north coast and numbered some 800 men. Like bearded replicas of the *mambises* from Cuba's revolutionary war against Spain, these warriors had flocked to Castro's banner from all over the island. Time and again, rebels told me that though this was the end of the rebellion, the real revolution was yet to come. Fidel, they said, had made that promise.

In Santiago, I met with twenty-four-year-old Carlos Chain, an ebullient, beardless M-26-7 veteran who had been Fidel Castro's civilian aide and had been named commissioner of civil affairs in the Oriente province. The city no long had a mayor and was governed by three rebel-appointed commissioners. Chain was hard at work in the municipal palace. He had quit his electrical engineering studies in Havana to join the revolution. Already, as he reported during my interview, work on repairing roads destroyed during the war was being carried out, mostly by individual volunteers aided by local construction companies. As for prisoners, he said that a military court would be convened to try those accused of war crimes. Asked about Castro's speech to Santiagoans on the night of January 1, stating that Santiago would become Cuba's new capital, he replied, "Why not?"

One of the men from the "Nicaragua" Column was an American whose war name was "Rex," added Chain; termed a good fighter, Richard Sanderlin, 23, was an ex-U.S. Marine hailing from Norfolk, Virginia. He had been badly wounded in a battle two weeks earlier, hit in the shoulder by an explosive bullet and was still listed in critical condition at Los Angeles Hospital.

Besides myself, another *periodista*[9] in town was actor Errol Flynn, who was there to film a documentary on the rebels. The fidelistas frowned upon liquor, and its consumption was prohibited in their fighting columns. With visible Quaker-like disgust and a thumb to the mouth, a pretty, gun-toting *Mariana Grajales*[10] veteran high signed that Flynn was a heavy drinker. "We are more than happy to assist newsmen whom we respect, but Mr. Flynn is not a real journalist." On Chain's desk was a copy of the new M-26-7 newspaper *Revolución*, which had been launched on January 2, replacing *Cubana Libre*.

The olive-clad, bright young female ex-combatant in Chain's office handed me my *laissez-passer*.[11] As I was a correspondent for the AP and the owner of the *Haiti Sun* newspaper, the pass stipulated that I had to be accorded major and preferential facilities to travel. It was signed in Spanish: "*Libertad o Muerte*,[12] Suzette Bueno R., in charge of Travel for *M. 26 de Julio*," and bore the 26th of July stamp.

Trucks were already bringing in fresh produce from the countryside, which had been under control of the rebels. My assigned M-26-7 helper, a fair-haired young female rebel originally from Havana, told me about a Haitian-born baker in a Sierra village; even though his original bakery had been bombed out by the batistianos, he had begun to bake bread again and "supplied us with his wonderful bread," said she.

*   *   *

Antonio Rodríguez Echazábel said we would move on to Havana to meet Fidel Castro, after his victory trip. Haitian consul Lamy Camille drove us to the Santiago's Antonio Maceo airport to catch a Cubana de Aviación flight to Havana. At the airport, we found Fidel's younger brother Raúl, who was having a hurried lunch with co-rebel Vilma Espín.[13] Rodríguez stepped forward and shook hands with the couple. I was introduced as the publisher of the *Haiti Sun*.

I quickly asked Raúl whether he might answer a few questions, perhaps in his first press interview since the end of the guerrilla war. It was by no means lengthy, as we had a flight to catch to Havana. Raúl had swapped his fighting cowboy hat for a black beret, and unlike the rest of his fighters, he had only a few hardly noticeable chin hairs, a slight mustache and wore his hair in a pigtail. Ms. Espín, dressed in matching olive-green battle fatigues, spoke excellent English. She had been a chemical engineer student in the U.S. at the Massachusetts Institute of Technology, where she did her post-graduate studies. The handsome young rebel from a wealthy Santiago family had played an important role in the rebellion from the very outset. She graciously helped with the interview, translating back and forth for us every now and then.

Raúl maintained that calm had returned to Cuba, and that everything was being done to speed up the country's transition to civilian life, after years of conflict. Asked what his own role would be in the new Cuba, he responded: "I will go where my experience best serves the country." Having been told that I had come from Haiti, Raúl said: "We know that Duvalier collaborated with Batista," and further charged that Batista had spread the word that the Castro brothers were a couple of land-owning *blanquitos*[14] who looked down on the blacks. Raúl denied this and pointed out that Cuban blacks who had fought in the ranks of the rebels were full-fledged members of the revolutionary army. Fidel's godfather, Raúl added, had been a Haitian.

*   *   *

In Havana, I joined Bruce Henderson, Caribbean bureau chief for *Time* and *Life*, who had been one of the few foreign newsmen present on January 1 when Batista fled. Bruce said he was elated to see me and to have my assistance on his reporting team. It was an exciting time. At the Havana Hilton hotel, soon to be renamed the Havana Libre, Bruce had coverage under control. The night of my arrived I visited with fellow New Zealander Ted Scott at the *Havana Post*. The old former World War II British secret agent was quick to hit the floor when a passing car of presumed batistianos fired a few volleys at pursuers.

Henderson assigned me to cover Fidel's arrival in Havana. I leaped onto a tank with a group of 26th of July female fighters and rode in Fidel's wake into Camp Columbia, once the bastion of Batista's army. It was January 8. Rodríguez Echazábel was already at the camp headquarters when I arrived; his presence, as well as my Santiago-issued laissez-passer, did wonders. I was introduced to bearded rebel *comandante* Maj. Camilo Cienfuegos, to whom I explained my challenging assignment. *Time* would want a full description of Fidel's first night in Havana. "Would the 26th of July leader choose to dance, date, or dive into bed after his arduous trip up the island from the Sierra Maestra to Havana?" I lightheartedly inquired. Camilo smiled broadly when I also told him that I needed to know the color of Fidel's pajamas.

Fidel and his entourage went into a reception room in the army's headquarters and when he came out to address a mixed crowd of former Batista soldiers, rebels from the Sierra and Camilo's men, I followed him to the podium. I had already heard Fidel's lilting *guajiro*[15] accent as he talked his way to Havana. By now Fidel's voice was nearly hoarse. Someone placed a glass of water on the podium to ease his throat.

A little way into his speech, an onlooker released four white pigeons out of a cage. The symbolic doves of peace were however hardly pristine white; in fact they were quite dirty, obviously from having been in their cage a long time. One of them settled on Fidel's shoulder, making for a good photo op. Another settled on the podium and put its dirty head into the glass of water. Fidel's bodyguards and I were suddenly transfixed by the pigeon's turning of the crystal-clear water into a muddy-colored potion. Then Fidel reached for the glass; his bodyguards and I instinctively cringed and couldn't help but to interject sonorous sounds of distaste. Castro stopped for a moment, looked around to see who the idiots interrupting his speech were, then drank the pigeon's bathwater.

After the speech, when I recounted the incident to Camilo Cienfuegos, he smiled and said: "Don't worry; he has been drinking dir-

Camilo Cienfuegos at Camp Columbia on January 7, 1959. He jokingly instructed the author to look angry, which he did!

tier water than that in the Sierra." He and I sat outside on a verandah at the officers' quarters, while Fidel received special guests inside. After a while Fidel's nine-year-old son Fidelito joined us and began playing around. Camilo, then twenty-seven, seemed comfortably on top of things and in control, despite his heavy responsibilities as commander of the Havana province. He favored a strong black tobacco cigar, and offered me one. With our smoke floating around his trademark cowboy hat, he opened up a little on his life and current activities.

Camilo was born in Madrid, too young to fight in the Spanish Civil War. He revealed that during his exile from Cuba he had spent three years in San Francisco, a city we both loved. He spoke English, which made him an obvious target of TV interviewers from the U.S. In fact, he was expecting a visit from the *Today Show* the next day. He joked that the media was harder to face than the batistianos, adding that journalists always asked the same questions, which he termed

Fidel Castro at his first press conference in Havana at the Hilton in January 1959. The *Haiti Sun* attended the conference.

annoying; for instance: "Are you a communist or Catholic?"

We talked on until nearly midnight. Then, he went inside, where Fidel had been meeting with a series of people, some friends and family. We had no clue as to their identity. When Camilo came back with the word that Fidel had left, he offered me accommodations that would allow me to stay in Camp Columbia for the night. I thanked him, but told him I was on deadline and had to report back to *Time* promptly. He thus offered his car and driver for me to get back to central Havana. He also asked me to take Fidelito with me; his driver knew where to drop the child off to his family. The car would pick me up in the morning and bring me back to Camp Columbia, where we could carry on with our talk. As we were heading into the city, Fidelito got Camilo's driver to turn on his siren. I instructed the driver to turn it off, telling the boy that we couldn't draw attention to us because there were still armed batistianos around.

As promised Camilo's driver picked me up the next morning at the

Castro jokes with the author after the press conference, where he autographed the author's notebook.

Havana Hilton, where I was lodged. Cienfuegos greeted me with a big smile and some important news I had queried him for: "He [Fidel] wore striped pink pajamas." "You are kidding?!" I asked, incredulous. He wasn't. Years later, a 1959 photograph appeared in Ann Louise Bardach's book, *Cuba Confidential*, showing Fidel Castro indeed wearing striped pajamas.

I spent the day with Camilo, again at his headquarters. The *Today Show* crew arrived, as did other interviewers. I stayed in the background. "What did you do in exile in California, comandante?" one newsman asked him. Cienfuegos responded that he had worked as a pearl diver. "Great!" exclaimed the reporter. "Was it a lucrative business, diving for pearls?" Deadpan, Camilo was quick with his response: "No, washing dishes at San Francisco's Fairmont Hotel was a poorly paid job." We all cracked up laughing.

Later that day, I shared the elevator at the Havana Hilton with several "bearded ones," along with the clean-shaven Jules Dubois of the

Chicago Tribune. One short-statured barbudo invited me to meet his commander, who turned out to be Ernesto "Che" Guevara, Fidel Castro's legendary Argentine-born rebel sidekick. I promptly accepted. Guevara had taken over command of the historic La Cabaña fortress, guarding the approach to the Havana harbor. The short barbudo, who said he was a doctor, took me to meet Che Guevara at La Cabaña, where batistianos accused of war crimes were being held to await their fate. Che could offer us only a few minutes of salutations, but vowed to provide us with a later interview. Unfortunately, he wouldn't be able to honor this promise, as I was about to fly back to Port-au-Prince via Miami. When he heard that I was from Haiti, he wished me luck in French.

Back home, after having traveled by Pan American Airways and suffering from lack of sleep and a bad cold, I put out the scheduled edition of the *Haiti Sun*, which however appeared more like a special edition. It was generously illustrated with photographs of the Cuban revolution, including Fidel's triumphant arrival in Havana, his first press conference at the Havana Hilton, Camilo Cienfuegos at Camp Columbia, and the 26th of July's first stand-in civilian president of Cuba, President Manuel Urrutia Lleó. Moreover, it broke with my tradition of printing only Haiti news in the *Sun*.

Our accompanying editorial from Sunday, January 2, 1959, warned:

> Developments in Cuba should be observed closely.
>
> Cuba's revolution should be studied with the utmost concern by this close neighbor. To all those who had the opportunity to observe this chapter of History, most are of the firm belief that it will have far-reaching effects on the future of the Caribbean nations.
>
> At a chance meeting in Santiago de Cuba, Raúl Castro told the Haitian Consul (and the author) that he hoped Cuba could count on the cooperation of Haiti. Dr. Fidel Castro, in a long press conference held Friday in Havana, was asked whether he saw any possibility of the entire

Caribbean linking together in a federation of sorts. He replied he didn't foresee any such thing, as he pointed out that countries like Jamaica and Haiti have much different cultures.

Although the cynics smile off another revolution as routine, the change in Cuba is startling and has all the earmarks of the beginning of a new era, unprecedented in Cuban history.

And indeed, at this writing, nearly five decades later, hindsight leaves little doubt that the *Haiti Sun*'s cautionary analysis stood the test of time.

Fidel Castro at his first press conference in Havana, held in the penthouse of the Havana Hilton.

CHAPTER 3

Late Night Meeting with Doc

On the evening of my return from Cuba, the grippe had taken hold of me. Ti Frère, the household majordomo, made me an extremely strong rum concoction to squash my cold. It was in fact strong enough to knock over a horse.

As I consumed the last drop of my "cold medicine" and prepared to retire, a car pulled up in front of my Mont-Joli residence. An officer of the presidential guard emerged from it and appeared at the door. He blurted out an order: "Diederich, President Duvalier wants to see you at the palace immediately." Needless to say, I was quite startled. Yet, and strangely, I didn't request that the military man give me more details, as to clarify the relevance and apparent urgency of such a nocturnal get-together. I guess the poor physical state I was in prevented me from behaving normally. Indeed, I would have otherwise been suspicious, distrustful even. By that time, I knew most of the army officers, at least by sight; I didn't know this one.

I asserted that I was ill, in no condition to meet with the president. "Maybe I would be in better shape after a good night's sleep." The officer wouldn't hear my protests. "Sorry," said he, "it's now; and the president's instructions are for you to come as you are dressed." The presidential car outside gave me some confidence that I wasn't being taken for a ride. At that stage, I was adventurous, liked taking chances and was always curiosity-driven. I reluctantly acceded and was chauffeured to the palace.

There, I was taken up the elevator and into Papa Doc's small bed-room office. Even at the late hour, the president was still dressed in his business suit, working relentlessly. He greeted me in a kindly manner and apologized for having sent for me in such tactless conditions and haste. We were alone. I suspected Doc wanted to know about Cuba, since he had provided the transport for my going there and I had just returned. I was right; my wits still proved adequate, despite intoxica-tion from Ti Frère's potion.

"Mr. Diederich, I am interested to know what is happening in Cuba," he said, directing me to a chair, while he sat on his little cot. It was just a personal chat, he explained. I thanked him for the plane ride to Santiago de Cuba.

Papa Doc then began interviewing me. He prodded me on, asking: "What do you think of the Cuban rebels?" Normally, I would have been more cautious and circumspect, but Papa Doc was wearing his convincing fatherly manner. I told Doc that this was no mere coup d'état but a true revolution. I explained that every rebel I had inter-viewed had insisted that the *rebellion* was over and the real *revolution* was about to begin. "Is it a revolution driven by ideology?" he asked, adding: "Some say they are communists." I answered that those inter-viewed had complained to me that it was the single question most raised by the foreign media. None had admitted being a Marxist-Leninist. "The population appears united behind the rebels," I point-ed out. He did not ask me to profile Fidel Castro. In fact, the leading rebel's name didn't even come up.

I cannot recall how long I talked, but Duvalier finally got up, and said: "Thank you very much, Mr. Diederich." He quickly pressed a buzzer, and the same officer who had taken me to the palace came back to take me home. It was the strangest of presidential audiences, in which the reporter did all the talking. I wondered if Papa Doc, who didn't drink, had suffered my spraying him with my rum breath, as our faces had been so close. I had spoken in Kreyòl, whereas Papa Doc had spoken in French.

*   *   *

I soon found out that my personal enthusiasm for the change taking place in Cuba didn't sit well with Duvalier. During my talk, his
eyes sometimes seemed to squint behind his thick glasses, and in spite
of his surface friendliness, I couldn't help feeling that he was hearing
news he did not wish to hear. Police Capt. Jacques Laroche, a diehard
follower of Papa Doc's, later confirmed this by confiding Doc's disappointment to me. Apparently, two days after our late-night meeting, Papa Doc had informed him that he had listened to me atten-
tively, but had been appalled. "During all that time, the vagabond
Diederich did not mention my own revolution once," he complained
to Laroche.

One of Duvalier's real concerns, I later realized, was that his enemies might now find in Cuba a base from which to attack him.
Caught in the middle of a fierce Havana-Ciudad Trujillo animosity,
he also had to be careful not to move too openly or too fast in trying
to placate Cuba's new revolutionary leaders. His old neighbor
Trujillo's violent opposition to Castro picked up steam, as El Jefe's
powerful radios increased their daily ranting and ravings against the
Cuban rebel leader. Yet, only eight days after Batista fell, the Haitian
president lost no time in recognizing Cuba's new revolutionary government, headed by President Manuel Urrutia Lleó.

In a remarkable turnaround, Duvalier lifted a death sentence he
had imposed on political exile Louis Déjoie and freed three newsmen,
Albert Occenad, George J. Petit and Daniel Arty, who had been given
five-year prison sentences by a military court. He also granted a full
pardon to Deputy Franck Séraphin after he had just begun to serve
his term in prison. Séraphin would later be rearrested and would die
in prison.

"Snatched from the jaws of death" was how the *Sun* described the
freeing of three other prisoners. Freed were "Yves Bajeux, Franck
Leonard and Holberg Christophe, three men given the death sentence
on August 25, when a military commission found them guilty of
being implicated in the Mahotières bomb plot."

"Robert Léger, a close Déjoie aide who had taken political asylum in the Spanish embassy on May 1, was given safe conduct to leave for Jamaica. Other asylees were also allowed to leave the country." Released also were Dr. Gaston Jumelle and his two sisters; they had not been charged with any crime, but had rather been imprisoned because they were Clément Jumelle's brother and sisters.

In Havana, Jules Dubois of the *Chicago Tribune* hailed Duvalier's release of the imprisoned newsmen as a positive step. Dubois headed the Freedom of the Press section of the Inter-American Press Association.

The wise political prisoners released from the National Penitentiary took advantage of the new climate, which they believed was temporary, and fled the country. Those who chose to remain in Haiti were to end their days in Papa Doc's gulag, Fort Dimanche.

CHAPTER 4

The Castro Effect

D ating back to his coverage of the Chaco war between Bolivia and Paraguay, *New York Times* correspondent Peter Kihss' reputation for thoroughness had spread from metropolitan New York to the Caribbean and South America. On January 15, 1959, he conducted an interview with President Duvalier that I also attended. Kihss straightforwardly asked Papa Doc when he would cease being a dictator and allow his special governing powers to elapse. Duvalier, in a seemingly casual manner, looked down at his watch as if checking the time, then retorted, smiling: "I am not a dictator. I consider myself a country doctor. I want to build up Haiti."

Speaking in English, he went on to say he would allow his special powers to expire at the scheduled end of their designated period, which was due in just two weeks, on January 30. But a state of siege would continue until lifted by the National Assembly, he added. He went on making a pitch for greater U.S. aid after stating candidly that Haiti was in a "financial mess." He then switched to the political sphere, adding: "I took everyone out of jail because I want to tell them that it is much better to think in terms of the nation, because the Haitian nation is for all the Haitian people, not only myself. I am only the chief. I did what I had to do as a Catholic."

Clearly, Papa Doc was now treading softly, as the new Cuba on his doorstep had changed the Caribbean equation. He made no mention of our bedtime chat — where I had done all the talking — about the

Peter Kihss of *The New York Times* and the author (pictured here) were not brave enough to take the medicine sent by President Dr. Francois Duvalier to cure their colds.

Cuban rebellion two nights earlier. He was all smiles, like the Cheshire cat.

Kihss was suffering from the same cold I had imported from Cuba, and our sniffling was all too evident during the interview. We left the palace and went straight to the Grand Hôtel Oloffson, settling at the verandah in one of its small bungalows. Hardly had we removed our ties and coats to begin comparing notes when a presidential limousine drove up. A Presidential Guard officer ascended the stairs and formally presented us with a small packet which, he explained, contained medicine that President Duvalier had sent us to cure our colds. Standing at attention, the young officer recited the learned lesson, explaining the dosage, which the president himself had prescribed for the both of us.

Startled, we told the officer to please thank "Monsieur le président-docteur" and added, politely if less than truthfully, that we much appreciated his medicine. The military officer saluted and left. Kihss and I sat there staring at the bottle and collapsed into laughter, knowing that neither of us was prepared to take Papa Doc's medication, not even a sip of it. Who knew what the effects might be?! The incident was so strange that we had photographs taken of us seated at the rattan table, transfixed by the little bottle containing Papa Doc's mysterious prescription.

Kihss and I were still laughing when we joined the lunch crowd on the Oloffson's main verandah. Among the group was George Beebe, then-managing editor of the *Miami Herald*. Beebe had just succeeded in interviewing both exiled Cuban dictator Fulgencio Batista in the neighboring Ciudad Trujillo, and Papa Doc in Port-au-Prince. Also present at lunch was Robert Sherrod, a celebrated World War II war correspondent in the Pacific, who at this time was managing editor of the *Saturday Evening Post*. Sherrod teasingly suggested that Kihss and I at least try Papa Doc's medicine. Asked whether he would like a drop, Sherrod quickly replied: "I don't have the cold." My fellow runny-nosed colleague and I weren't overcome with an excessive feeling of bravery, and so we ultimately consigned the unopened bottle to the garbage tin.

Peter Kihss' next interview was with Clément Barbot, Doc's wiry, mustached secret police chief. Neither Brooklyn mobsters nor Haitian bullies scared Kihss. He seemed immune to fear, and his only concern was the story. Thus, he treated the *tonton makout* chieftain Barbot to a straightforward news interview, which I once again attended. Barbot wore a dark suit, an outfit he greatly favored. Between us, we both agreed the interviewee resembled a sharp businessman, and that he could well have been the manager of a funeral parlor. Of course, he reportedly provided them good business... The man had sharp features and his straight face gave away nothing of his thoughts. He refused to take off the trademark dark glasses that completely hid his eyes and which set the fashion for his makout followers; the latter, however, graduated from dark glasses to the even more intimidating reflector spectacles.

Predictably, Barbot disclaimed the title of chief of the bogeymen, or even that of secret police commander. He professed that he was just another supporter of President Duvalier, and stated that as all other Duvalierists, he was always on "alert" against Doc's enemies. Seemingly as an afterthought, he agreed that being on "alert" indeed involved collecting intelligence on Doc's enemies. Asked about his famous calling card, which had identified him as secret police chief, Barbot admitted: "Yes, it is true they said that." But the cards, he hurriedly explained, had been wrongfully printed. "They were recalled," he added.

Ti-Barb Morrison, posing with some of Barbot's men at the national palace.

Many Haitians had not even heard of Barbot until the military made him a wanted man with a price on his head, as he was accused of involvement in the 1957 bomb plots. Duvalier denied at the time that he even knew Barbot. Yet, after his electoral victory, Barbot suddenly came out of hiding, quickly became Duvalier's most powerful henchman, and by 1959, he was already the second most important man in the makout machine. I knew from my reporting that he did a lot more than just gather intelligence on Duvalier's opponents.

In order to finance "intelligence gathering," Barbot had moved quickly to take over the capital's International Casino on Harry S. Truman Boulevard, officially the only gambling establishment in Haiti. The Italian group that held a thirty-year concession to it was unceremoniously bounced out of both the casino and the country. In repayment for financial backing during his presidential campaign, Duvalier had then handed the Casino to Corado Salimbene, a long-time Italian resident businessman in Haiti. However, Doc saw to it that Barbot also be a silent partner.

Then, on January 9, 1959, the International Casino, which was only a few blocks from the *Haiti Sun* offices, became front-page news. Franck Legendre, the casino's manager, had mysteriously disappeared. Legendre, who had once headed the National Lottery, had seemingly vanished without a trace. His car was found at the bottom of a steep ravine. It had no evidence of blood.

In his Italian-accented Kreyòl, Mr. Salimbene told the press that money indeed was missing from the casino. A doubtlessly orchestrated rumor surfaced, alleging that Legendre had taken off with a young woman. The missing casino manager's photo, published in the *Haiti Sun*, was that of an ordinary-looking middle-aged man, who hardly appeared the type to suddenly desert his family and take off into the unknown with the casino money and a young female.

For the Haitian media, including the *Sun*, the case remained a mystery. It was not until many years later that a ranking casino employee explained to the author what he said were the circumstances surrounding Legendre's disappearance. According him, after Legendre refused to explain the disappearance of $40,000 in missing casino money, he was shot four times and his corpse disposed of in a grave in the countryside.

Clément Barbot kept the rumor mill buzzing, particularly promoting tales about himself; his reported exploits, true or false, made him the most feared man in Haiti. In mid-January 1959, Captain David I. Carter arrived in the country; he was one of eight U.S. Marine Corps

Ti-Barb, the flamboyant press agent of Papa Doc, was also a shadowy character.

officers assigned to the new U.S. naval mission. The officer's meeting of Mr. Barbot, which he recounted to the author, was quite unusual, verily worthy of a Hollywood screenplay. While house hunting in Montagne-Noire, above Pétionville, Capt. Carter knocked on the door of a house he believed might be for rent. A well-dressed man answered the door. "No, this house is not for rent," the man told Carter. He then invited him to enter. To Carter's surprise, the room was full of men. The man in charge introduced himself as Clément Barbot. Carter found Barbot to be extremely friendly but puzzled by the fact that the house was full of men.

Several months later, Carter received an invitation from Barbot to spend the weekend with him at a holiday house in the pine forest, on the high mountain of Morne La Selle. The secret police chief, Carter recalled, spent most of the time at target practice amidst the pine trees. At night, before they retired, Barbot would methodically place a loaded pistol in each corner of the living room; he explained that in the dark, one could always hit on a corner of the room and find a gun there, in case of an attack. Good thinking, conceded the U.S. Marine officer — though the fact that his host feared a possible attack somewhat disturbed his vacationing.

*   *   *

Herbert "Ti-Barb" Morrison wore the only beard in town. Duvalier and Barbot utilized the clownish American scrounger as a token *blan'* (foreigner) for many purposes. He boasted to the *Haiti Sun* that he had brought a management group from Las Vegas, Nevada, to take over Haiti's International Casino. The team was headed by Clifford E. Jones, 46, former Lieutenant-Governor of Nevada. The tall, lanky Jones had previously run the Havana Hilton casino in the Cuban capital. Along with his associate, Jacob Kozloff, he received an eight-year lease on the Haitian gambling institution and its nightclub, for a reputed sum of $175,000. A percentage of the revenues would go to the government; every night, an officer from the government's Superior Court of Accounts would be present to supervise the nightly take.

Besides this profitable transaction, the Las Vegas group also received a lease on the nearby Beau Rivage hotel, which the aforementioned Italian group had reconditioned. Ti-Barb, as well as two of Barbot's Syrian-Haitian associates, was given a lucrative post at the casino.

There was no escaping the brash and boastful Herbert J. "Ti-Barb" Morrison, whose birth name was really Jerome Breitman. The young Jewish song-pusher from Brooklyn, New York, was a newsmaker; he was riding high on Duvalier's coattails. Ti-Barb would ostentatiously cruise the capital in his late-model white Corvette, the only one in Haiti, with twin Great Danes as passengers. The huge canines consumed more meat in one meal than many a Haitian did in a year or a lifetime. His outrageous wardrobe included an often-worn outfit: plaid wash-and-wear jacket and shorts. The pith helmet, which regularly covered his bald pate, competed with that of the U.S. Marines, who wore similar colonial headgear. This strange sight was completed with a slightly trimmed red goatee; Ti-Barb cut a bizarre figure, which caused Haitians to stop in their tracks and wonder. Accentuating his movie-plot persona, Ti-Barb also carried duel, pearl-handled .38 caliber pistols.

Morrison's rise to fame and fortune in Haiti was phenomenal. Press releases under his name, as director of the Bureau des Relations Publique Palais National, were grammatically akin to the script of a non-English-speaking American immigrant. However, nothing appeared to bother Ti-Barb as he flaunted his official clout. A high point came when he hosted a dinner for President Duvalier and a group of junketing American travel writers at his Diquini residence. During the soirée, Duvalier made his case for U.S. financial aid. Haiti would be grateful, said the president, to receive as much as $200 million in assistance, which could improve the lot of the poor. Beaming, he disclosed however that he had written to his counterpart, President Eisenhower, suggesting a more modest figure of forty-three or perhaps fifty million dollars. He reported having received "a very nice reply." Ti-Barb applauded wildly, and his visiting newsmen guests followed his lead in the gesture.

A photograph of the dinner, available from Ti-Barb for a price, showed him posing grandly behind Duvalier, his wife and son Jean-Claude, as well as Clément Barbot. We used the picture in a *Time* magazine story featuring the eccentric American. By this time, Morrison/Breitman was garnering more free publicity than the president, and it didn't reflect well on his powerful boss. Some Duvalierists saw Ti-Barb as a sleazy character who was degrading the Duvalier presidency.

Ti-Barb branched out into broadcasting in English over the government radio. His ill-informed, spontaneous outbursts, delivered in a heavy Brooklyn-accented and questionable English, startled even loyal Duvalierists, who included in their ranks a number of prominent mulattos. "Haiti is a black country and there is no room for mulattos!" shouted Morrison into the microphone, once. Among his early targets was Franck Magloire, the mulatto owner of the newspaper *Le Matin*. On the airwaves, Ti-Barb accused Magloire of being a blackmailer, among other things. Magloire demanded to know what he had done to deserve this disservice from a foreigner on government radio airwaves. Though furious, he was mostly restrained in his reply, but nonetheless ended it with a less-than-subtle warning to Ti-Barb;

by a refined metaphor, the latter was threatened with a swift kick in the rear. It was Ti-Barb's turn to become furious when several Duvalierists teased him about Magloire's riposte.

Ambassador Drew threatened to lift Ti-Barb's U.S. passport. Morrison in turn tried unsuccessfully to have Drew recalled, but had to ease his attacks on the ambassador, as Clément Barbot's own relations with the embassy and Marine officers improved. Barbot was reportedly tiring of Ti-Barb's "constant whining and demands for attention," according to one of the top aides to the secret police chief. Barbot shared his National Palace office with Morrison. Needing his space for interrogations and in order to shift his roommate out of the palace, he found the latter a reconditioned government building, off Harry Truman Boulevard. The building was also close to the International Casino, where Morrison also had a hand in business.

A large sign with yellow letters sprouted on the structure, advertising "Ti-Barb Enterprises: Art Gallery, Port-au-Prince Times" as well as "Caribbean Anti-Communist League." Ti-Barb bragged that he had launched the "CACL" as a non-profit organization with "the president's blessing." He insisted that there were 3,000 Communists in Haiti, but found it difficult to name any.

At my suggestion, a husband-and-wife radio team from NBC News sought out Ti-Barb and requested that he arrange an interview with President Duvalier. Wilson and Lee Hall were received by Morrison at his new downtown "gallery." Their radio report ended up as a special on Ti-Barb, in which they reported: "Morrison explained his role in Haiti very simply: 'I'm Duvalier's Jim Hagerty [U.S. President Eisenhower's then-press secretary]. You want to talk to President Duvalier, you talk to me. Drop over to the casino and I'll give you the word....'" "In Port-au-Prince, this wasn't an invitation to drop a few quarters in those slot machines that never seem to pay off. It was the way I was to find out whether or not I had an appointment to see President Duvalier," Lee Hall reported in his story.

Lee Hall noted that "Americans and Haitians view Morrison's meandering and maneuvering in Haitian politics and economic life with a combination of fear, disgust and even perverse amusement.

For a man who came as a tourist three years ago, Morrison has muscled or finagled his way up to the powerful position of President Duvalier's public relations counsel and press secretary."

"He yelled for a boy, ordered a Coke for us and took a spoonful of a red medicine," reported Lee. "He suggested we take a look at the rest of his layout. 'Ti-Barb Enterprises' consists of Haitian paintings on the walls and some Hong Kong rattan furniture. 'I've got five Haitian artists sewed up,' he explained. Nodding toward the rattan bar set and lounge chairs, he said he planned to import the line from Hong Kong. 'Don't buy nothin' 'til you hear from me,' he told a visitor. 'Don't worry,' he told us again, 'drop by the casino.' He called his chauffeur and told him to drive us back to our hotel."

The NBC duo observed that most Haitians and Americans they talked to could not explain why Duvalier showed such loyalty to Morrison, or why the palace paid Ti-Barb a reported $25,000 a year, a hefty sum at the time. My own conclusion was that the wily Papa Doc deemed it a sly device to have an American citizen — even one as unsavory as Ti-Barb — beating the drums for Duvalier's regime and criticizing the U.S. embassy in Haiti at every opportunity.

The Halls didn't get to interview Papa Doc; the promised answer from the Ti-Barb never came, as he didn't show up at the casino on the appointed night.

We too, at the *Haiti Sun*, became tired of the thirty-seven-year-old song-plugger's radio ranting and raving, yelling his crude English over the airwaves as if he were involved in a brawl at a seedy Brooklyn barroom. In an editorial, the *Haiti Sun* asked whether Morrison was "public relations or public enemy," and described him as a "gibbering sower of discontent." We also cautioned him in Kreyòl: "*W'ap' fouyé zo nan kalalou, a pas vrais. M'ap' ba'w yon ti konsèy, tandé: zafè kabrit' pa zafè mouton, pwovèb-la di'w. Bat' chen, tann' mèt-li. Ca m'wè pou ou, Antoine lan gommier pas wè'l.*"[16]

The logical and proper attitude from the nation's president would have been to make sure Morrison be reined in, especially as the general outcry grew. Instead, Papa Doc awarded Ti-Barb a medal, whereupon the decorated jester promptly issued a press release to make it known. Said he, Duvalier had honored Herbert J. Morrison with a decoration from Haiti's new Toussaint-Louverture Order of Civil Merit, in a special ceremony at the National Palace. Moreover, President Duvalier himself had supposedly handed Morrison the insignias and diploma of the Haitian Order of Chivalry with rank of "commander."

Following an assignment in Haiti, John Kobler returned to the U.S. determined to uncover Ti-Barb's police record — the U.S. embassy and other American sources had told the then-contributing editor of the *Saturday Evening Post* that Morisson had a rap sheet and a shady past. But Kobler didn't succeed in finding anything on "that certain American in Haiti who throws a good deal of weight around," a formula he used in a piece published in March 1959.

*   *   *

It was a time of saying goodbye to a Good Samaritan. Doc Reser, though he appeared as robust as ever, had come "home" from Miami to die. On the last Sunday of January 1959, the seventy-one-year-old former U.S. Navy pharmacist and warrant officer was stricken by a heart attack at his new three-room home in Plaine du Cul-de-Sac, outside Port-au-Prince. He was driven the twenty miles to the capital's General Hospital but had gotten there too late. Both his son Charles "Sonny" Reser, a Pan American Airways purser, and his daughter Marie-Claire flew in from the U.S. for the memorial service and burial at the Port-au-Prince cemetery. I assisted as a pallbearer. Nine days following his funeral in the city, the Haitian country folk, among whom Doc, had chosen to hold a special Vodou ceremony for him.

Decades later, Doc Reser is still remembered in the Plaine du Cul-de-Sac area, where he had resided. And, strange as it may seem, on the very site where he lived stands today the home and temple of *mambo* priestess Lolotte, one of the finest and most caring Vodou priestesses in Haiti. It is as if Doc Reser's spirit never left that piece of land next to Pont Beudet. As *oungan*, priest Gwo Roche of Lilavois later told me: "Reser was more than just a Vodou priest." He didn't elaborate, but the high esteem in which he held Doc Reser was still evident, a quarter of a century later.

*   *   *

In early 1959, there was still some flickering of hope that things might get better for the common people of Haiti. Papa Doc's feared *Tontons Makouts* notwithstanding, Haiti had retained much of its ineffable character. Pre-carnival bands still filled the streets on weekends, with dancers prancing to the irresistible rhythms of drums punctuated by the staccato of *vaccines.*[17] Tourists still came. American singer Harry Belafonte and his family divided their ten-day vacation between Cap-Haïtien and Pétionville, where they stayed at the El Rancho hotel; Belafonte boned up on Haitian songs to add to his popular repertoire.

On the political scene, Duvalier rid himself of Madame Lucienne Heurtelou Estimé, the widow of his former mentor, President Estimé, and a precious ally during the electoral campaign from which he got his crown. To thank her for her vital assistance, he gave her the post of Haiti's ambassador to Belgium, which in Papa Doc language, meant that he felt more comfortable with her being an ocean away from his power.

Public Health Minister Dr. Auguste Denizé received Dr. Nathan S. Kline, an eminent American psychiatrist and pioneer of psychopharmacology, at the opening of a new government psychiatric health center in Port-au-Prince. The clinic, which Dr. Kline had helped set up, not only bore his name, but also benefitted from his advice and expertise. It provided supplies of the latest drugs for treatment of the mentally ill. Some of us remarked that the psychiatric center had arrived just in time.

Unfortunately, by March 1959, the glimmerings of optimism were ebbing. Constraints on Haiti's press had grown to a point where self-censorship was the order of the day. Because the *Haiti Sun* was in English, we could still get away with printing more relevant news than could fellow outlets.

CHAPTER 5

Caribbean Cold War

The Caribbean was by now roiling with intrigue, increasing the already sharp tension. Assembling in Castro's Cuba, revolutionaries of every stripe were putting old-line dictators on notice that their days were numbered. In the *Haiti Sun*, we produced a new weekly page openly entitled "Caribbean Cold War News." In so doing, we competed with the *télédjol*, Haiti's version of the bush telegraph. Rumors of what had been said by Haitian exiles over Cuban radio were quickly embellished by the *télédjol* and spread throughout the country. Without perhaps realizing it, Haitian exiles were thoroughly waging psychological warfare against Duvalier. The capital became increasingly nervous as the exiles' threats grew increasingly menacing. Their hatred and contempt for Duvalier had no limit. Papa Doc responded in kind. In Haiti, listening to anti-Duvalier jeremiads over Trujillo's powerful Voz Dominicana, or to the exiles' Kreyòl and French broadcasts on the Cuban shortwave Radio Progreso, was a subversive act punishable by jail or worse. Before tuning in to any foreign broadcast, one had to be sure of the safety of his or her surroundings.

The anti-Duvalier transmissions from Radio Progreso began on February 24, 1959, barely eight weeks after Fidel Castro came to power. Haitian ex-presidential candidate Louis Déjoie personally spoke through its airwaves, and ex-President Daniel Fignolé, for his part, sent tapes to Havana from Brooklyn, New York. Déjoie, along

51

with ex-Col. Pierre Armand and Maj. Maurepas Auguste, was in the first group of Haitians to arrive in Havana after Cuban strongman Fulgencio Batista fled. They recruited Fignolé and declared themselves "The Haitian Revolutionary Front." Other Haitian exiles organized themselves into the "Liberation Committee of Haiti."

, "Liberation" was in the air in Havana, and besides Trujillo and Duvalier, Nicaragua's Luis Somoza and even Paraguay's Gen. Alfredo Stroessner were targets of South American exiles flocking to Cuba. One of Castro's top commanders, Argentine Maj. Ernesto "Che" Guevara, facilitated "The Haitian Revolutionary Front" with a military training camp at Jamaica, a Cuban town some 30 kilometers from Havana. Both Cuban and former Haitian military officers were in charge there of a three-month training course aimed at building a force capable of dislodging Duvalier.

Some thirty-two Haitian exiles — most of whom, sadly, considered themselves leaders — arrived in post-revolutionary Havana. They opened a recruiting office on Refugio Street in Havana, but most of the volunteers were non-Haitians, but rather Cuban officers and soldiers of Castro's rebel army. However, Déjoie was said to have personally secured arms and munitions, along with a landing craft that had a capacity of 300 men.

Meanwhile, Antonio Rodríguez returned to Port-au-Prince from his trip to Havana, not merely to oversee things at his Oso Blanco butcher shop, but mostly as the new Cuban ambassador in Haiti. Eager to appease the new Cuban government, Duvalier quickly accepted Rodríguez' accreditation, in a formal ceremony at the National Palace, although he knew the new ambassador "hated his guts."

*   *   *

Examples of what the *Haiti Sun* printed on its "Caribbean Cold War" page:

- Duvalier declared to United Press International that "Haiti is ready to defend itself with its army of 5,000 men who are now being given adequate preparation, and also with its civilian militia of more than 8,000 men."

• A group of retired Dominican generals were given the job of preparing Trujillo's "Anti-Communist Foreign Legion." They announced that the Legion would accept foreigners and Dominican recruits who were not on active service. Each and every applicant would be carefully screened to ensure he is "truly anti-Communist."

• The Dominican "Anti-Communist Foreign Legion" would have a total strength of 25,000 men. It would be headquartered along the Haiti border at the town of Restauración (pop. 2,000).

• In a petition to the Cuban president, immigrant Haitian agricultural workers (cane cutters), at nine sugar mills in Cuba's Guantánamo province, demanded the expulsion from Cuba of Haitian exile Louis Déjoie.

• Cuban rebel Maj. Camilo Cienfuegos was quoted as stating that fighters against Latin American dictatorships would get a friendly hand from Cuban revolutionaries.

• U.S. Rep. Victor Anfuso (D-Brooklyn) has been enlisted by Dr. Elmer Loughlin, an advisor and friend of President Duvalier, to the Haitian president's cause in Washington. Dr. Loughlin arranged for his Brooklyn congressman, Mr. Anfuso, to visit Haiti and meet with Duvalier. Anfuso called for the OAS (Organization of American States) to police the Caribbean, in an effort to prevent any invasion of Haiti. Anfuso quoted Duvalier as saying that in his opinion, it was the role of the United States to maintain peace.

• *Time* magazine declared that Haiti "is caught in a bind between Castro's Cuba, only 50 miles to the northwest, and Rafael Trujillo's bordering Dominican dictatorship." *Time* disclosed that in Cuba, preparations by Castro's bearded rebel veterans to invade the Dominican Republic are indeed underway. Col. Alberto Bayo, a sometime Spanish loyalist soldier who has trained Castro in Mexico three years prior to the revolution, has been put in charge of strategy and training for the Dominican venture. But since hitting the beaches in Trujillo's well-armed police state could prove suicidal, *Time* reported, the invaders want to slip in through Haiti.

- René Chalmers, Secretary General of the Haitian Foreign Ministry, refuted charges broadcast in Caracas and Havana that Dominican forces were occupying Haitian villages on the border.

- Frank H. Bartholomew, President of United Press International, stated after an interview with Duvalier that the United States has another Balkans on its doorstep that could erupt in warfare. (Bartholomew had asked me to string for UPI but I had declined, as I worked for the AP.)

- According to UPI, Trujillo has begun dispersing his air force, the most modern in the Caribbean and his primary defense, amid rumors that American soldiers of fortune, friendly to Castro, have assembled surplus warplanes on an island in the British West Indies in hopes of destroying the Dominican air force in a single raid.

- The United States, according to a long article in the *New York Times* from its Washington bureau, has decided on the backing of Duvalier's regime, "which has opposition at home and aboard," as the "safest policy." (At the *Haiti Sun*, we were constantly tempted to test just how far we could go in ferreting out the truth, but the danger in doing so was ever present.)

- "If the aggressors want to see brains and beards flying like butterflies, let them come near Dominican shores in a hostile attitude," declared Generalissimo Rafael Trujillo.

• Fidel Castro told a huge crowd in Santiago de Cuba that if there were a call for volunteers to fight the Trujillo dictatorship, not a soul would be left in Cuba. But, he added: "The Dominican people will do it on their own." Castro also charged that Trujillo has not returned the five planes that Cubans fleeing with former dictator Batista used to escape to the Dominican Republic. "Trujillo does not want to return them because he will need them when he flees the Dominican Republic from the revolution that will overthrow him."

*   *   *

While traveling by jeep in Haiti's northwest, I was treated to a preview of Haiti's state of preparedness to ward off any invasion force. Driving through Môle St. Nicolas, I passed its crumbling, old, British-built forts that date back to the 1793–98 British invasion and occupation of parts of Haiti. I sped towards the sea across a wide, denuded field. It was noon. Under the shade of an ancient, French-made 75-mm. Howitzer, which was pointing in the direction of the close Cuban coast, the Haitian army artillerymen slept soundly. Awakened by the rare intrusion — few people visited this forlorn area — the soldiers angrily ordered me to get away. Waving their rifles, they yelled: "*Vou zan! Vou zan!*"[18]

From Cuba came world-famous playboy Porfirio Rubirosa, Trujillo's last ambassador to Havana. Stopping off with his pretty, young and French (fifth) wife, he was in transit in Port-au-Prince towards the Dominican Republic. Rubirosa partook of a hurried rum-and-soda at the airport bar. Waylaying him, I asked the celebrated bon vivant whether there was any truth to the rumor that he had been the victim of an abortive kidnapping in Cuba. The ruggedly handsome Rubirosa laughed, patted his wife's arm and told her in

Author interviewing Porfirio Rubirosa, the Dominican ambassador to Cuba, who was in transit at Port-au-Prince's Bowen field.

French: "*Quelle histoire!*"[19] Ten days later, we met again at the Port-au-Prince airport. Rubirosa was returning to his post in Havana, in spite of the war of words between Trujillo and Fidel Castro.

In an effort to halt his enemies from using Cuba as a launching pad for another invasion, Duvalier dispatched a special mission to Havana, headed by Haitian poet Roussan Camille, a friend of Cuban poet Nicolás Guillén and of other influential Cubans. The delegation did its best to convince the Cubans that Déjoie was no revolutionary and that by supporting him, they were in fact supporting an extreme right-winger. But Che Guevara, who was in charge of assisting exiles fighting for their home countries, had learned during the Cuban rebellion that to succeed, it was sometimes necessary to make short-term alliances, even with one's ideological enemies. An invasion of

Haiti, Che hoped, would open the path to an invasion of the Dominican Republic. At least, this was his rationale in helping Déjoie and the "Haitian Revolutionary Front."

Back in Haiti, it was becoming an increasingly dangerous time. The gun-toting Makouts had the jitters and many partisans of Déjoie and Fignolé were emboldened by broadcasts auguring that liberation was near.

Papa Doc needn't have worried; once they had flocked into Havana, the Haitian exiles, many of them Déjoie followers, merely renewed the inherited, traditional penchant for bickering among themselves. This attitude had always prevented any concerted and serious effort against Duvalier. Meanwhile, their wives, who had accompanied them, were more concerned with finding the best addresses in Havana that could help them sustain the very constructive activities to which they had devoted their time back home; while their refugee husbands wrestled with one another's egos and political ambitions, most of these ladies vehemently sought the best hairdressers, for instance, as one Haitian present complained at the time.

Trujillo was for his part well aware that Dominican exiles wanted to land first in Haiti and then infiltrate his territory across the border. *El Jefe*'s navy began patrolling Haiti's coastline and his army reinforced the Haitian-Dominican border with more troops. The Dominican frigate Presidente Peynado berthed in Port-au-Prince during the week of one expected invasion. It was not only to show Trujillo's flag, but also to "defend Duvalier" against an invasion from Cuba.

In one Radio Progreso broadcast which we, at the *Haiti Sun*, monitored, the Kreyòl-speaking announcer declared that thousands of Cubans were seeking to join an international brigade to restore democracy in Haiti. "Duvalier must go!" heard we.

While some news reports stated that there were 120,000 Haitian laborers in eastern Cuba, the Haiti exile coalition in Havana could count on fewer than 400 rallying to their cause. Washington officials, the *Haiti Sun* noted, were telling reporters that Castro had as little in common with the Haitian exiles as they had with each other. The

Cuban leader's real purpose, these U. S. officials agreed, was to help foment rebellion in Haiti to create the opportunity to use Haiti as a base of guerrilla operations against Trujillo.

On February 11, 1959, a provoked and angry François Duvalier promised Armageddon if attacked. "All citizens must be vigilant during the next few days, the next few weeks, and the coming months," he declared at a gathering of Haiti's Association of Chauffeur-guides members. Given at the Savoy restaurant, on Port-au-Prince's Champ-de-Mars, it was Duvalier's first such incendiary speech. In the *Haiti Sun*, we referred to it, citing Duvalier's "firebrand declarations." *Le Matin* quoted the president, who had warned that at the first cannon shot sounding the alarm, "all the sons of the fatherland must repeat the gesture of Christophe at Cap-Haïtien"; Christophe had burned down the city as Napoléon's forces were landing....

In *Le Jour*, columnist Rodolphe Derose stated another declaration of Duvalier's: "The total triumph of the 1957 revolution requires that we sterilize the efforts of the bourgeoisie to once again take power." Duvalier further stated that it is with "the political lever that we must be able to tear the secular capitalist tenants of this country away from their formidable economic apparatus."

Referring to "anti-patriots," Papa Doc warned Haitians training in Cuba that "you shall not pass." And, "if you have the misfortune to attempt a new July 29 [Pasquet's invasion], you will have provoked against you the total revolution, which will leave only stones upon stones in this city." In his speech to the chauffeurs and tourist guides, Duvalier invoked Dessalines' famous war cry: "*Coupé tête! Boulé caille!*"[20]

The following day, President Duvalier issued an official protest to the Cuban government, not only against the training of Haitian exiles in Cuba, but also against the use of Cuban radio stations by Haitian exile leaders.

Meanwhile, the Caribbean Cold War was attracting foreign correspondents and other assorted literati. Norman Lewis, correspondent for the *London Sunday Times*, made his third visit to Haiti. Martin Agronsky, of NBC, succeeded in interviewing Duvalier, thus one-upping his network colleagues Wilson and Lee Hall. Columnist Drew Pearson, after a very brief visit, published a column relying heavily on *Haiti Sun* material. Historian James McGregor Burns, whom I had met through Anne Bancroft at director Arthur Penn's home, arrived with his family, declaring that they were on vacation.

At the same time, Haiti's brain's drain was well underway. René Depestre, one of Haiti's top writers, packed up and left the country. The *Haiti Sun* noted in a cover story that Depestre was off to Paris, where he would return to his work at Présence Africaine. In fact, he was bound for Cuba, where he was to begin his long exile. Depestre was among the young La Ruche militants of the 1946 uprising, which had led to the overthrow of President Elie Lescot but also had stirred an irreversible wind of change and lucidity amongst Haiti's intellectuals. Subsequently to these events, he went into exile, studying at the Sorbonne. He was not able to return to Haiti until 1958.

Prior to his departure for Havana, Depestre told me he was leaving for many reasons, one of which was the belief that harassment by the Duvalier police would soon become intolerable. Another reason was the ridiculous and frustrating method of pleading and even paying to be published in daily Port-au-Prince's daily press, he said. In Havana, he became a regular contributor to the official M-26-7 newspaper *Revolución*.

CHAPTER 6

"Disappearing" Critics; Trujillo Agents Active in Havana

In late March 1959, the Associated Press and then *Time* magazine requested that I look into the disappearance of a naturalized Mexican national. The preceding February 20, the man in question had flown from Port-au-Prince to Ciudad Trujillo on a Pan American Airways flight; normally, the journey from one capital to the other is less than an hour. Officially, he had not arrived in the Dominican Republic. When I learned that the missing person was the export manager of Hormona Laboratories, a Mexico City pharmaceutical company, all I could think was "here we go again."

Alfredo Pereña had arrived in Port-au-Prince for a two-day stay at the Hotel Riviera, where he was to arrange for the placement of a new representative of his drug company in Haiti. The former representative, local pharmacist Joseph C. Valmé, explained that Pereña was in the process of transferring the agency to importer Lelio Bailly, as Valmé himself was suffering ill health and had his hands full with his thirty-five-year-old rue des Miracles pharmacy. Mr. Bailly agreed to represent the drug company.

On February 20, after completing his business in Haiti, Pereña had evidently taken the afternoon PAA "clipper" to Cuidad Trujillo. His name appeared on the flight's list of departing passengers, but

Dominican authorities said their immigration and customs records showed no trace of it.

Two days after Pereña's documented departure, Haitian pharmacist Valmé received a cable from Hormona's Ciudad Trujillo representative, José Roldam, asking for news of their export manager. Astounded, Valmé checked with Haitian immigration and PAA officials; the search corroborated that the missing man had left on the airline's afternoon flight of February 20. To further enquire into Pereña's movements and possible whereabouts, Hormona's director in Mexico City communicated with Valmé on February 26, asking him to confirm the information he had given Roldam.

Pereña made it a practice to send telegrams to his family and company each time he arrived in a new destination city. His wife Mercedes, 40, had initially accompanied her husband to the Mexico City airport, where he had caught a Cubana de Aviación flight for Miami, via Havana. On February 23, she had received a letter from him, sent from Haiti and dated February 19. He had written that he was leaving for Ciudad Trujillo the next day, on the last leg of his business trip. When no telegram arrived from Ciudad Trujillo, Mercedes was alarmed; she telephoned executives at Hormona's home office. Executives there informed her that they too had no news from him and that they would cable Jose Roldan in Ciudad Trujillo. "Waited at the airport for Pere but he didn't show up" was Roldan's reply. Mercedes became hysterical. "Something has happened to my husband!" she frantically explained to Dr. C. Krumm-Heller, the technical director at Hormona. The pharmaceutical company promptly hired an investigator to trace every step of Pereña's trip after his departure from Mexico. The Mexican consul in Ciudad Trujillo, Alberto Reyes Spindola, consulted the Dominican authorities, who declared to him that there was no record of Pereña having arrived in Ciudad Trujillo. His name didn't appear on any Dominican hotel registry, they said to the diplomat. In March, the Mexican government sent Dr. Melchor Cardenas Gonzalez to Port-au-Prince to investigate Pereña's disappearance. Cardenas was on duty from their Foreign Office's *Sección de Justicia.*[21]

Alfredo Pereña was born in the Lérida province of Cataluña, Spain, on September 13, 1915. At age twenty-four, after graduating from the University of Barcelona with a law degree in 1939, he married Mercedes Gili, a twenty-year-old Spanish red-haired beauty. Subsequently, the young couple fled the horrors of the Spanish Civil War to Bordeaux, France, where they found a ship bound for Ciudad Trujillo. Pereña sailed from his homeland with empty pockets and a pregnant wife.

The couple arrived in the Dominican Republic in 1939 as immigrant Spanish refugees, but were well received,[22] as had been other Spanish exiles at the time, including Jesús de Galíndez.[23] Mercedes was provided the best hospitalization facilities for her pregnancy. When the Pereñas opened the Academia Cristóbal Colón, a private school in Ciudad Trujillo, Dictator Rafael Trujillo's son Ramfis was among the students. However, the school was reported to have been a financial failure, and Pereña thus closed it after a year. To make ends meet, he gave private English and literature lessons to wealthy Dominicans. But insecurity and poverty badgered the exiled pair.

Daughter Heidi was born in 1940. The following year, the young family got visas for Mexico and left the Dominican Republic. In Mexico City, Pereña worked as a translator and then got a job at a publishing company. A year later, he became manager of an export-import company and remained in that post for four years. In 1947, he obtained work with Hormona Laboratories' export division. He became a Mexican citizen in 1950 and four years later was promoted to manager of sales and export for the pharmaceutical firm.

Port-au-Prince pharmacist Joseph Valmé described Pereña as a tall, quiet, sober-sided man devoted to his job and family back in Mexico. He wore horn-rimmed glasses and a customary grey business suit. With four daughters by now, the family was happy and had finally made it in Mexico. Perhaps significantly, and unlike many of his exiled countrymen, Alfredo Pereña did not consider politics one of his interests.

Unfortunately, even I managed to confirm to my satisfaction what everyone troubled by the case suspected: Pereña never got to the immigration counter in Ciudad Trujillo. According to a Dominican airport employee who had witnessed the arrival of the Pan American Airways flight from Port-au-Prince that afternoon, an official-looking automobile had met the plane directly on the tarmac and had left with a passenger. At the time, the airport employee thought the passenger must have been some kind of dignitary or other VIP, entering so the country without having to go through immigration or customs. PAA, for its part, refused to speculate publicly and forbade its employees to talk to reporters.

From all indications, Pereña was liquidated by Trujillo. He was never seen again and his body was never found. Was it a mix-up in targeted victims, or was there some unknown reason why he disappeared in such a cloak-and-dagger scenario? There was one possible, if inconclusive, clue: in 1957, Hormona Laboratories had held a contest among their salesmen. The prize was an all-expense paid, fifteen-day trip to Mexico. The winner was a young Dominican, Jose Mejia, an employee of Jose Roldan. Mejia was received in Mexico City by Hormona's export sales chief, Alfredo Pereña, and ensconced at the Hotel Del Prado. Together, they toured the city, visited the nightspots and even took a trip to Acapulco. When Mejia returned to Ciudad Trujillo, he was arrested. For six months, his whereabouts were a mystery. When he finally reappeared after having been released, he told Roldan he no longer wished to work for Hormona; he gave no reason. The *Haiti Sun* was unable to locate Mejia, who might have shed light on this strange case, which, to this day, has never been solved.

*   *   *

This disappearance from the Dominican Republic wasn't the first nor the last. The missing-person mysteries brought unwelcome notoriety to Trujillo's *Servicio de Inteligencia Militar*, its boss Johnny Abbes Garcia and the Caribbean country. A change of pattern consequently occurred; from then on, perceived enemies of the Dominican State would have to disappear from somewhere else. No longer would there be any trace of the person's vanishing from Dominican soil, even if he or she had been killed there and fed to the sharks. Instead, for example, an imposter would travel to Haiti and then magically fade away, leaving behind the real victim's passport and other evidence, "proving" that the latter had gone astray while on Haitian soil.

One such case occurred the following May. A man identifying himself as Raphael Jesus Velasquez traveled to our island of Hispaniola from Bogotá, Colombia. He checked into the El Rancho hotel in Pétionville upon his arrival from Ciudad Trujillo, and disappeared the following day, leaving his personal effects, his passport and the plane ticket he had for his return to Colombia. On the eve of his disappearance, the man, the *Haiti Sun* learned, had dined with the Dominican military attaché, Col. Luis Trujillo Reynosa, and two females. The Dominican embassy counselor, Dr. Fred A. Didier Burgos, said the report of the missing man dining with Col. Trujillo Reynosa was erroneous, and that we inquiring newsmen should "seek explanations at the Colombian embassy," which we did. There, a representative responded that they had no leads, but off-the-record, another embassy spokesman told the *Haiti Sun* that the Dominicans were somehow involved in the man's disappearance. The Dominican ambassador's residence was located next door to the El Rancho hotel.

Velasquez or his imposter was the third visitor to have disappeared from Haiti during the year. The second of the missing trio was Vittorio Radeglia, an Italian-born private secretary to ex-President Juan Perón of Argentina. The circumstances surrounding the vanishing of "Velasquez" followed closely that of Radeglia's. The latter, or his stand-in, had arrived in Port-au-Prince in mid-July from Ciudad Trujillo, where Perón then resided in exile. He had checked into the Castelhaiti hotel in the Haitian capital. From there, he had disappeared, never to return. An airline ticket to Rome with his personal effects and a half-bottle of whiskey were left behind. The police failed to turn up any identification papers other than the Haiti tourist card.

Haitian police finally established that the man who had registered at the Castelhaiti under the name "Radeglia" was an impostor who wanted the world to think that the former private secretary of Juan Perón had disappeared in Haiti.

CHAPTER 7

Chasing Zombies

As often happens during a crisis in Haiti, there was a zombie scare in early 1959, mostly concentrated in the famine regions. Our editorial line at the *Haiti Sun* was to respect the Vodou religion, but we did not accept the popular belief in the existence of the living dead. Since the late 1980s, scientific theories have appeared, mostly emanating from the botany, pharmacology and physiology fields of biology and medicine, and which credibly indicate what biochemical processes could disrupt a pathologist's examination of an ostensibly lifeless human body. Yet, so deeply ingrained has the country's zombie myth become over the centuries, it seemed at the time imbedded in the Haitian psyche — and among some resident foreigners' as well.

The fear of zombies can seriously be considered the outgrowth of a strong mystical fear harking back to the days of slavery. In the minds of many Haitians, and not only peasants, there is nothing so frightening as the idea of being made a slave with no will to resist, no power to react. According to legendary superstition (and actual medical theory), a *bòkò*,[24] using a secret powder, can allegedly make someone fall into a state of catatonic-like lethargy. The victim's vital signs being imperceptible under examination, he or she is then pronounced dead and is buried. Once unearthed and taken from his grave, the "zombie"[25] is kept in a submissive state with powder made from the white flower of a plant called *konkonm zonbi.*[26] As it appears in some

67

novels and other written accounts,[27] it is believed that the tasting of salt by the poisoned captive can trigger a partial reversal of his or her condition. But usually, awakened or not, the alleged victims of zombification end up with severe neurological damage, supposing they hadn't already been so afflicted before.

The fear of being targeted by such a ghastly procedure is so high, that it is not uncommon for the deceased, before burial, to have a poison poured down their throat, or to be buried face down with a knife in hand to defend themselves in case some *malfétè*[28] tried to dig them up and make them into a drugged slave. This terror, of course, enhances the power of the bòkò. It is not rare to find a Haitian somewhat informed on the making of a zombie and how the latter reacts and is used as a slave. The Haitian judicial system takes the matter very seriously; Article 249 of its *Code pénal* declares such a procedure "will be termed murder."

«VOICE OF PEOPLE BRANDED ME ZOMBIE MAKER; ZOMBIE WAS CRAZY RELATIVE» SAYS ENACIER

3 HOUR DONKEY RIDE FROM BOMBARDOPOLIS ENACIER APPEALS TO REASON

Several weeks ago the story that a tobacco farmer in the northwest was keeping zombies and making them work in the fields after dark broke in the that area. Supposedly one zombie was picked up by police and then given back to the bocor after he «bribed» the corporal with 400 gourdes. The corporal is now being

(continued on page 11)

Enacier: Never even seen a Zombie

Curé Laroche: Interviewed that Zombie

Haiti Protests Embassy Incident And Threats To Throw Grenades On Edifice

An energetic protest and a demand for protection of the Haitian Embassy in Havana was made to the Cuban Government this week following several incidents which included threats to throw grenades upon the edifice. Haiti's Chargé d'Affaires, Mr. Jacques Dorismond presented the note of protest to Cuban Minister of State, Dr. Roberto Agramonte.

(Continued on page 13)

The author decided that Enacier was no zombie-maker. Father Laroche, the Canadian-born Roman Catholic parish priest on Bombardopolis, was convinced that the farmer was a zombie-maker.

During my first decade in Haiti, there were only a couple of publicized zombie sightings, and upon investigation, we twice proved that the creatures involved were actually very real, mentally ill persons. Both of these poor souls recited the same "experience" of having died, having been buried, dug up and taken to a place where they worked with other undead slaves and from which they finally escaped.

A report stated that in Bombardopolis, a small village in the mountains of the northwest corner of Haiti, a tobacco farmer was keeping zombies and making them work in the fields after dark. Supposedly, one of the victims was picked up by the police and then given back to the farmer, who, so it was said, had bribed a corporal with 400 gourdes.

However, no one had asked the tobacco farmer for his side of the story. No one in the village had gone to his land and searched for any evidence of the tale. By this time, the entire Northwest had maligned the farmer, whom they referred to as a bòkò. At the *Haiti Sun*, we decided it was a story that needed investigating. We would search for the farmer and learn the truth.

Bombardopolis had been a German farming community in the eighteenth century; it had since fallen on hard times. Accompanied by a reporter and photographer from the *Miami Herald*, I arrived there in the middle of the night. A huge spike from a cactus made a hole in one of our jeep's tires near the town's old cemetery. As I struggled to change the tire, the atmosphere was so spooky that if someone had touched me on the shoulder, I would have been airborne in a half a second. The next morning, we met with the local priest at the town's big Catholic church. Rev. Father Laroche was a Canadian who had served in Haiti since 1948. Astoundingly, he had interviewed the zombie, according to a quoted statement of his. Father Laroche had the look of a business executive and was known for his flare in road building. His apparent lucidity only accentuated our surprise, as he was quite adamant about the zombie being real. He even produced from his church office a book on herbs, leaves and other nostrums that were used, he believed, in zombification. He had obviously become haitianized, and thought as did the rest of the little town. The inhabitants had completely ostracized the farmer. Father Laroche truly believed the farmer had committed the terrible sin he was accused of, and so refused baptism to the man's grandchildren.

As we stayed and probed, the story began to unfold before us: a group of young men had been playing cards one night — there being little else to do in the town — when a wasted, naked man with long matted hair appeared at the door, asking for water. His hands were tied behind his back. He complained that he was hot from digging up a man from the Bombardopolis cemetery, another victim that the tobacco farmer wanted as slave. We checked the cemetery. The grave in question had not been disturbed.

Cards flying, the players fled the house by the window and arrived at the police post shouting, *"Zombi! Zombi!"* The gendarme, described as extremely hesitant to go hunt and jail whatever or whomever the card players saw, told them bluntly: "You found him. You keep him." The men thus returned, found the naked man and tied him to the porch of a house opposite the police post. But during the night, he managed to gnaw through the ropes binding him. When he appeared at the police post at around 3 a.m., stating, "I must now go for water," the soldier on duty vanished in fright.

The following day, the naked fellow was taken into custody and when the people began to comment on how withered he was, he replied: "You should see the women." He went on to tell the locals that he and five others, including two women, were kept in caverns on the side of a cliff and given nothing but sour oranges to eat. Father Laroche went to the police post to interview him. The priest recounted that he had found him lying on a bench, his body so thin that it did not even overlap on either side of the bench. With his head in his hands, the poor man slowly looked up. He then told the priest that he recognized him from his own burial three years earlier in a farming district near the town. The good father didn't need any further proof. Unfortunately for the Canadian's wits, he had been in rural Haiti too long.

It turned out that three years earlier indeed, a nephew of Énacier, the accused tobacco farmer, had been buried; the alleged zombie may have attended the funeral. The police sent for Énacier, who identified the walking skeleton as his crazy nephew and promised to send him back to his father. Happy to be rid of the undesirable character, the police released him to his uncle's care.

It was a long trip for the *Haiti Sun* and the donkey to find the zombie maker.

The *Herald* team was excited by the prospect of our interviewing farmer Énacier, and perhaps the zombie himself, to learn the truth. A youthful guide named Michel agreed to accompany us on the three-hour mule ride over rough, barren hills, only if the rural policeman came along. When we finally arrived on a rocky cliff top, Énacier was working with his hoe near a trickle of river. Our meeting took place out of the cruel sun in one of five small latticewood huts on the cliff ledge above the river Henne. The thin, poker-faced man said his deranged nephew was no zombie and that mental illness ran in the young man's family. When he began to talk, Énacier made a Mark Anthony-like appeal to his visitors. His hypnotic eyes blazing, and with demonstrative hands, he pleaded his cause with senatorial eloquence and made his audience forget their thirst, the three-hour mule ride and the long return trip we'd have to tackle...

Énacier said that the nephew, for the past ten years, had forsaken clothes, food and lodgings given to him by his relatives, preferring to live naked as an animal in the wild; he would occasionally appear in nearby localities, terrifying the entire population. "He's horribly, horribly thin.... We would give him clothes and he'd throw them away

....Understand, some people in small rural communities like ours don't have any wits."

It was difficult to comprehend that this illiterate farmer was making a case as any high-powered legal defender could make. "What I

Father Laroche was so convinced of Enancier's use of zombies that he refused to baptize the man's many children and grandchildren.

should have done was to leave him there and make the crazy people from nephew's side of the family come from Jean-Rabel to pick him up. That was my mistake. The voice of the people has forced this on me, but I want to fight it. Let anyone come and look in my house, my garden or any place; I'll dare them to say that they can find a zombie working here. I myself have never seen such a being.... If I had done something like this to one of my relatives' children, they would have been the first to come and protest. The last time I saw my nephew was when I gave him food, put him on a mule and gave him to a boy to take to his brother. As for bribing the corporal, why I've never given him a mere cigarette!"

Énacier, who claimed to have fathered thirty-one children, twenty-nine still living, sighed and declared: "there is no lack of crazy people in Haiti." The population of Bombard', as he called the village, "has sinned against me in saying I am a zombie-maker." Lowering his voice for the first time, Énacier declared: "I am not a bòkò. I used to dispense medicines with the leaves but I have long since given up because it's a thankless task. It takes you away from your own garden and if your cure doesn't work, you have problems." Perhaps what upset him the most was the fact that Father Laroche, at St. François church, had refused to baptize his grandchildren. Convinced of the farmer's case, upon our return to town, I pleaded his cause to the good priest, try-ing to persuade him to finally baptize Énacier's grandchildren. Father Laroche smiled and shook his head in refusal.

Shortly after our story appeared, news reached the *Sun* that the zombie had died of natural causes.

Author examining the Bombardopolis cemetery to solve the mystery of the zombie story.

CHAPTER 8

Let Them Starve

The more the Haitian exiles' broadcasts from Cuba threatened Duvalier, the more Papa Doc tightened the screw of intimidation. Unexplained deaths of non-Duvalierists were happening more and more frequently. Police shot and killed one man "while he was trying to escape arrest." He had been accused by a Duvalierist neighbor of telling people that Déjoie would soon return. He had been listening to a radio broadcast from Havana.

It became dangerous in Haiti to wear a beard, as did Fidel Castro's guerrillas. A young Haitian returned home from Paris, where he had been studying art. Bearded, he was quickly arrested and detained at Ft. Dimanche; he lost only his beard in the old prison, but the cold water shave he received traumatized him so badly, he chose exile.

The *Haiti Sun* began publishing regular lists of individuals, both military and civilian, who had taken refuge in Latin American embassies and who were seeking safe conduct to leave the country. As our reporting of such cases increased, especially of those involving persons imprisoned at the National Penitentiary, we decided at the *Sun* to refer to the Port-au-Prince prison by a series of veiled appellations, such as "Sandstone College," "Hotel Rue-du-Centre" or "The Hotel of Many Bars."

Lt. Jean Tassy, a member of the new presidential guard, was driving recklessly at high speed on the new Delmas highway when he nearly struck a car driven by Roger Denis, a well-known Haitian businessman and sportsman who had carefully stayed out of politics. What could have been a fatal accident was avoided in extremis, but that was not the end of it; the arrogant young lieutenant heard Denis mutter something along the lines of "Well, you do *own* the road...." Infuriated by the close call and the comment, Tassy arrested Denis on the spot and carted him away, leaving the latter's wife and young son helpless in the car; both were non-drivers. At police headquarters, the fifty-year-old Denis later recounted to the *Haiti Sun*: "They tied me with my hands under my knees, and then Tassy invited two fellow officers to join in beating me." Denis lost consciousness and awoke in the military hospital. I interviewed him later, at the Canapé Vert hospital. His posterior, groin and thighs were a mass of bruised flesh. The doctors were fearful of gangrene. When I published the story, I was sure Duvalier would reprimand Tassy for his abuse of authority; I was wrong. Duvalier promoted his lieutenant, who in turn suggested that I watch my own "arse."

*   *   *

In March 1959, Uncle Sam came to the rescue of the Duvalier government; the U.S. poured $6 million into the Haitian budget in support. There was no longer any doubt that Washington had decided to back Papa Doc for reasons of realpolitik. It didn't matter that the Haitian president — and it was no secret to the Americans — was reaping off-the-books money to the tune of millions, from the Régie du Tabac slush fund. It was a time when anti-Communist ideology excused many sins. Duvalier had already made arrangements to purchase a beautiful villa in the hills of Desprez that overlooked the city, and had also built a country home in Arcahaie, on a large track of land adjacent to the northern highway. All this on the president's meager salary of some $14,000 plus expenses, of course.

While reinforcing its military defenses with the help of the U.S. Marines, Papa Doc's government also spent $338,000 on the services of two U.S. consulting firms, hired to carry out studies and submit recommendations on how to facilitate Haiti's financial and economic recovery. Whether or not Duvalier had any intention of following their proposals, or whether he was just window-dressing for Washington, no one knows. One thing is certain: he did not carry them out.

*   *   *

So lamented by the "country doctor" Duvalier when he was campaigning for the presidency, the misery of his less fortunate fellow-citizens didn't seem to have much visible effect on the newer "Papa Doc" Duvalier. "Half the population of the northwest faces death by starvation," the *Haiti Sun* warned in a bannered story on March 1, 1959. Our dramatic first-hand description of "walking skeletons" in the dry, parched mountains of that region was heartrending. The area hadn't received a drop of rain since Hurricane Hazel had passed through it in 1954. Leafless tree branches drooped and hovered in the breeze. Even weeds had disappeared; donkeys desperately licked the tips of acacia branches. Heavy winds along the coast and low tidal basins had hindered, and then ended the salt-making trade, as saline reservoirs became fouled. Rivers and streams were reduced to a trickle in La Gorge, a locality where Columbus had found an abundance of water in 1492. Guinea fowl had vanished and native pigeons were being enticed into traps with one seed. Our *Sun* editorials begged for aid to this region.

Traveling through the drought-stricken area, above the once-busy banana port town of Jean-Rabel, was a shocking experience. Skin hung in folds from bony children. Many were endeavoring to survive on a diet of hard-as-marble, unripe green mangoes. One photograph I took in a little hollow called Fond-la-Loi was quite representative of the people's situation: the youngsters of a family were naked, and their elders were dressed in scraps of clothing.

Elsewhere, a farmer, his wife, brother and seven children were slowly weaving baskets from *latanier.*[29] They would strive to sell them for one cent each. The farmer doubted that he would find a market for the baskets in Port-de-Paix, the main town some thirty miles away.

This was a typical picture of poor farmers and their families in the northwest during the terrible famine of 1959.

Adding to the distressing sight were burns on two of the children, who had accidentally fallen into an open fire on which nothing was cooking.

In another area called Poirier, farmer Estilen Vital, 53, prodded a fire over which a tin of small green mangoes boiled, while his tiny pot-bellied son slowly shelled a little handful of peas into a small can. This would be their only meal of the day. Asked why he hadn't sold his pig, Vital replied: "Look at it; it's thin and dried up. Nobody would want to buy it."

His fifteen-year-old son had died of fever the previous week. Had Vital been able to sell the pig, he would have given his son a proper funeral. Instead, as no money was available, the boy had been buried at night without service; just put under the ground. Such shameful circumstances had targeted many other families in the region. This was a terrible thing, the inexorable result of *force majeure*. It was strictly against Haitian custom, which calls for a service and rites for the deceased.

Father Marcel Cornet of the Jean-Rabel parish routinely toured the hungered area accompanied by Dr. Painson, of the town's small hospital-dispensary. Father Cornet said the most discouraging matter was the people's loss of hope. They were resigned to their fate. Even if rain finally came, few had any seeds left to sow, and most no longer had animals left to sell for seeds. Diseases, explained the French priest, were hastening the end of many who suffered from severe malnutrition. In one family, he reported, four had died of typhoid. He gave us a list of needed medicines.

Children with spider legs and haggard eyes, their hair turned red

from kwashiorkor, sat listlessly around thatched family huts with the tired attitude of old people. Asked how they were, some lied; "Not so bad, thank you." Skeletal men and women seemed to be hiding themselves inside their humble dwellings, as if starving was a sinful thing. The crops of beans, peanuts, manioc for cassava bread, bananas, coffee and millet had been scant. Livestock, along with the typical farmer's prize possession, the fighting cock, couldn't be seen nor heard anywhere. Yet, we found no one begging.

Ambassador Drew, who had doubts about the severity of the famine, called in the editor of the *Haiti Sun* to explain what he had seen.

A Duvalier deputy along with merchants in the town had food for sale; they were only too happy that the relief supplies were slow to arrive.

During my inspection trip, the contradictions and complexities of Haiti were illustrated by the regular Sunday cockfight in a secluded corner of the town of Jean-Rabel. The mood was festive, offering no hint of the misery that existed but a few miles away in the country-side. Excited onlookers and gamblers peered down on the fighting cocks. With shrill cries, vendors sold bread and little candied peanuts, amid two gambling tables. Life here was truly a gamble, in more ways than one.

After our initial story appeared in the *Haiti Sun*, U.S. Ambassador Gerald Drew invited me to the embassy to discuss the situation in the northwest. Grumpy, he complained that I was exaggerating the situation, and added that he had dispatched his consul, who was mandated to report on conditions. The latter had returned saying that there was plenty of food in the Jean-Rabel marketplace. I suggested he send the consul back to visit the countryside above Jean-Rabel, this time. Certainly, there was food in the market, but who could buy it, and with what?

At the time of my visit to the mountains above Jean-Rabel, Duvalier was in nearby Cap-Haïtien, where he delivered in French a long, prepared speech, lavishing praise on the American administration in Washington and personally lauding President Eisenhower for aiding the Haitian government. He virtually gushed over with implications that U.S.-Haiti relations were wonderful. By now it had become difficult to predict Papa Doc's politics and policies, as they tended to zigzag, from one day to the next. However, following his "Off with Their Heads" address, he had evidently decided that moderation in his rhetoric was advisable, so as not to give ammunition to his enemies abroad.

Doc always found it difficult to speak extemporaneously, and the words he uttered on public occasions were usually drafted by one of his speechwriters. In his Cap-Haïtien speech, the text of which the *Sun* reprinted in its entirety in an English translation, Duvalier portrayed himself as a caring "Papa" determined to remake Haiti. He declared that the country was "at war, in an effort to alleviate its most pressing problems." It was a "sacrosanct war against ignorance." Victory would come from his anti-illiteracy campaign, said he. "Total war has also been declared against disease, unemployment and wretched housing conditions...," he intoned, ratcheting up his hyperbolic expression. "General mobilization to cultivate the soil is decreed throughout Haiti. The life of the nation depends on it." His government had opened the "battle on all fronts." And it was thanks to the "U.S. financial aid I have obtained that we will be victorious." Duvalier nearly sang *The Star-Spangled Banner.* But in reality, what he wanted was Washington squarely on his side. He continued to worry about Haitian exiles training in Cuba. "The steps taken by my government have not been undertaken for the benefit of a sector of the nation or a portion of the country," Doc continued in his Cap-Haïtien oration. "They are in the interests of all Haitians, without distinction, whatever their political credo, their profession, their religion, the color of their skin. I desire only the happiness of my people and the health of my wounded fatherland." Citing the words of French writer Remy de Gourmont, Duvalier said: "No, there is no place for hatred in us even when we are hated." If only it had been true...

It was a strange setting for such an optimistic, stylized French speech, when not so far away, thousands of desperate creolohones were starving. He made no mention of the predicament of hungry farmers who were selling all their meager possessions to flee towards the British Bahamas islands. Indeed, in what was one of the major boatlifts of that time, an estimated two thousand people took to the sea.

The *Haiti Sun* noted that food supplies to the area were being furnished, as news of the desperate plight of the population spread outside Haiti. The Catholic Welfare Organization and the Protestant Church World Service Organization began to distribute emergency U.S. foodstuff, followed by CARE and the Pan American Health Organization. Under the U.S. emergency aid regulations, the Duvalier government was to pay for internal distribution of the American food from the capital to the Northwest department. However, it did not come up with the money; Papa Doc's officials objected to paying the four-dollars-a-ton cost of transportation. They gave no reasons or excuses for not furnishing the funds, and decided that the churches themselves should provide the shipping. The U.S. authorities eventually had to waive the clause requiring the Haitian administration's contribution, and thus permitted church organizations to provide the transportation funds.

In early April, Duvalier received a $4.3 million development loan destined to the completion of an agricultural project in the Artibonite valley; 80,000 acres needed to be irrigated there. Consequently, Duvalier and his American friend Dr. Elmer Loughlin were eventually to go into the rice-growing business.

*   *   *

Haitian poet and Kreyòl playwright Félix Morisseau-Leroy returned from a trip to the African nation of Dahomey[30]; the *Sun* ran a three-part series on his trip to the ancestral home of most Haitians. Little did Morisseau, a supporter of Clément Jumelle, know at the time that within a short while, he would return to Africa where he would spend the rest of the Duvalier years in exile with other prominent Haitian writers, including Jean Brierre and Roger Dorsinville.[31]

Meanwhile, seventeen members of opposition parties, labor leaders and journalists who had run to the safety of the Venezuelan embassy in Port-au-Prince were finally permitted to depart on April 1, 1959, for exile in Caracas. They included well-known writer-historian Stephen Alexis, who was to die in exile.

CHAPTER 9

First Plane Hijacked to Cuba

here was often personal anguish in reporting many of the stories in the *Haiti Sun*. For example, on Sunday April 12, 1959, I gave the headline on page one to a fine pilot and friend: "'Cowboy' Guilbaud dies; Cohata [DC-3] hijacked"; "Cuban Govt. considering asylum for six 'RIH' men." Photographs on page one included the smiling aviator, Maj. Elberle "Cowboy" Guilbaud, forty-two years old, and the army's most experienced pilot. Why had the hijackers killed him? Did they have a choice? Questions that were never answered.

Inspired by Castro's triumph, six young Haitian men had successful hijacked the vintage DC-3 of Cohata, the twenty-one-year-old domestic airline operated by the Haitian air force. They aimed to land in Santiago de Cuba. It was one of the first cases of air piracy with Cuba as intended destination. The unfortunate incident cost the life of a fine Haitian; it was ironic that Guilbaud should die at the hands of anti-Duvalierists, as he himself was not happy with the regime.

The DC-3 had left Port-au-Prince on the morning of April 7 and picked up twenty-one passengers in Les Cayes. George Salling, a U.S. aid worker, was one of them. He recounted that fifteen minutes into the flight, "a scuffle suddenly broke out." The American official said that the airplane went out of control during the wild free-for-all between the Haitian gunmen and the crew, and it plunged to within seventy-five feet of the sea. "I held onto my life jacket and expected

Haiti Sun

VOL. IX — SUNDAY, APRIL 12 1959 — No. 28 — PORT-AU-PRINCE

«COWBOY» GUILBAUD DIES; COHATA HIJACKED DC3 EN ROUTE TO CAPITAL

DC3 Transport plane of TA, Raizan Island Airmade a perfect take-off the airstrip outside the Southwestern town of Aux and the twenty-five passen- the crew of six settled for the forty-five minute Port-au-Prince. As the of the plane part of the on by the Haitian Airpopular Major Eberle age 42, one of the most skilled pilots of nine children, two men who had the plane there was new from their seats the door, and entered cabin with drawn They ordered Guilmake for Cuba. were red arms bands others who had plane twenty minuat the town of Jerealso drew revolvers the passengers to

Funeral Services For Popular Pilot Today

Suddenly there was a shot and Guilbaud slumped in his seat, shot through the head. One of the men took over the controls.

The following morning Haiti's Foreign Minister, Dr. Louis Mars, told the press that the plane had landed in Santiago de Cuba and all the passengers, including a Canadian nun, Sister Marie de la Visitation, British Major John Munroe and two U. S. citizens were safe.

The kidnappers had been arrested and extradition was being sought.

Word from Havana indicated that the leaders of the kidnapping gang were ex-Haitian Army Officer Airforce Adjudant Daniel Georges and Robert Victor.

The names of other members of the hi-jackers were given as Hubert Dupuy, Carl Bellard, Jacques Laforest and Jn.-Claude Bourand.

Foreign Minister Louis Mars told the press that the arm bands had the letters «M. D. I.» (Movement Revolutionnaire Interval for the Communist Caribbean organization known as the «Movement for Internal Revolution».

«There is no Communist Party. (Continued on page 2)

Pilot Guilbaud had close to 8,000 flying hours.

CUBAN GOVT. CONSIDERING ASYLUM FOR SIX «RIH» MEN

SANTIAGO DE CUBA.— The Cuban military government to Santiago with 22 persons aboard.

Five passengers were fugitives.

The plane, a DC-3 was en route from Aux Cayes, Haiti, to Port-au-Prince when the revolutionists whipped out pistols and announced they were taking control. A brief fight between the rebels and plane crew followed in which the pilot, Eberle Guilbaud, was

and forced the copilot to fly it to Santiago with 22 persons aboard.

killed. Upon arrival at Santiago the rebels wore armbands which read «RIH» for Haitian Interior Revolution and shouted «Viva Fidel Castro».

A Cuban Army communique listed the rebels as Daniel Georges, Jean Claude Bourand, Jacques Laforest, Hubert Dupuys Nouille, Carol Nellicade and Robert Victor.

The Haitian rebels were held at Moncada Military Head. (Continued on page 2)

Life Of Clement Jumelle Still Believed In Balance At Cuban Embassy Asylum

Former candidate brought from kidney-place in critical state — complications high blood pressure and uremia.

Very little improvement is reported in the condition of Mr Clement Jumelle who is at present under the care of a corps of Medical Specialists at the residence of the Cuban Ambassador, in Bourdon. Two Cuban medical special

day from Havana on a special Cuban de Aviation chartered plane, examined Clement Jumelle who is critically ill in asylum at the Cuban Embassy here since Tuesday night. At the special request of Cuban Ambassador Antonio Rodriguez Echazabal, the specialists, Doctors Rodrigo Bustamente Marcaydo and Antono Barquet (Continued on page 2)

EXILED BATISTA BACK TO FORMER JOB

President Dr. François Duvalier decorating flour Mill owner, Texas Multi-Millionaire Industrialist Clint Murchison Jr. (Story on page 2)

COOP Formed Jean Rabel

operative for the articles and production as aid to a fine

Turnball, vp for the past called a meeting of the Cenesand the Unevs Mission of the last Sunday. representatives a they elected a mittee for their association — Unis du Jean-Ra.

ed on page 14)

At Ambassadors Meet
No Immediate Invasion Seen In Caribbean

SAN SALVADOR, April 10 United States Ambassadors and officials of the State Department today discussed the activities of groups of exiles in the Caribbean and arrived at the conclusion that there does not seem to be any immediate probability of an invasion against any country of that region.

The 12-ambassador meeting is presided over by Loy Henderson, Subsecretary of State, Roy

(Continued on page 2)

Reds In School Close Down

A Government communique, on Thursday, announced that due to Communist infiltration into the Teachers Corps, particularly the professors at Lycée Petion, here, it was obliged to close down the establishment for one week in view of its complete reorganization.

An earlier Communique on Thursday, regarding the same (Continued on page 2)

Former Cuban Strongman Fulgencio Batista photographed last week in his room in Hotel Jaragua where he has returned to his former job of stenographer.

to be swimming the next minute — if I was lucky," Salling said. The five Haitian crewmen aboard the plane were armed but the hijackers managed to disarm them. Two of the gunmen forced their way into the pilot's cabin. Salling didn't hear the shot but was sure it was at that moment that Guilbaud was killed, as the plane went seriously out of control. Some of the passengers got up and tried to help the crew but the confusion was such that one could not tell who was fighting whom. "Then, just as suddenly, we leveled off and started climbing. The rebels held pistols on the crew and some of the passengers, and we were flying again."

Returning from inspecting two sugar mills, John Munro, a sixty-five-year-old British engineer from Kingston, Jamaica, was also a passenger on the hijacked plane. "It looked like we were all going to die," he related. Munro said he glimpsed the "scuffle in the cockpit, then the door slammed shut and the plane took a nasty dip down. We had been at about 1400 feet and then dived to about 150 feet. Because the noise of the engine muffled the shot, it was not until we arrived in Santiago de Cuba that we learned that the pilot had been killed."

One of the hijackers, identified as Daniel Georges, was an ex-Air Force adjudant; he reportedly took over the controls and diverted the plane to Santiago de Cuba. The six hijackers arrived in Cuba and stepped off the airliner wearing red armbands with the lettering "RIH". They told the Cuban authorities that RIH stood for *Révolution Intérieure d'Haïti*.[32] Haitian Foreign Minister Dr. Louis Mars told the press in Port-au-Prince that the RIH was a Caribbean Communist organization. There was no evidence that the armbands were anything other than homemade, merely created to meet the occasion. The six rebels, who were eventually granted asylum in Cuba, were named as Daniel Georges, Jean-Claude Bourand, Jacques Laforest, Hubert Dupuys Nouille, Carl Béliard and Robert Victor.

A U.S. aircraft ferried the shocked passengers back from Santiago de Cuba, while arrangements were being made to return the hijacked DC-3 to Haiti.

That week's editorial in the *Sun* pointed out the need for more passenger planes to fulfill the Cohata's task. With the hijacking of the last DC-3, and with another plane in Miami having an engine changed, air travel was paralyzed. A third plane had recently burst into flames on takeoff; its crew and passengers had miraculously escaped, unhurt. Road travel was time-consuming, hazardous and sometimes impossible. And only Jérémie had a passenger boat service.

Two young Haitian exiles, student Fritz Thébaud and mechanic Max Munro, had recently been allowed to leave diplomatic asylum in Haiti and go into exile. The same week, during which the hijacking had been perpetrated, they set out in a small boat from the Oriente province, twelve miles west of Santiago de Cuba, in a plan to invade Haiti. They were accompanied by twenty-eight armed Cuban volunteers, had automatic weapons and 140,000 rounds of ammunition. The group was intercepted at sea by the Cuban navy and forced ashore at Siboney beach, not far from the chicken farm from which Fidel Castro had launched his own revolution, in 1953.[33] Upon their return to Santiago, the officer in charge of the province, Comandante Manuel "Red Beard" Piñiero, lectured the two Haitians about abusing Cuba's hospitality. Jacques Riché, a leader in Cuba of the "Haitian Revolutionary Front," denied his group's involvement in the failed invasion. The two Haitians were released, and the Cubans who had assisted them were officially reported to having remained in jail.

*   *   *

Other news and headlines printed that week:

- "Life of Clément Jumelle still believed in balance at Cuban embassy." Those who helped hide the former presidential candidate told me he had died of a broken heart upon learning of the murder of his two older brothers by Duvalier. He never smiled again, they said.

- At an U.S. ambassadors' gathering in El Salvador, it was decided that there would be "no immediate invasions in the Caribbean."

- Duvalier said that there were Reds in the Lycée Pétion school, and so had it closed down.

- At the bottom of page one was a photo of exiled ex-President Fulgencio Batista of Cuba seated at a typewriter in his hotel room in the Dominican Republic. The caption noted that the dictator Batista had returned to his original job, army stenographer.

- Clint Murchison Jr., a Texan millionaire who had built Haiti's flour mill, was awarded Haiti's high decoration by President Duvalier; the photo got the centerfold in the *Sun*.

CHAPTER 10

Doc the Body Snatcher

On the evening of April 6, 1959, a Tuesday, about 7 p.m., Cuba's Ambassador Rodríguez recounted to the Haitian media that he heard a noise on the front patio of his residence and a car drive away. There, on the patio, he found his friend Clément Jumelle lying on the ground semi-conscious and Clément's wife kneeling beside him. The couple was clad in tattered peasants' clothing. It was difficult to recognize Clément, this onetime handsome, heavy-set man, Rodríguez said. The technocrat who proposed to, and could have, modernized Haiti was a frail, dying man. This political leader who aspired to give Haiti its first government of technicians lay inert on the ground. His wife cradled his head in her lap.

With difficulty, the Cuban reported, he and the servants carried Jumelle to an upstairs room, which was quickly transformed into a sick room. The ambassador didn't explain how the former presidential candidate, declared an outlawed with a $5,000 price on his head, had managed to reach the embassy without alerting the Makouts or Duvalier police. Rodríguez would say only that Jumelle and his wife had obviously managed to elude capture by hiding out disguised as peasants. The outlawed ex-presidential candidate had steadfastly refused to take asylum even when he became seriously ill. When his wife decided to take him to the embassy he was too ill to resist. That Jumelle's wife should have turned to Cuban ambassador Rodríguez was not surprising. Not only was his diplomatic residence secure, as the home of an ambassador; Rodríguez was a devoted friend and supporter of Jumelle.

Six Haitian medical experts and a member of the Haitian Foreign Office were summoned to the Cuban ambassador's residence. The doctors diagnosed Jumelle as critically ill suffering uremia complicated by hypertension. He was placed on oxygen and administered blood transfusions. The Haitian doctors worked around the clock to save him.

Duvalier ordered extra police to keep watch on the embassy, as he feared that Jumelle might make a recovery, and according to a presidential aide, there was no politician that Papa Doc feared more than Jumelle, with whom Duvalier had worked and had once had close ties.

Four days later at Rodríguez's request, two Cuban specialists, Drs. Rodrigo Bustamente Marcayda and Antonio Barquet, arrived from Havana. It was too late.

The end came at sundown on Saturday, April 10. Father Etienne Grienenberger, rector of Petit Séminaire St. Martial, the country's largest Roman Catholic secondary school, administered Jumelle's last rites. The death of Duvalier's last major opponent was officially confirmed.

Ambassador Rodríguez, who among Haiti's diplomatic corps, was unusually well informed, had been tipped, he later revealed, that an attempt might be made to seize Jumelle's body. The ambassador decided to deliver it instead to Jumelle's eighty-five-year-old mother.

As a group of Tontons Makouts knocked on the ambassador's front door – with orders from the palace to claim the corpse – Rodríguez was taking down a back door to allow the large body of the dead man to be carried out to the ambassador's car. Rodríguez sat the dead Jumelle — who had been dressed up in a suit — in the front seat and secured him in an upright position. As the Cuban ambassador drove down the steep driveway past policemen and Makouts he was seen "talking" to his passenger. The police and Makouts saw nothing strange about the occupants of the embassy car. Mrs. Jumelle, having been granted political asylum, remained behind in the safety of the Cuban embassy residence.

"I did all I could," the ambassador later told Jumelle's mother at the home of her exiled son, Dr. Gaston Jumelle. The next day, Sunday, hundreds of Clément Jumelle's friends and partisans ignored the Makouts who were keeping watch on the Jumelle house on Avenue Magney just off the Champs de Mars, in order to get a last glimpse of their beloved candidate. It was an extraordinary emotional scene and I was listening to Haitian Poet Jean Brièrre deliver a stirring eulogy to Jumelle when a military officer arrived from the palace. He informed Mrs. Jumelle, the aged mother and her five daughters that for security reasons — the situation could become violent – no funeral procession would be permitted. Some mourners became agitated, crying out defiantly, "Jumelle lives." Krèyol Poet Felix Morriseau-Leroy arriving with his wife and daughter was hailed by one mourner, "Brother Antigone, look they are again refusing to bury Polince." Many of the mourners had seen Morriseau-Leroy's Krèyol version of the Greek tragedy *Antigone* played by an all-peasant cast. They understood.

Despite the palace warning, hundreds of wailing mourners filed out into the street and began to follow the hearse carrying Clément Jumelle's coffin towards the nearby Sacre Coeur church. The funeral procession had reached the first intersection when army troops appeared and barred the way. Army officers crouched behind machine guns mounted on tripods on each of the intersection's corners. Undaunted the mourners sang, "Clément Jumelle is not dead, he lives." Dr. Georges Rigaud, a prominent dentist and leading liberal, marched defiantly on, as did many others. Infuriated Poet Felix Morisseau-Leroy hastened up to each of the officers manning the machine guns and shouted at them: "Vultures!" Overcome with emotion the poet collapsed on the sidewalk just as the hearse reached the intersection.

Suddenly a black-and-white police wagon, its siren wailing, screeched up and expertly cut off the hearse from the mourners. To the shrieks of the bereaved and with floral wreaths flying, a police officer, Maj. John Beauvoir, waving a Tommy gun, jumped on the running board of the hearse and ordered the driver to speed away.

Police then began scattering the mourners with swinging rifle butts. One frantic man screaming at a soldier invited him to shoot him but the soldier chose to use his rifle butt rather than a bullet and the man collapsed in the street with a bleeding skull.

As no one knew where the body had been taken, everyone's imagination ran wild. The bloodied mourners, as they limped home, took vengeful relish in spreading word that Duvalier had stolen Jumelle's corpse to use it in some diabolical act of black magic.

Port-au-Prince Police Chief Daniel Beauvoir later announced that the family had been forewarned that the burial could take place only in St. Marc, Jumelle's hometown. He confirmed that the police had been forced to do just that.

In St. Marc the population had expected that their native son would indeed be buried there. Thousands waited in vain at the church. Police had sealed off the cemetery. When the hearse finally arrived, the casket was unceremoniously lifted by soldiers, hurriedly placed in the family tomb in the St. Marc cemetery and sealed. There were neither pallbearers nor any ceremony. *La Phalange*, the Catholic daily, reported that a priest had ridden on a bicycle to the cemetery and asked permission to bless the casket. The army officer present told the cleric, "It is not necessary."

The quasi-clandestine burial quickly set off new rumors that Duvalier had extracted Jumelle's heart and other vital organs to make powerful Vodou oungas. Members of political opposition fanned the rumors in order to discredit Duvalier. Even Vodou priests and priestess were shocked by the fact that Jumelle had been deprived a Christian funeral.

Before Clément Jumelle died, he had asked to see Father Etienne Grienenberger, to whom Jumelle entrusted his last testament to his partisans. That Sunday the French Catholic priest read Jumelle's testament, which he had jotted down word for word, over the radio. It took Duvalier completely by surprise and he placed Grienenberger on the regime's growing list of allegedly dangerous adversaries; the French priest was later expelled from the country.

A dying Jumelle had whispered his last words to Father Grienenberger.

"May younger generations make no mistake about it. My appeal is directed especially to them. They will remember that a man cornered by night and chased by day has faced the risk of death every second in order that . . . this piece of land continues to be a land of liberty. My enemies have slandered me. They have compelled me to live the life of a hunted animal. Today I am poor, naked and dispossessed, face to face with death, having as my only comfort the pureness of this ultimate sacrifice. Conditions of political struggle in Haiti have never been so hard, worsened by the mischievousness of the men presently ruling the country, and whose eagerness it is to cause more and more bloodshed in order to stay in office. I am leaving a party, the National Party that should be a weapon. The party will name my successor."

Jumelle's final utterance was "May my death be an example for humanity."

It was another sad chapter in Haitian politics. Jumelle's party would eventually disappear into the mist of history. The man himself would be remembered less for his contributions than for the manner in which Duvalier had snatched his body. It was a tragic ending for such a young and vigorous man who, as a modern-day economist, had so much to offer his country. His became just another name on the growing list of Papa Doc's victims.

In the *Haiti Sun,* we printed a lengthy article headlined: "The Drama of Clément Jumelle," and signed it with a *nom de plume,* "Baron Von Holbache." (It was an outrageous Germanic name from out of the blue.) It was a time when precautions had to be taken concerning not only what we published in the *Haiti Sun* but also what I reported to my news clients abroad. Associated Press stories usually appeared with my byline but as they were straightforward news reports they didn't at the time worry me too much. As for NBC News, radio network was not broadcast in Haiti and no one concerned seemed interested in tuning in to domestic U.S. radio broadcasts. Nor did television footage bother the palace unless it was an interview with the president. And as for the *New York Times* and *Time* magazine, in those days a "stringer" didn't get a by-line and thus remained anonymous. (Exceptions for the *New York Times* were annual surveys of the economy and travel-section stories.) *Time* files from the field tended to be long reportages running many pages as the editors required not only a recounting of events for the story but also an abundance of substantiating facts along with plenty of "color" and analysis. "Color" was the journalistic jargon for descriptive details that often required exhaustive sleuthing for such seemingly insignificant minutia as what a story subject wore or didn't wear. *Time* founder Henry Luce believed that a certain detail by itself could bring a story alive. Luce's formula likewise required that all the information filed by correspondents to New York headquarters be compressed, written, and edited there, frequently down to a column-long published report. If it were a political story, *Time*'s Washington bureau would be expected to file and often the administration's spin on a story would conflict with the correspondent in the field.

*   *   *

Nevertheless, the bizarre public snatching of Clément Jumelle's body had its effects. This incident, combined with the killing of Clément Jumelle's two brothers, was the last straw for some onetime Duvalierists who feared that the president was acting irrationally and leading the country into an abyss. Thus Duvalier's fifty-first birthday, April 14, 1959 was not a happy one. He was already looking older than his years. His legislative branch did not have the rubber-stamp bounce he believed it should have. At least six Duvalierist congressmen were taking their parliamentary roles too seriously for Duvalier. Senator Jean Belizaire, presiding over the opening session of the 38th legislature, was too candid in Duvalier's opinion. The *Haiti Sun* ran a full translation of Belizaire's French-language speech, in which the senator had declared in part: "Without respect for the constitution, there is no democracy . . . there is no respect for the dignity or the rights of citizens and without which there is no political stability and consequently no progress." He went on to warn, "It is the accumulation of small unconstitutionalities that breeds totalitarianism and absolutism." Belizaire, from north Haiti, went on to criticize the legislature's suspension of constitutional guarantees in declaring the May 2, 1958, state of siege and granting full powers to the president on the following July 31, "for the purpose of thwarting a political crisis." In doing so, Belizaire asserted, the legislative branch "had abused the letter of the constitution."

A lot was bothering these newly independent-minded Duvalierist senators. Some were true believers in democracy, and although Haiti had never truly known democratic rule, Haitian congressmen had a reputation for taking their work seriously. They had shared the election ticket with François Duvalier because he had stood as "the candidate of 1946," Dumarsias Estimé's successor; now they were no longer sure of Duvalier and the direction in which he was headed. They didn't want to be accomplices, in what they now sensed was a new dictatorship, and they tried without success to apply pressure on the president to act within the constitution.

They were further bothered by an incident that had proved to them that Duvalier had little or no esteem for the legislative branch. In late 1958 a legislative commission had gone to the palace seeking an audience with the president, only to be figuratively tossed out of the palace by an arrogant, bad-tempered young lieutenant of the presidential guard, Lt. Franck Romain. The rude and abusive treatment brought an outcry from the congressmen. They demanded an apology and asked that Romain be disciplined. Far from it! Duvalier, upon hearing of the young lieutenant's action, considered he had done the right thing and promoted him. Romain was one of the cadres of policemen who had been shifted to the palace after the election because of their sworn loyalty to Duvalier. These zealous young officers formed the hardcore of Duvalier's palace security and support and the president cultivated them as a mobster would his best triggermen.

There were more symptoms of Papa Doc's increasing paranoia and tightening fist. As the congressional dissension stirred, Duvalier decided that Venezuelan *charge d'affaires* Enrique Jose Miliani was too eager to grant asylum to the government's enemies. Doc declared

Miliani *persona non grata,* and the diplomat was soon on a plane back to Caracas.

Duvalier also ordered a close watch on students, who traditionally launch Haiti's anti-government process. When at the end of March 1959 the Lycée Pétion (along with the Lycée de Jeunes Filles) went out on strike, he announced that he had been forced to close the former – his old alma mater – because of "communist infiltration" in the faculty. He ordered the arrest of the school's principal, Marcel Gilbert. Duvalier knew that an ideological accommodation with the United States was a simple matter of painting his opponents as Communists.

In a surprising Cabinet shakeup in April, Duvalier dumped three loyal, hard-working ministers: Interior and National Defense Minister Frederic Duvigneaud, the man who had helped the president secure his rule; Father Jean-Baptiste Georges, who had been Haiti's first Roman Catholic priest to hold a cabinet post – that of education – and who had hidden Duvalier in the cleric's home during Doc's days in the underground; marquis (hiding) and Henri Marc Charles, agriculture minister, who had been a popular and influential employee of the U.S. Point Four's agriculture and rural education program, and who had garnered rural votes for Duvalier. The president called the trio "incapable." Gratitude was not Duvalier's strong point. In fact gratitude in politics, he often said, was cowardice.

A literacy campaign was launched on May Day, 1959 and Haitians learned that "DDD" stood for "Dieu" (God), "Dessalines" (hero of Haitian independence), and Duvalier. A sign that materialized before the workers' city on the edge of the capital, which had been built by ex-president Paul Magloire, further stated that God was the great worker of the Universe; Dessalines was the supreme artisan of liberty; and Duvalier –architect of the New Haiti. Duvalier's name was beginning to proliferate on roads and streets. To support the literacy campaign, $140,000 worth of stamps was issued.

CHAPTER 11

Barbudos and U.S. Marines

Meanwhile, Cuba's new Ambassador Rodríguez had returned to Port-au-Prince with his own four-man military mission. The bearded, neatly uniformed "diplomatic" contingent were veterans of Castro's guerrilla war and members of the new Cuban Revolutionary Army. Capt. Armando Torres, the new Cuban military attaché and his assistant, Capt. Luis Perez, led them. The two other Cuban soldiers were classified as their aides. Under normal diplomatic protocol, a military attaché assigned to an embassy would hardly go about armed to the teeth, as did the new Cuban envoys. But there was nothing normal about Haiti's existing situation, and Papa Doc didn't object, as he was still trying to court Castro.

A curious sight at the time was that of U. S. Marines sharing the sidewalk in front of La Belle Creole department store in downtown Port-au-Prince with Castro's officers. The Marines wore tropical colonial pith helmets and were unarmed, while the Cuban army officers in rakish black berets and olive-green uniforms, with matching ammo belts and holsters, carried submachine guns. The Cubans also packed holstered pistols with extra-long ammunition magazines and were reported to possess an assortment of hand grenades. (About this time, the commandant of the U.S. Marine Corps had declared the swagger stick obsolete. Colonel Heinl defied his superior's order and continued to carry a swagger stick throughout his Haiti assignment.)

Papa Doc was delighted to have the U.S. Marine Corps back in the palace. Following the formal dinner, he autographed a picture of the event for each of the American officers. (Courtesy of Col. James T. Breckinridge)

(The Dominican military attaché, Col. Luis Trujillo Reynoso, and his men were also armed and dangerous. However, they were careful not to flaunt their weapons. Dominican Spy Chief Johnny Abbes habitually carried a small arsenal along with him in the trunk of his car whenever he visited Haiti.)

And there was little doubt that Castro's contingent meant business. One night shortly after the arrival in Port-au-Prince of the Cuban Revolutionary Army attachés, there was an alert at the Cuban ambassador's residence. A small group of armed men probed the embassy grounds. The embassy barbudos in seconds fanned out into the garden in defensive positions prepared to repel the enemy. The intruders quickly fled.

Whereas the U.S. Marines were referred to by anti-Duvalierists as Papa Doc's *Tontons Makouts Blancs* ("white Tonton Makouts") radicalized Haitians worshipped the Cubans as revolutionary heroes. There was a strange feeling of elation among many young men in Port-au-Prince. They crowded around and watched every move of these famous guerrillas, members of the new Cuban Revolutionary Army. There was no question as to which of the two military contingents were the idols of Haitian youth. Fidel Castro had become an inspiration to the youth of Haiti as well as young Dominicans. At last there seemed an undercurrent of excitement that things were about to change. Some began to refer to it as liberation fever. Six months after Fidel Castro's success in Cuba, liberation fever gripped not only Hispaniola but also the republics of Central America.

Many Haitian exiles who had flocked to Cuba, looking back on their home soil, adopted what almost became a mantra among them: "If Fidel could do it, we can do it." They referred to the fact that Castro had managed to gain the Sierra Maestra with only a dozen followers, after eighty members of his landing force were killed or captured, and still go on to fight his way to victory. However, many exiles were to learn just how deadly liberation fever can become if the right conditions do not exist.

By mid-June 1959, the Caribbean was boiling. On June 12 Venezuela broke diplomatic relations with the Dominican Republic. That same day a small group of pro-Déjoie supporters in Haiti's pretty seaport town of Jacmel tried to emulate Castro by launching an attack on the military post guarding the little grass landing strip that served the town. They failed. But instead of fading into the nearby mountains to launch a guerrilla war, they fled into hiding in Port-au-Prince. Among this group was a twenty-year-old rural schoolteacher, Fred Baptiste, from an old Jacmel family, whose fight was just beginning. His brother Renal also participated in the attack and his wealthy uncle, Leon Baptiste, an important Jacmelian political figure and coffee speculator, was jailed along with other suspects. The Duvalier government announced that the assault was part of a plan which had been elaborated in Cuba and was suppose to coincide with the landing of an expedition whose departure from Oriente Province, Cuba, had been reported to the *New York Times* by its Havana correspondent, Ruby-Harts Philips.

A fragmentation grenade exploded on the night of June 14 at Port-au-Prince's International Casino waterfront open-air nightclub, killing four persons and injuring five. The culprit was not found.

CHAPTER 12

Papa Doc Is Dead?

During the spring of 1959, there were signs that it was going to be a very hot summer, in more ways than the weather. Political suspense grew as both sides of the island of Hispaniola waited for their respective exiles in Castro's Cuba to make good on their threats of invasion. In Haiti, Duvalier seethed with anger at his parliament for not doing his bidding, while students turned restless as the palace tightened the reigns of power. In the Dominican Republic, dictator Trujillo tightened his own screws on the Cuban embassy, which he suspected of subversion.

Covering the opening of the second session of Haiti's 38th Legislature in late April, I had to marvel at Papa Doc's thespian talent. A poor speaker, he read his prepared text but betrayed no hint of his fury at six parliamentarians who had dared to challenge him. Papa Doc gave them no telltale glances but his palace Makouts in attendance stared at the six-contrarian legislators.

Duvalier launched his speech promising a revolution that he declared would do nothing less than cure Haiti's many ills. "The Duvalierist revolution," he intoned, "your revolution!" However, already seventeen months into his scheduled six-year term, he pleaded that his revolution still needed time. (The talkative Lucien Daumec, who had become the president's brother-in-law after marrying First Lady Simone Duvalier's sister and acted as his private secretary, bragged that he had written Duvalier's speech.)

A friend of mine, Senator Yvon Emmanuel Moreau, then 39, who was also an Episcopal priest later told me privately that he was deeply troubled by Duvalier's autocratic drift. A Papa Doc partisan elected with his pro-government colleagues on the Duvalier ticket, Moreau could not see how Duvalier, without the necessary popular backing which the government lacked, in his limited constitutional time frame would possibly achieve any worthwhile changes let alone a revolution. Even Duvalier's political base, the middle-class, Moreau noted, was small and more divided than ever. The senator also worried that many of the president's circle appeared interested only in patronage — which in Haiti is traditionally bestowed by an election winner on his partisans allowing them to share the fruits of victory and furthering corruption.

The maintenance of order and public peace, which Duvalier referred to as "total security," had been, he said, his major worry, long before the events of July 28–29 of 1958 (failed filibuster invasion) thus he had not hesitated "to use the axe on the army, an institution" that had "lost the sense of its mission."

Papa Doc likewise bemoaned "the countless ills" afflicting Haitian society, "where inequalities reign and persist, where shameful exploitation of the ignorance of the great majority of our citizens has remained the sovereign rule . . . Such are the intrinsic factors of . . . more than a century and a half of a mode of life, which the Duvalierist revolution . . . intends to change, to overthrow and to destroy."

Once again he noted that Haiti was no longer just an island nation but there was need for the hemisphere to work together. And in a nod to Uncle Sam, Duvalier added: "I do not hesitate to affirm the choice of the people and of the Haitian Government in marching shoulder to shoulder with their great friends of the United States of America for better or for worse."

*   *   *

"Good night, Mr. Ambassador": That May Day evening, as I dined with a friend at Buteau's Rond Point restaurant, we witnessed an attempt on the life of the Cuban ambassador. The former butcher, Antonio Rodríguez, was parked across the street in his embassy Buick Roadmaster with his Haitian wife and pregnant daughter, receiving curb service from the Nobble-Bondel restaurant. In Haiti during those days, automobiles and their owners were still easily recognizable. The Dominican embassy Land Rover with diplomatic license plates cruised by and parked a short distance up Rue des Casernes. As we watched, a man alighted from the Land Rover and walked toward the Nobble-Bondel restaurant. Suddenly an explosion rocked our restaurant. It came from in front of the ambassador's car.

I rushed over to help if necessary; fortunately no one was hurt. I then interviewed Rodríguez, whose wife had restrained him from giving chase to the assailant and the Land Rover. The Cuban ambassador described his assailant as a Dominican. The man, Rodríguez said, had approached his car, greeted him with, *"Buenas noches, senor embajador,"* tossed an object into passenger side and hurried away. Rodríguez's reflexes averted tragedy. The ambassador recognized the object as a hand grenade that had literally landed in his lap, with the pin withdrawn. Scooping it up, he hurled it out the window against a wall. It exploded harmlessly.

"I know by the accent, he was definitely Dominican," the Cuban diplomat repeated. He likewise had little doubt that because the assailant had acted with such impunity on a well-lighted busy restaurant corner, the Haitian government was involved.

Partisans of Disaster: Haiti's important anniversary of Flag Day, May 18, had its principal celebration in the little town of Arcahaie, some thirty miles north of Port-au-Prince. Haiti's original flag had been born in Arcahaie 156 years earlier. Dutifully paying tribute, Duvalier visited the historic town, and as the presidential entourage walked across the town's square to a newly built rostrum, I photographed them. Papa Doc wore his traditional black fedora. Shepherding the group was Secret Police Chief Clément Barbot whose dark glasses hid his eyes but whose head movements and tight grip on his British-made Sten-gun made him appear akin to a leopard ready to pounce. As I snapped their photographs, I noted that Barbot's right forefinger was on the trigger.

Listening to the president's strong nasal voice carried over the town square by a loud speaker, even I found his words beautifully patriotic (even though they were tailored to the occasion by a speechwriter). Duvalier's speeches presented a perplexing problem for future researchers because while they often reflected a keen sense of Haiti's problems, they did not always reflect reality. They were likewise usually politically expedient. And some were pure demagoguery and untruths.

Papa Doc recalled the historic gesture when, in Arcahaie in 1803, Jean-Jacques Dessalines created the first Haitian flag by ripping the white from the French tricolors, and asking Haiti's version of Betsy Ross to sew the blue and red together. However, Duvalier already espoused changing the flag from the equal bands of blue and red placed horizontally, which symbolized the union between black and mulatto, back to the black and red flag standing up vertically. For the *noirists* the black band of the flag next to the mast symbolized that the blacks, the most numerous were also the most powerful. Following Dessalines' assassination, when the nation was divided, King Henry Christophe in the north continued with the black and red flag while President Alexandre Pétion in the south chose the blue and red flag. Duvalier in 1964 felt powerful enough to change the flag back to black and red. His act only exacerbated the country's deeply ingrained tensions between those of different skin shades. Nevertheless, in his Flag Day address, Papa Doc called on his countrymen "to remember the 'Old Haiti' which, taking inspiration from the respect of God, was able to grow by conscious labor, by unfailing courage and an ardent love for the fatherland." Duvalier went on to refer to "the grandiose and perilous task of the nation after eighteen months of battle with itself and with . . . the partisans of disaster."

As then, however, such exhortations were falling on deaf ears. The country's youth and even some of Doc's own partisans saw him heading for disaster. Resistance to his rule was growing. Students were agitating. Two newly-founded clandestine Marxist parties were competing for popular favor with an anti-government Catholic cell working out of Petit Seminaire St. Martial. Threats of invasion by Haitian exiles from Cuba were real. Random exploding bombs were now a regular nightly occurrence in the once-tranquil capital of Port-au-Prince.

The rainy season had begun in earnest. Tropical downpours hammered the mountains sending avalanches of mud (mostly precious topsoil) into the city and sea. There were the usual casualties. Poor people who had built their makeshift huts in ravines were washed away along with their meager possessions. And more and more Haitians, eyeing the increasingly isolated National Palace, wondered who the real "partisans of disaster" were.

A CIA Party: Yet in the *Haiti Sun* we did our best not to allow politics to dominate our columns. Haitian jazz trumpeter Alfonse Simon was making a name for himself in New York. International celebrities continued to visit, albeit less often. Columnist Drew Pearson ("Washington Merry-Go-Round") dropped by the *Sun* office and asked to be briefed. I was becoming more and more cautious about talking to visiting colleagues. When Stanley Meisler of The Associated Press, who dropped by the *Haiti Sun* after visiting Cuba, asked, "What's new?" "Nothing," I replied. I didn't wish to be a source for every newsman who visited Haiti. One misquote could lead to tragedy.

Moreover, politics had not unduly affected Haiti's always-active social scene. Cocktails and dinner parties continued. One May evening, I attended one of the many farewell cocktail parties for Rudolph Landreth and his pretty wife. The other half of Mutt-and-Jeff, a local CIA team, tall, curly-headed Robert Frambrini was hosting the social event. Frambrini's wife was known for her superb Italian cooking. It was a strange gathering as it was no secret that Landreth was the Central Intelligence Agency's first station chief in Port-au-Prince, but everyone was pretending that he was only an embassy political officer.

As I munched on Mrs. Frambrini's scrumptious canapés, a U.S.

embassy political officer approached and asked a now-familiar question: "As a newsman, what do you think of our Marine Mission?" Clearing my throat, I replied that while the Marines were a wonderful body of men, and I had personally known members of the Marine first division who trained in New Zealand for their first attack on the Japanese at Guadacanal, theirs was a "Mission Impossible" in Haiti. Col. Robert Debs Heinl, the mission's commander, and several other Marine officers were in attendance. Noting their white dress uniforms, I asked the political officer if he was aware that the Marines were known among Haitians as Tontons Makouts Blanc (in this case, white Makouts). Even illiterate Haitians, I told him, knew that Papa Doc was using the Marines as a sideshow to warn his opposition that the powerful United States was on his side.

Unhappy with my assessment, the embassy official responded with a curt rebuttal: "You think like a Haitian." "Thanks," I replied. "I take that as a compliment!" Irritated, the diplomat walked away, adding over his shoulder an old colonial phrase: "You have been here too long."

Indeed, by now I considered Haiti my home. And as publisher of a Haitian newspaper, my loyalty was to my readers who were mostly Haitian.

Diplomatic Gift: At the time my principal sources in the diplomatic community were the representatives of Argentina, Venezuela and Cuba. All had an anti-Duvalier bent and thus were more willing to share sensitive information. One night, the three diplomats spent the evening at my home discussing Papa Doc. Before leaving, the Argentine charge d'affaires, Frederico Massot, asked whether I was armed to defend myself. "No, I am a journalist. I have no weapons nor will I carry one." On the morning tray of coffee and orange juice lay a nasty-looking .45-cal automatic pistol. "The ambassador left it for you," Ti Frère, my housekeeper, informed me. "Quick, bury the damn thing," I instructed Ti Frère. I never asked where he buried it.

The U.S. Marines had settled into their training NCOs and new recruits principally at Caserne Dessalines and the NCO Camp Lamantin on the coast, south of Port-au-Prince where the manatees once existed peacefully. But in those early days, the Marines complained privately that, "nothing was routine." Colonel Williamson was later to write in his book on the mission that the Dessalines barracks resembled more like an "ill-tended barnyard than a military post." The army had provided the Marine (Naval) Mission with the second floor of the Chrysler Building on the Champ de Mars. On the ground floor was an empty automobile showroom. The building itself was well located, a brief walk from the Haitian army headquarters, National Palace and the American embassy. Once settled in his office, Col. Robert Debs Heinl Jr. launched into a campaign to rearm Duvalier's troops. He privately described the Haitian army as being in "shocking state." All but hardened Duvalierists wish it would remain in that state. However, Heinl had a job to do and his frontal attack often dismayed Haitians. In interview after interview with the foreign media, Heinl made his pitch. He was a gracious host, as was his wife Nancy, at their lovely rented home in the hills close by the Hotel Montana with a splendid panoramic view of the city below. They had a lovely blonde daughter, Pamela, and a son, Michael whom the colonel appeared to treat like a Marine recruit. "Michael, stop flat-hatting!" Heinl once snapped to his son while the boy was romping on their verandah.

A congenial language instructor James L. Oberstar (in 1974 he was elected congressman for the eighth district of Minnesota) arrived under contract with the U.S. Navy on loan from the English Language Services in Washington to teach members of the Naval Mission French. He also taught Haitian army officers at the Military Academy English and in no time, was himself speaking Krèyol.

The arrival of note, Prof. Sydney Mintz, an anthropologist from Yale University, was with fewer fanfares but nevertheless very important, as his studies into the culture of Haitian market women were to prove. The thirty-six-year-old Mintz had already published an enormous amount of material in academic journals on the peoples and cultures of the Caribbean and Latin America. He had been accepted as a *bon blan* by the *marchandes* (market women) of Fonds des Negres, an important market town in the Southwest as well as by the

Haiti Sun. Professor Mintz's engaging essays on market women soon filled columns of the *Haiti Sun.*

Journalist Aubelin Jolicoeur had begun to write a regular column for the *Haiti Sun* covering mostly passenger arrivals and departure by both ships and planes. To their delight, Aubelin, with his liberal use of adverbs and adjectives, turned ordinary tourists into VIPs.

Chicoms & the FBI: One day, while emptying my post office box, I was surprised to find a coarse brown envelope, its faded red Peking postmark barely visible. The *Haiti Sun* had become the recipient of free English-language dispatches from *Xinhua,* the New China News Service – official news agency of the Communist regime of mainland China. Regularly, the brown envelopes arrived at my post office box from Red China.

Chairman Mao's English-language service supplied us with photographs of sporting events and important accomplishment of the Communist regime. As we published only Haitian news, the material was unusable. My only possible explanation for receiving it was that a fellow New Zealander, Rewi Alley, teacher and writer and an old-time "China hand," might have put me on Xinhua's list. No one at the Port-au-Prince post office or in the Haitian government appeared to have become aware of the brown envelopes. If they had I was sure someone would use the mailing against me, accusing me of being a Maoist.

As the *New York Times* wanted to see some of the China sports photography of table tennis that I had recently received from Peking, I asked a female colleague from *LIFE* magazine heading home to New York to carry a packet of the pictures to the *Times*. On the evening of her departure, I received a distress call came from San Juan, Puerto Rico. The U.S. Federal Bureau of Investigation had apprehended my courier in San Juan with the Chinese Communist photographs. The woman was extremely upset. A quick call to the *Times*'s foreign editor, Manny Freedman, to intercede with the FBI did the trick; both my female courier and the photographs were released and I heard no more on the matter. In June, in an effort quite frankly to clear the *Haiti Sun* and me with the FBI of any suspicion, I ran a complimentary profile by Hearst columnist Bob Considine on the FBI under its powerful controversial director J. Edgar Hoover. In an editorial after the profile, we noted that my newspaper and I had been honored by a personal letter from J. Edgar Hoover commending us for our effective reporting on an U.S. citizen "involved in the traffic of dope." The *Haiti Sun*'s publication of the unusual FBI story convinced some Haitians that their suspicions were correct, that I was indeed a FBI agent. There was always a need in Haiti, with its ambient blend of suspicion and doubt, to believe that someone was something other than he was.

No Rubber Stamp: Meanwhile, the Haitian senate continued to try to carry out their role as solons. They endeavored to apply checks and balances to Papa Doc's rule, challenging his cabinet members as deeming necessary when they came before parliament. Cabinet members, the senators pointed out, were required by the constitution to explain their actions to the representatives of the people. Sen. Candelon Lucas, from the famine-wrecked Northwest, demanded to know what was happening to food aid earmarked for his thousands of starving people. He was particularly sarcastic about the government's delivery of famine relief: fifty bags of peas. The two-year plan of the six-member economic board, known as the Grand Conseil Technique, collapsed after senators criticized and ridiculed it. For Duvalier, angry, tired and overworked and suffering from diabetes, the political pressure was reaching the breaking point.

A surrealistic atmosphere had descended on the capital. In the capital, a new and dangerous novelty was the flaring up in pre-dawn darkness of flaming Molotov cocktails thrown at pro-Duvalier targets. Deep in the narrow passageways of Bel Air, Fignolists huddled together in certain huts at night to hear, "midnight Mass," as they called exile Krèyol-language radio broadcasts over Cuba's Radio Progreso and Venezuela's Radio Continente. It was a risky pastime inviting possible death. A well-known Fignolist labor leader speaking from Caracas called for outright revolt. A Krèyol-speaker in Havana promised: "political freedom and social advances. Why should ninety percent of the Haitian people continue to be illiterate? Nothing is being done to change this shameful situation."

Haitians who hadn't smiled for months were buoyed by talk of a biological solution — Duvalier's imminent death from natural causes. (A conjecture that proved highly premature.) Invasion rumors increased. There seemed to be no end of anti-government leaflets that literally fluttered through the capital; new ones were on my desk virtually every morning. The anti-government mimeographed tracts carried high-sounding letterheads: *Bureau General Pour Coordination du Mouvement Insurrectionnel de Liberation.* The MIL declared: "Fignolists! Arm yourselves and be ready!". . . Long live Haiti free of Duvalier and Trujillo." One night leaflets appeared tossed from an automobile, urging, "Patriots, fight the Duvalier clique. Hit them hard!"

Students were preparing to eventually face Duvalier. They had won their first round when fifty-one of the fifty-three teachers at Lycée Pétion, the president's old alma mater, had gone on strike. It was the jailing of Marcel Gilbert, the legendary school's principal and president of the National Union of Secondary School Teachers, that touched off the threat of a nationwide teachers' strike. Duvalier backed down and released Gilbert after a forty-eight hours' detention. The students and Duvalierist were now on a collision course.

Papa Doc Is Dead?: On Monday morning, May 24, 1959, I had arrived at my office early and was in the act of writing a letter to Peter Kihss at the *New York Times*, when a friend arrived with word that that Duvalier was ill and may have died. I closed my letter to Kihss telling him of the rumor and wondering if Papa Doc had taken the medicine he so recently had offered us to rid us of our colds.

Suddenly the town was filled with rumors. Duvalier had attended the wedding of the Port-au-Prince police chief, Col. Daniel Beauvoir, on the preceding Saturday night. Late Sunday night or early Monday morning, he had reportedly suffered a heart attack, or some other physical collapse, and was said to be gravely ill — lingering between life and death, perhaps paralyzed. However, no one knew for sure. As the rumors multiplied, ever-suspicious Haitians even suggested it was a political booby trap: Duvalier was feigning illness to flush out overly ambitious Duvalierist rivals who sought his job. By nightfall, he was supposedly dead. However, no Haitian newspaper rushed to prepare his obituary. It was prudent to be extremely cautious. In the streets, the Makouts became noticeably less arrogant. They were obviously worried about their own health if in fact Papa Doc had died.

Finally in the early afternoon, a medical bulletin signed by Dr. Jacques Fourcand, one of Duvalier's physicians and head of the Haitian Red Cross, announced that the president was "progressively recovering from an attack of the grippe [influenza]." All eyes continued to be focused on the palace. It was worth a motorist's life to blow his car horn in the palace vicinity.

"Grippe Confines President," was our front-page headline. The government communiqué on Duvalier's condition intoned that "this is the first time in eighteen months of working almost around the clock that President Duvalier has been ailing." But the palace had a credibility problem. Few if any Haitians by this time believed any official statement. "*Yo manje li.*" "They ate him" was the reaction of many typical Haitians who concluded that Duvalier had been a victim of malevolent magic.

No official report on what actually transpired has ever been published. However, from sources close to the palace, we did learn the following: On Sunday night, Duvalier, a diabetic, had gone into a hypoglycemic coma, a condition caused by extremely low blood sugar level due to the fact he took his insulin without eating. Dr. Jacques Fourcand, called to the palace, reportedly made a mistaken diagnosis of his condition. He administered a massive insulin shot, which provoked a moderately severe coronary occlusion. Papa Doc remained in a coma. The palace was in a state of panic. Mrs. Duvalier prayed. Secret Police Chief Barbot, who had only recently recovered from a bout of malaria, had rushed to Papa Doc's side. When he found the president unconscious, "he cried like a baby," Fosy Laham, one of Barbot's Haitian-Lebanese associates, recounted this to the author.

Barbot called in Dr. Jean Bartoly, a general practitioner, son of a Corsican immigrant. When told that Duvalier needed glucose, to offset the insulin shot, Barbot screeched at high speed through the darkened capital to the Castera pharmacy. It was closed. Breaking in, the secret police chief loaded up on glucose. Even after glucose was administered, Duvalier continued in a coma. Two top Haitian cardiologists, Alix Theard and Gerald Desir, were called. Barbot was reported ready to shoot Dr. Fourcand, on suspicion that the brilliant U.S.-trained neurosurgeon couldn't make such a life-threatening mistake. Another physician also present was likewise suspicious of Fourcand's action and confided the fact to Madame Simone.

Barbot had quickly alerted U.S. Ambassador Gerald Drew of the president's grave condition. The ambassador called Colonel Heinl. According to Col. Charles T. Williamson, USMC, in his book, *The U.S. Naval Mission to Haiti 1959-6*, Heinl took prompt action. Within hours, an U.S. Navy cardiac team was en route by air to Port-au-Prince from the U.S. naval base at Guantánamo Bay, Cuba. Fortunately for Duvalier, Commander Jack T. Jones, USN/MC, executive officer of the naval hospital at Guantánamo, headed the team. "He was a cardiac specialist and was available to treat Duvalier as an attending physician," recounts Williamson in his book. "Duvalier was in a coma for nine hours before the U.S. Navy team of specialists resuscitated him," according to the account published by Col. Williamson. On Thursday, May 28, four days after Papa Doc was stricken, Doctors D. Kispel and Lawrence Cone, two New York diagnosticians, arrived from New York to examine the patient.

With the strong-willed Duvalier fighting for his life in his second-floor east wing palace bedroom, which had been turned into a hospital room, the strong-willed Barbot stepped into his shoes and ensured continuous one-man rule from the palace. The new Minister of Interior and National Defense, Jean A. Magloire, was technically in charge of running the government and became head of a Ministerial Counsel. But he dared not cross Barbot and spent his time signing papers.

Words to Bullets: On the night of June 6, 1959, Barbot left the patient to go out and allegedly shoot the Cuban ambassador. It was reportedly a cross-border collaboration between Barbot and his Dominican counterpart, Johnny Abbes Garcia. Both sides knew that invasions of Haiti and the Dominican Republic by exiles in Cuba were imminent. They presumed that the Cuban embassies in both Ciudad Trujillo and Port-au-Prince were actively involved in preparing the terrain. On the same Saturday of the grenade attack in Port-au-Prince on Cuban ambassador Rodríguez, a mob attack on the Cuban embassy in the Dominican capital had been staged. Two persons were killed during the melee and one wounded.

Footnote: Jean-Magloire, a longtime journalist, a mulatto and no relation to the former president, Magloire, was of small stature and belonged to the Anglican Church. In 1931 he had accused Duvalier in print of plagiarism – more specifically, of lifting lines from French thinker and essayist Ernest Renan. Magloire, in his own newspaper *Oedipe*, wrote that Duvalier had cited Renan without quoting him. Duvalier counter attacked in *La Presse* and a polemic ensued as "*An affair of plagiarism.*" Duvalier ingenuously explained that he admired the lines of the French writer so much that he knew them by heart, which would justify the absence of quotation marks. An Estimeist, Magloire was loyal and not known to make waves.

Personally, Barbot detested Antonio Rodríguez whom the secret police chief had once jailed in Rodríguez's earlier political life as a rabid Jumelle supporter. Rodríguez had won his revolutionary spurs against a tough and bloody Cuban dictator, President Gerardo Machado (1925–33). Now enjoying diplomatic immunity, he was blatantly active on behalf of Castro's revolutionary regime. (A year earlier, Barbot had tried to locate the transmitter of an anti-Duvalier clandestine Radio Liberty. He had failed to find it, even with the help of U.S. Navy ships tracking equipment. In fact the small radio transmitter with a not very strong signal was operated out of an upstairs room of Rodríguez' Oso Blanco butcher shop, across from the National Palace.)

Early Saturday morning, June 7, I received news of a new attack on the Cuban ambassador. The story as published in the *Haiti Sun*:

The Cuban Ambassador Antonio Rodríguez Echazabal narrowly escaped death early Saturday morning when gunmen ambushed him at the entrance to his Bourdon home.

The gunmen, firing submachine guns, wounded the chauffeur, Celhomme Pierre, in the head, shoulders and stomach and the ambassador's Buick was riddled with 52 bullet holes. The chauffeur is still in critical condition at the Canapé Vert hospital.

Wearing a bloodstained suit, Saturday morning at eight, the ambassador refused to make a statement saying he was in touch with his foreign office in Havana.

He was believed to have fought off the assailants with his automatic pistol. Three empty magazine clips were noted on the back seat of the window-shattered automobile. Señor Celestino Fernandez Suarez, former coordinator of the *26th of July Movement* [Fidel Castro's original group] in the Caribbean and newly designated head of the Cuban Sugar Workers Retirement Fund, was nicked in the right arm by a bullet.

Sr. Fernandez, who spent a week here, returned to Havana by Delta Airlines in the afternoon lucky to be alive. He gave all the credit to cool, courageous old-timer Ambassador Rodríguez who it was hinted mortally wounded one of his attackers who were believed to have numbered a dozen and traveling in three vehicles. Interior Minister Jean Magloire, chief of the Ministerial Council, made a call on the ambassador and presented his regrets and sympathies. Army General Staff officers and Police Chief Daniel Beauvoir visited the residence and examined the bullet-punctured automobile.

Later that day, Rodríguez had to have his gun hand tightly bandaged because he had sprained his wrist using his .45-pistiol to ward off the attackers. That evening Cuban State Minister Roberto Agramonte recalled Rodriguez to Havana to give a first-hand report of the attempt on his life. The chiefs of foreign diplomatic missions residing in Haiti called a meeting and charged its dean, British Ambassador Sydney Simmonds, to hand their formal protest to the Haitian foreign minister.

The gravity of Haiti's political situation aside, all of these events made for compelling news in the *Haiti Sun*. Under a banner headline on the attack on the Cuban ambassador, I carried photographs I had taken that Saturday morning of Rodriguez still in coat and loosened tie, and Fernandez in shirt sleeves before their shattered automobile. Another front-page story was the unprovoked beating of a hapless tourist guide, Carl Henri Fombrun, by Army Lt. Jean Tassy. Fombrun was dragged to Ft. Dimanche prison and charged with refusing to dance a meringue that sang the praise of President Duvalier at the International Casino.

Under the fold, on the front page of the same issue of the *Haiti Sun* smaller item: "U.S. Envoy Sees President: President Duvalier received Ambassador Gerald Drew of the United States in a brief audience Monday (June 8). The envoy reported he had found the president in good spirits. Rumors about the president's health have been circulating increasingly since he was stricken May 25 with what the Ministry of Information described as grippe."

Drew later said that Duvalier had requested some movies including one of President Eisenhower's inauguration.

Inside, sharing page six was a story that Caribbean Mills (Murchison Flour Mill) had offered to give the town of Cabaret an electric generating plant. (This pretty little town soon disappeared and was replaced by a concrete monstrosity called Duvalierville.)

The edition of Tuesday, June 9, 1959, was to be the last edition of the *Haiti Sun* for five months. The final edition of my newspaper before it went into a forced eclipse carried an editorial commemorating Freedom of the Press Day.

Eclipse of the *Haiti Sun*: For the ordinary Haitian, *"L'Etat"* (The State) is an all-powerful tyrant. The common saying is "After God, the State!" In Haiti, L'Etat traditionally preys on its citizens like vultures on the defenseless. There is no recourse. An official document from L'Etat with its threatening black typewritten script on flimsy paper and names of half a dozen government lawyers ready to pounce, is designed to put the fear of God into the average citizen whose name, like mine, was often misspelled. And the paper with which the recipient is served is in a language the majority of Haitians do not understand: French.

It was in June 1959 that I experienced the average Haitian citizen's fear and frustration of being literally hit by L'Etat! I was served not once but three times with demands for payment of supposedly outstanding bills owed the state, under the threat of six months in jail for non-payment. The written demands were no love letters.

It began on June 11 when *L'Imprimerie de L'Etat* (the State Printing Office, conveniently located next to the National Penitentiary) demanded payment of $975.00. The State Printing Office published *Le Moniteur*, the official gazette, and also solicited private printing jobs. For several years I had been a good customer and used their presses to publish the *Haiti Sun*. The contract stipulated weekly printing payments and they were made in cash. At the time there were only two banks in Haiti, the State Bank and Royal Bank of Canada, and cash rather than checks was the main method of payment. Mrs. Laporte – an American married to Justice Christian Laporte – the *Haiti Sun*'s capable and efficient office secretary had all the payment receipts.

We protested the State Printing Office's claim and presented proof of payment to no avail. While the disputed payments were being argued, my contact was pronounced null and void. The door was shut. With no other presses available, the *Haiti Sun* abruptly ceased publication. Readers couldn't even be informed of the shutdown, as the edition of June 9th was our last. However, when delivery ceased suddenly, they understood.

On June 24, the first of three documents arrived from the *Directeur General des Contributions* (the ineffable French term for taxes). The official Tax Office document stated that as proprietor of the *Haiti Sun* I was to pay $975.00 to the Tax Office, owed to the State Printing

Office, without delay. On the advice of my lawyer and over my protests I paid $500.00 (cash) on June 25 to the Tax Office and was allowed time to pay the purported balance. On July 7, to the surprise of my lawyer and me, the Tax Office sent a new demand to pay $975.00, the same amount, and threatened me with six months in prison for non-payment. There was an added 1,000 gourdes ($200.000 added to the bill for so-called "dommages" – damages and interest).

On July 30 we received yet another bill that displayed a flare for the imaginary even by bureaucrats. This outlandish Tax Office document stated that the *Haiti Sun* owed an additional $503.00 for unpaid printing at the defunct, government confiscated daily *Le National* during December 1956. Complete invention. I had, at a time, published at *Le National*, but not during the period they specified.

It had always been my practice to pay all taxes, patents and even income tax — which some wealthy Haitians ignored. It appeared that the *Haiti Sun* had displeased a person or persons of the regime in power and the squeeze was on. One possibly explanatory case was the following.

The month before, in early May, an expatriate American named Atherton Lee had come to the *Haiti Sun* literally fuming with anger and indignation. Lee had established, in the mountains near the holiday village of Kenscoff above Port-au-Prince, the Chatelet des Fleurs, a plant nursery and flower-growing business. His story was that after attending the New York Flower Show where he had won an international trophy for his Kenscoff flowers, he had returned to learn that vandals had wantonly pulled out some two acres of his flowers and seedbeds. Lee had been a trustworthy source in the past and several persons in Kenscoff confirmed his account. He had given a similar version to the French-language newspaper, *Haiti Journal*. In publishing the article under the headline, "Flower Farm Hit By Vandals," we made several errors. We regretted not having interviewed the individuals cited by Lee; nor had we attributed the vandalism accusations to him as our source, and put his charges in quotes.

Our story stated that, "the most incongruous feature was that the vandalism was directed by a Justice of the Peace, Rene Raphael, and an employee of the Department of Information and Coordination, one Michel Auguste." The story continued:

> Lee says he buys land when he can and also has long 18-year leases for other gardens. There was litigation for ownership of some of the leased lands, which did not concern him, and this atrocity was on land in litigation. The irony of the deed was that some of the flowers that gained the International Trophy were produced on the lands where this wanton destruction took place.
>
> President Duvalier, appreciating that such an act of vandalism on investments of a foreign enterprise will kill off such foreign investment, payrolls and employment for years to come, has directed that the lands be restored to the leaseholder of Chatelet des Fleurs according to contract, and quick indemnification is expected in government bonds for the vandalism by public officials.
>
> Chatelet des Fleurs has an investment of $125,000 in land and its gardens and in the relatively short life of the company has brought revenues of $500,000 US to the small town of Kenscoff.
>
> Employment, which was suspended immediately following the vandalism by Government employees, will be resumed with completion of the indemnification negotiations.
>
> The *Haiti Sun* wonders what punishment will be meted out to the men who dared to abuse, using the cover of their functions to perpetrate such an atrocity.

It was the *Haiti Sun* that was punished. We had stuck our neck out just a little too far. In the following edition, we published a correction issued by lawyer Michael C. Auguste, who vehemently denied the facts as presented by Lee. Auguste said that he had been at Kenscoff as a lawyer representing the owner of the land, and that the justice of the peace was there to see that the land was returned to its owner.

Auguste accused the *Sun* of defending the interests "of one of their own." "Consistent with the press law which requires that a rebuttal must appear in the same space in the newspaper," he wrote and we published, "I have noted the great care with which you have chosen to name only government employees as the sole authors of this false act of vandalism."

As for the government, while Papa Doc appeared to tolerate the *Haiti Sun* (we published English-language translations of his speeches) many of his underlings did not. Being basically in English, the *Haiti Sun* had more leeway as it was seen as an instrument in the promotion of tourism. Duvalierists were no different to their predecessors. If you are not with me, you are my enemy. No political middle existed. But as I had been booted out by Dejoie in 1957 the bullies tolerated me a little more than others.

The Tax Office squeeze had come at a difficult juncture. Over the years, while having to print the *Haiti Sun* elsewhere under contract, I had managed to build my own print shop behind the editorial office on property on which I had a 99-year lease.

Purchasing printing machinery had been a slow process. By the end of 1958 I had located a good second-hand Linotype in New York for $4,300. Even my savings from my "stringing" work for American and British publications did not suffice to cover the costs. An American friend, Harold Connery (his wonderful Connecticut family had invited me to their home while passing through New York during World War II), owner of the Georgetown, Connecticut, general store stepped in and guaranteed a partial loan to purchase the machine from the Manhattan Linotype Supply Company.

Thus, one of my most exciting days occurred in January 1959 when the *SS Cristobal*, a combined passenger-freight ship of the Panama Line (operated by the Panama Canal Company), serving New York and Panama with calls at Port-au-Prince, arrived with a large crate addressed to the *Haiti Sun*. The crate contained my precious Linotype machine. (It would take until the end of 1959 to locate a Kelly B automatic printing press at the General Printing Equipment and Supply Co. in Miami, Florida for the handsome price of $1,690 and make my newspaper completely self-sufficient.) In the mean-while, with my linotype I could at least prepare each issue of the newspaper in my own shop and print it on another press. From *La Phalange*, the Catholic daily, I had purchased an ancient but effective guillotine weighing more than a ton. It was a superb paper cutter.

In the end, I reluctantly paid the Tax Office the total amount in installments. I recall that when I paid the last installment, in cash, the recipient at the Tax Office, smiling to himself, put the money in his pocket.

While I kept our editorial office open and staffed during the *Sun*'s hiatus, I suffered grief at not being able to publish. However, it may have been for the good; with Barbot and his Makouts out of control, those were highly unpredictable times. I might have been forced to challenge them in the *Haiti Sun* with unforeseen consequences. With no newspaper of my own to publish all my efforts for the ensuing four months, I went into reporting for news outlets abroad. Every penny I earned from being a resident Haiti correspondent saved to defray the cost of purchasing my own printing press. And there was a lot of news to report with the Caribbean Cold War moving into the shooting stage.

CHAPTER 13

Resurrecting Papa Doc

My angered at being forced to close the *Haiti Sun* quickly abated because in June 1959 I had a month filled with major stories for foreign media. I was also convinced that the closure of my newspaper would be temporary – as everything seemed surreally kaleidoscopic in Haiti that summer. Called upon to cover one crisis after another not only in Haiti but also in the Dominican Republic, I had little time to mull over my loss; in fact, reporting and interpreting news stories from Port-au-Prince and Ciudad Trujillo served as an antidote to my frustration at not being able to publish my newspaper.

The only way I found to straddle both sides of an island firmly in the grip of violent dictatorships was to routinely meet the daily flight from Ciudad Trujillo and "interview travelers" passing through Port-au-Prince. As for covering Haiti itself, I must concede how different our coverage in the *Haiti Sun* was from the foreign news stories I reported. Looking back today at my yellowing bound copies of the *Haiti Sun* and comparing the content with my stories published abroad, I am reminded of the lamentable but unavoidable content. Like other Haitian publications, the *Haiti Sun* reflected prudent self-censorship. Publish and perish applied to any newspaper that stepped too far out of line. However, we often used code words and subtle double-entendres to communicate what was really happening. Although from time to time I did write some obliquely critical editorials — and the fact that they were in English buffered us somewhat — we all knew where the line began and ended. For instance no one dared to speculate negatively in print about the state of Duvalier's health. Nor could anyone publish a straw poll on just how many, including ambitious Duvalierists, wished him dead. There were relatively few who wanted him to survive.

One major impediment to reporting under a Port-au-Prince dateline was getting the news out. By now the new telex machine had arrived to replace the old cable method of transmitting abroad. Sometimes employees at the local RCA office would allow me to type out my stories on their telex machines that had a keyboard much like a typewriter. Once the story was transmitted, friendly employees destroyed the original copy and tape. Army censors checking outgoing messages would find no press reports. Another way was to "pigeon" the story abroad by a trusted airline passenger or, on rare occasions, a pilot, steward or stewardess who, against regulations, would carry a "mailer" and see that it got to New York.

Writing from his Mexico City base, Paul Kennedy of the *New York Times* said in a letter: "I've been intending to send this along to you all these days and have just now gotten around to it. Thought you'd like to see how Mexico's biggest paper treats the editor of Haiti's biggest paper. I would certainly appreciate getting a note from you on your evaluation of the situation. Meanwhile all remembrances to Laura and Roger [of the Hotel Oloffson] when you see them and all best fortune to you." (My AP dispatches had made the front page of *Excelsior,* Mexico's leading daily newspaper.)

While Kennedy thought I would be happy to see the play my stories received, I was only too aware of the risk. Fortunately, the AP was the only media outlet to use my correspondent's byline. The other publications for which I reported did not. I subsequently became much more cautious in my AP reporting. Meanwhile as Haiti's crisis deepened, interest among foreign publications intensified and my workload increased commensurately.

When the news first seeped out of the palace that Papa Doc was alive but gravely ill, some of his Haitian opponents tried to invoke the *lwas* (gods) to push him over the edge. A *Time* Magazine story to that effect appeared in the Hemisphere section of the June 18, 1959 issue. In colorful *Time* style, the article – written in New York and based on my surreptitious dispatches – reported that Duvalier had suffered a heart attack after he had worn himself out with a succession of twenty-hour days at his desk, and also that he had just turned fifty and was fighting both diabetes and high blood pressure. The President's enemies, *Time* declared, "went after what was supposed to be one of the strongest *oungas* (spells*)*: the grave of his father who died last year. Grave robbers pried open the above-ground family tomb in Port-au-Prince's cemetery, hauled out the coffin, defiled the body. The outrage was kept secret from the bedridden President."

Indeed Papa Doc's enemies had cut out Duval Duvalier's heart and smeared his corpse with human excrement. The desecration bore all the trappings of black magic, the work of a *bòkò* (witchdoctor*)*. In fact, the men who stole into the cemetery late at night to perform their strange deed were the most unlikely witchdoctors. They included a prominent Déjoie partisan who detested Vodou and later confessed that he had learned all he knew about black magic from Hollywood movies. The culprits were not caught but one of the ringleaders was to die in a Duvalier prison. However, he was not accused of black magic but of more worldly misdeeds – being anti-Duvalier.

A week after Papa Doc's near-death crisis one of my more sensitive sources – a palace photographer who secretly sold me an occasional photo and whose confidence I assiduously protected – told me that Papa Doc was still alive. I decided to wait for the official resurrection. The most improbable witness to that miracle was Paul Kennedy. The Duvalierists, including Papa Doc, considered the *New York Times* correspondent to be an enemy as they decided he was pro-Déjoie. One day Kennedy advised me by open cable from San Jose, Costa Rica that he would be arriving for a reporting visit. (From San Jose, Kennedy had reported on June 12, "Nicaraguan Revolt Shakes Somoza Dynasty." Dictator Tachito Somoza's regime was putting down an invasion by a rebel band that had landed by plane and taken on Somoza's Nicaraguan National Guard.)

At Bowen Field airport, I was caught by surprise when a palace officer stepped forward and led Paul Kennedy away. I was left holding his bottle of Barbancourt rum. Fearing the worst I followed the presidential automobile.

When it turned into the National Palace grounds, I anxiously drove on to the Oloffson to await the outcome of what appeared to be an official kidnapping. Not long afterward, a jaunty Kennedy arrived at the grand old hotel in the presidential limousine. The barrel-chested Kennedy was laughing his head off and could barely talk until after barman Cesar had handed the correspondent his second Barbancourt rum on the rocks. Continuing to shake with laughter, Kennedy explained: "The goddamndest thing happened. They picked me up and drove me to the palace. I thought I was in deep shit. They escorted me into the presidential chamber and there was Papa Doc propped up in bed. He was cordial and said he was happy to meet me. It then dawned on me that I was to report to the world that the old bastard was still alive!"

Following his celebratory libations at the Oloffson, Kennedy sat down at his battered old typewriter and did just that. He wrote:

> This reporter was met at the Haiti airport by an army colonel   and taken directly to the National Palace. With no explanation he was ushered into the presidential apartments and warned not to ask any questions of the stricken president. He was taken into Duvalier's bedroom and allowed to shake hands with the president and talk briefly. It was apparent then that the gesture, this first visit of a newspaperman, was primarily to head off swiftly accumulating rumors. The president was in good spirits and joked about his struggle with his medical staff to keep him in bed. The president is a physician himself. Dr. Jacques Fourcand, his chief physician, said it is difficult to keep the president from getting out of bed but thus far he had been successful in this and in a lesser degree to keep him from attending to any political duties.

Interestingly, it was also the first confirmation that Dr. Fourcand still had the confidence of the president in spite of Fourcand's original incorrect diagnosis, which was said to have nearly caused Papa Doc's death.

Kennedy's story ran in the *New York Times* on Sunday, June 14, 1959, headlined: "Haiti Faces Crisis As Economy Slips and Intrigue Rises." The front-page article story was not one to please Duvalier. Kennedy's lead paragraph noted that, with its chief of state critically ill, Haiti "is torn by internal and international intrigue." In addition, the correspondent wrote, the country "is on the verge of bankruptcy. The long history of graft in public places and inept administration has caught up with the country."

Kennedy added: "The nation is being run by a cabinet while the president is bedridden," noting that Duvalier's illness couldn't have come at a more critical time as the country was faced with "the smallest coffee crop in years [and] the economy is bumping along on bedrock." (Coffee accounted for about two-thirds of Haiti's foreign exchange and about one-fourth of the government's revenue.) The U.S. administration, Kennedy reported, had given Duvalier an outright grant of six million dollars. In a follow-up story, the *New York Times* published an analysis, also written by Paul Kennedy of Haiti's budget problems.

Duvalier utilized other ploys to prove that he was still in this world. Col. Charles T. Williamson, USMC, retired, relates how as a U.S. Marine captain and newly appointed advisor to Duvalier's Presidential Guard, he was invited by its Haitian commander, Maj. Claude Raymond, on June 25, 1959, to meet with the president. In his book, *The U.S. Naval Mission to Haiti 1959-1963*, Williamson writes that he found Duvalier "dressed in pajamas and robe resting in an easy chair with his bare feet propped up on a stool. Piled around him were books and papers. In his lap was the paperback book he had been reading – a western adventure novel written by Max Brand." Duvalier, Williamson reported, "contrary to all rumors is quite alert and far from physically infirm or mentally incompetent."

Papa Doc needed to be alert as Caribbean geopolitics was heating up and about to boil over into Haiti as it already had spilled into the Dominican Republic. However, Duvalier's reading a book about American cowboys hardly seemed in character for the noirist ideologue. The book could well have been a prop. Besides being a consummate actor Duvalier was somewhat of a *metter en scene*. With Haiti's home Island in the eye of an ideological hurricane, Papa Doc might have been expected to be reading maps and boning up on the Cuban revolution. Then again Duvalier knew that the United States was assessing its Caribbean neighbors in terms of their ideological leanings, and he was sitting pretty in Uncle Sam's geographical lap. With Washington on Papa Doc's side, U.S. warships could be counted on to ward off any serious attempt to invade Haiti. Duvalier also even asked Capt. Williamson about the health of Marine mission members, citing their names. Some of the Marines had suffered dysentery, "Dessalines' revenge," as one Marine called it. Duvalier commiserated and told Williamson that during his, Duvalier's, first month studying public health in Michigan he had also suffered the curse but that he had quickly recovered. It all had to do with a change of diet.

CHAPTER 14

Killings that Sealed
El Jefe's Fate "June 14, 1959"

There were rumors on June 14 that the long-awaited invasion of the Dominican Republic from Cuba had begun. There was no confirmation. Trujillo's usually vociferous propaganda machine continued its regular programming. There was no mention of an invasion. However, during the ensuing week, air travelers from the Dominican Republic in transit at Port-au-Prince's Bowen Field confirmed that "something was happening," that the country had been invaded but no one had details. One American businessman from Ciudad Trujillo said that travel to the north of the country had been halted. Ciudad Trujillo at night was described as morgue-like. Military vehicles patrolled the Dominican capital.

I was asked by the Associated Press as well as the *New York Times* to proceed immediately to the Dominican Republic and report on the situation. But the new Dominican ambassador to Haiti, Dr. Ernesto Sanchez Rubirosa, said he couldn't issue a visa at that time. An important story went uncovered. None of the other large news organization believed it was worth staffing. Some forty rebels for instance had just surrendered in Nicaragua. Invasions and rebellions were too frequent that summer for news organizations to devote their resources to every reported invasion.

On June 15, "The Free Dominican Radio Hour" in Havana

announced that fighting had broken out in the Dominican Republic. The *New York Times* the next day quoted the broadcasts as stating that on June 14, a truckload of Dominican soldiers had been killed by a group of revolutionaries near the mountain town of Constanza, sixty miles northwest of Ciudad Trujillo. "No other details were available," the exile radio said. In Ciudad Trujillo, *El Caribe* editor Rafael Herrera stated: "Authorized sources have made a statement that complete tranquility reigns throughout the entire country."

On June 21, I filed a story to the *New York Times* (which was edited down to a three-paragraph "coat-tail" with other world reports) to the effect that the Dominican radio monitored in Port-au-Prince had given unusual instructions to pro-government irregular forces. The radio declared that, "Troopers [Riders] of the East *(Los Jinetes del Este)* must attack any rebels with machetes." The official communiqué advised the private Dominican militia force in the east of the country not to use "firearms against foreigners or citizens found in rebellion but to use machetes." (Long-bladed knives used especially to cut sugar cane.)

Meanwhile, officials of Dominican embassy in Port-au-Prince confirmed that one of their country's Vampire fighter jets had crashed and burned near the Haitian town of Jacmel. There was no explanation as to what the Dominican air force plane was doing in Haitian air space. On June 22, *New York Times'* Ruby Harts-Phillips filed a brief story from Havana reporting that increased fighting between rebels and government troops was going on in the Dominican Republic, according to reports from Santiago de Cuba.

"Travelers reaching Santiago de Cuba from the Dominican Republic, stated the Havana report, have said that more than 100 soldiers have been hospitalized at a Dominican air base as a result of the fighting." *The New York Times* quoting rebel sources went on to state that "seventy well-armed Dominicans and Cubans had landed on the Dominican coast recently."

Finally, on Sunday, June 21, the *New York Times* managed to contact Ciudad Trujillo by telephone from Manhattan and learned that the Dominican Republic had officially declared that it had frustrated an attempted invasion. Editor Rafael Herrera, at *El Caribe*, confirmed that a Ministry of War communiqué had been issued on Saturday, June 20, to that effect. The communiqué also declared that a Dominican air force pilot Captain Juan de Dios Ventura Simo had pretended to join the exile conspirators' abroad and had lured them back to the Dominican Republic. The government further stated that the captain had returned with information that aided government troops in trapping the invaders.

The facts were slightly different. What really had happened was that Captain Ventura Simo, a young Dominican pilot, had defected to Puerto Rico in April in his Vampire jet and then fled to Venezuela. Roundly denounced by the Trujillo regime, Capt. Ventura didn't request political asylum in Caracas but instead joined fellow Dominican exiles in Cuba. Returning on the invasion plane, he was captured alive near Constanza and taken before Trujillo. A master of the double-cross, Trujillo seized upon Ventura Simo's capture to sow doubt in the ranks of the regime's enemies in exile.

Few observers were fooled by El Jefe's legerdemain. *The New York Times* intoned in an editorial: "The most talked-about country in Latin America in the last few weeks has been the Dominican Republic. A cloak-and-dagger drama seems to have been taking place in the obscurity that normally blankets the country. Everyone has been asking: What is happening there? Yesterday, at last some light was thrown on the still mysterious developments in that tightest of all dictatorships in the world."

The *Times* editorial added that not only had the Dominican Republic announced that a group of invaders had been wiped out; the government had also produced a Dominican pilot who it claimed had done a good job of spying for them. "This rings true since it is just the sort of plot to be expected from the lurid dictator," the *New York Times* had concluded wrongly. The Ventura Simo story had Trujillo's sticky hands smeared all over it.

Captain Ventura Simo was "promoted" to the rank of lieutenant colonel and given a military medal for his devoted work for the Fatherland. Dominican Foreign Minister Porfirio Herrera Baez subsequently invited foreign diplomats in Ciudad Trujillo to 'a reception" at his ministry. He gave no other reason for their summoning and the envoys, as per diplomatic custom, shook hands with various foreign ministry and military officers gathered at the Ministry. A photographer busily snapped pictures. U.S. Ambassador Joseph S. Farland was still mystified as to why he and his fellow diplomats had been called to the ministry. The next day he was furious when he found out why.

One of the military officers with whom Ambassador Farland shook hands, unknown to him, was none other than Trujillo's supposed "agent" Lieut. Col. Ventura Simo. The photograph of the U.S. ambassador gripping the pilot's hand was splashed across the front page of *El Caribe* as if the U.S. envoy were congratulating Ventura Simo for a job well done. The photo was made available to news wire service and transmitted to newspapers throughout the Western Hemisphere, appearing in *El Mundo* of San Juan, Puerto Rico.

However, like many amateur dramatists Trujillo overplayed his hand. A storm of protests from Dominican exiles erupted across the Americas. Exile leaders demanded that U.S. Secretary of State Christian A. Herter and Ambassador Farland disassociate themselves with the repressive Dominican regime. On June 24, the *New York Times* published the picture in question with details of the trick photograph. Ambassador Farland, a former FBI agent, was no friend of Trujillo and this episode stiffened his opposition to the Dominican dictator.

Few Dominicans themselves were fooled by the Ventura Simo story. Trujillo had used the same scenario before. On being captured, Ventura Simo had been given a choice: play the part Trujillo had scripted for him or die. The renegade pilot played his part and died anyway. One day, not long afterwards it was announced that Ventura had died in an air "accident."

The Latin American embassies in Port-au-Prince were helpful sources concerning events in the Dominican Republic and passed on the sketchy news they had from their embassies in Ciudad Trujillo. The U.S. embassy under Ambassador Drew was not always helpful in such matters. It was Cuba's Ambassador Rodríguez who told me that an invasion had taken place in Trujillo's fiefdom but I couldn't quote him.

An invasion had long been expected. It was no secret that Dominicans were being trained in Cuba. Like the Haitians, they had left their studies, their work and some their wives behind to heed the call to liberate their country from the ferocious dictatorship of Rafael Trujillo. The majority came from New York City. It was the hour of the exile. Fidel Castro, as a student had joined the famous Cayo Confites venture. Assembled in August–September 1947 on the tiny island off the East Coast of Cuba it was the largest such amphibious invasion ever conceived in the Caribbean but after mobilizing a fleet, planes, men and munitions to ouster Trujillo it collapsed. Over a decade later, Castro was in agreement with his fellow rebels Che Guevara and Camilo Cienfuegos: that all possible should be done to help their Dominican revolutionary brothers, some of whom had fought with the Cubans against Batista, and thus to return the favor. Even President Romulo Betancourt of Venezuela had provided funds, arms and munitions. A contingent of Dominicans in Caracas had joined the invaders. But Trujillo was no Batista. He controlled his fiefdom like a hermetically sealed fish tank, allowing only sufficient figurative oxygen for the occupants to stay alive. He had built the most powerfully equipped armed forces in the Caribbean. He had been receiving regular shipments of munitions from Europe, which he was stockpiling to ward off any invasion. Besides a regular army of 20,000 men, there was his much-touted, newly-formed Anti-Communist Caribbean Legion as well as the *Cocuyos de la Cordillera* (Fireflies of the Cordillera), a militia made up of *campesinos* armed with old rifles and machetes in the feudal-like Bonao mountains, and commanded by Jose Arismendi (Petan) Trujillo, El Jefe's brother. *Los Jinetes del Este* (Riders of the East) were a mounted militia in the eastern part of the island that had been organized by cattlemen and a former Dominican consul general in New York, Felix Bernadino. Trujillo's modern air force counted sixty planes, including thirty-eight British single-engine Vampire jets, plus American-built P-51's, P-47's and AT-6 advance trainers. Stationed at the Presidente Trujillo air base at San Isidro were the troops of CEFA (*Centro de Ensenanza de las Fuerzas Armadas*). This elite armored unit wore WWII steel German helmets making them look like a German SS battalion. They were equipped with Swedish as well as U.S. made tanks and other armor.

Nor could the invaders count on any simultaneous internal uprising. El Jefe's secret police chief, Johnny W. Abbes Garcia, saw to that. His feared SIM (*Servicio Inteligencia Militar*) agents in their Volkswagens roamed the streets and back roads, efficiently tracking down, and eliminating any cracks in Trujillo's all-knowing surveillance network. "We had no arms, we had nothing," a Dominican youth recalled later in the year, tears filling his eyes. Some young Dominicans tried to reach the invaders only to learn that the roads were blocked.

Even the cleverly conceived rebel airborne landing in the mountains at Constanza, designed to draw Trujillo's troops away from the beaches and establish a guerrilla foothold, enjoyed little more than the element of surprise. On Sunday, June 14, 1959, navigating the established commercial air route from Havana, the C-46 cargo plane piloted by a Venezuelan and a Cuban rookie co-pilot landed in the saucer-shaped Constanza valley near Japanese gardeners' fields of flowers and vegetables. The rebel contingent of fifty-four men – Dominicans, Cubans, Puerto Ricans, Venezuelans and an American named Charles White (a World War II army veteran and expert in explosives) – jumped into a firefight on landing. After a short skirmish, they broke off the engagement with the Constanza garrison and moved rapidly off into the misty Cordillera Central. There they hoped to gather forces and duplicate Castro's success in Cuba's Sierra Maestro. (The plane meanwhile managed to make it back to Cuba landing in Santiago de Cuba.)

Alas, the Dominican Cordillera Central was not the same friendly environment that Fidel encountered in Cuba's Oriente Province, where there had even been an ambulant Haitian baker who supplied Castro and his small band with bread. The Dominican mountain range was not only sparsely populated, but the Dominican peasantry had been heavily indoctrinated by the Trujillo regime for years concerning the danger of aiding the "heathen Communists." The *campesinos* had been organized to resist any invaders and anyone caught harboring or assisting subversives was summarily executed. That was an order.

An early rumor, heard in Haiti, was that Maj. Ernesto (Che) Guevara commanded the Constanza rebels. In fact, their leader was Enrique Jiménez Moya, a Dominican who had reached the rank of major fighting in the Sierra Maestra with Fidel Castro. The top-ranking Cuban rebel with the force was Maj. Delio Gomez Ochoa, who had made a name for himself as a fighter in the Sierra Maestra as well as having taken the Havana airport at the end of the rebellion. It was he and Jiménez Moya, according to Juan Delancer's excellent book, *Desembarco de la Gloria,* who had purchased the C-46 cargo plane in Miami, Florida.

Meanwhile the 138 sea-borne invaders did not even enjoy the precarious initial luck of the Constanza contingent. At least the latter managed to touch down on Dominican soil whereas many on the launches didn't even reach the target beaches of Mammon and Estero Hondo, some fifteen miles southeast of Luperon. Whether the sea-borne rebels wanted to duplicate Castro's invasion of Cuba in the motor launch *Granma* with eighty-two men, their effort proved just as disastrous.

The Dominican invasion force packed aboard two launches, *La Tinina* and *Carmen Elsa*, had chugged off in the direction of the Dominican Republic from Bahia de Nipe on the southern coast of Cuba. The *Carmen Elsa* lost contact with *La Tinina* and finally, experiencing a motor problem, called for help. Three Cuban navy frigates appeared, and with the aid of the Cuban frigates, both launches finally got within sight of the Dominican coast. The *Tinina* managed to land sixty men at Estero Hondo, but the *Carmen Elsa* became the target of an intense aerial bombardment and shelling from Trujillo's Coast Guard. The bombs, rockets and shells finally set off ammunition aboard the *Carmen Elsa* and it was little more than a hull when it finally beached with the few alive left to fight.

In a matter of days, the incessant aerial bombing and shelling wiped out most of the invaders. Some were driven by hunger and thirst to approach campesinos for food and were quickly taken prisoner or immediately killed for the bounty offered for their heads. The twenty-five to thirty rebels who were taken prisoner were ordered to be sent to San Isidro air base. Trussed up like animals, they were flown to the air base and dumped out the door of the aircraft onto the tarmac. There were many stories of the atrocities committed on them before they died under torture. Only three of the Dominican prisoners were allowed to live.

Dominican rebel leader Jiménez Moya, who suffered health problems, didn't last long and was killed in the early days of the landing. But twenty-seven-year-old Maj. Delio Gomez Ochoa, the Cuban veteran of the Sierra Maestra, was well trained and a tenacious fighter and he lasted twenty-six days in the mountains. He was captured on July 11 along with his thirteen-year-old adopted son Pablito Mirabel who had stowed away aboard the invasion aircraft, and as the Dominican soldiers said admiringly, "he fought like a tiger."

When Dictator Rafael Trujillo had received word of the invasion, he had gone ahead with a planned military parade in Ciudad Trujillo commemorating his June 19, 1949 victory over an earlier incursion. His forces had wiped out all but five of fourteen rebels who landed an old seaplane at Luperon on the Dominican north coast. (It was not until June 21 that Trujillo permitted mention in his media that the country had been invaded again. Naturally the press release was limited to praising the heroic defenders of the Fatherland.)

However, the invaders of June 14, 1959 involved in this latest effort to topple Trujillo did not die in vain. Their invasion was like a clarion call. The executions and atrocities committed against the invaders helped seal the regime's own fate. Out of the blood of the invasion came a force to be reckoned with: the youthful *Movimiento 14 de Junio* (MR-IJ4) that took its name from the date of the ill-fated landing.

Thirty-eight years later, I had the pleasure of standing with the few survivors including Maj. Gomez Ochoa during a celebration in Santo

Domingo at the Monument to the Heroes of Constanza, Maimon and Estero Hondo. The occasion was the publication of Dominican writer Juan Delancer's book, *Desembarco de la Gloria* ("Debarkation of Glory"), for which I had written the foreword. Dominican President Lionel Fernandez and other officials of the government and armed forces attended the event. It was remarkable how many knew the words when it came time to sing the *14 de Junio* hymn:

> *Llegaron llenos de patriotismo*
> *enamorados de un puro ideal*
> *Y con su sangre noble encendieron*
> *La llama augusta de la libertad*
> *Su sacrificio que Dios bendijo*
> *La Patria entera, glorificara*
> *Como homenaje , a los valientes*
> *que alli cayeron por la libertad.*

(They came imbued with patriotism,
in love with a pure ideal.
And with noble blood lit
The majestic flame of liberty.
Their sacrifice, blessed by God,
The entire country will glorify
As an homage to the valiant ones
Who fell there in the cause of liberty.)

*　　　　*　　　　*

Back in Haiti, on June 21, 1959, an already nervous Port-au-Prince was thrown into a panic when cries of *"feu! feu!"* (fire! fire!) echoed through the capital city's streets and clouds of smoke billowed over the National Palace. Army tanks and soldiers took up defensive positions around the palace where Papa Doc was still convalescing. At first it seemed as if the huge pillars of black smoke were coming from the National Palace. It soon proved to be a wing of the Caserne

Dessalines behind the palace that was on fire. For two and a half hours, firemen fought the blaze but the barracks's wing containing the cinema was totally destroyed. The government announced that the blaze had been caused by a short circuit in an air conditioner. The U.S. Marine advisers concurred that it was an accident. However, as armed Tontons Makouts sped around in cars in a show of force and searching for the invisible arsonist, the general public believed it was another act of Papa Doc's enemies.

Haiti's short, squat interior minister, Jean Magloire, didn't offer a large target nor did he appear to be an obvious target of the opposition. Yet someone lobbed a grenade at him as he paced along the second-story balcony of his home. He was only slightly injured in the back and legs and the following day was present at a military parade on the palace grounds marking the official return of Papa Doc to his presidential duties. As with any bureaucrat, Magloire was highly efficient in signing papers. We, at the *Haiti Sun,* could attest to that fact. As specified in the country's law of the press, we had notified the minister of interior of the fact that the *Haiti Sun* had changed its *Gerant-Responsable.* The person who was by law is responsible for what the newspaper prints. In reality his or her name was published on the masthead of the paper to conform with the law. At the time, we had deemed it prudent that Paul Najac, a promising young writer who sometimes contributed a colorful folktale for our Bouqui and Malice column, not continue as the person technically responsible to the State for the *Haiti Sun.* Rony Chenet, a close friend who was working with his father at the Sun Life Insurance Company of Canada had earlier relinquished that post for the same reason. Mauclair Labissiere, who had been a long-time employee, volunteered his own name. Minister Magloire promptly replied that our letter had been received and that the change had been noted. He personally signed his letter of confirmation.

Under the tightest security, Papa Doc was "welcomed back to life" (as some Haitians joked at the time). Attired in his habitual dark suit and hat, he sat on a special reviewing stand, constructed on the palace steps, with U.S. Ambassador Drew and Marine Colonel Heinl. For forty minutes Duvalier sat there, occasionally addressing Heinl and Drew while watching a full-dress parade by his presidential guard. Tanks and armored cars had been positioned on the palace lawn, and manned anti-aircraft batteries, newly installed, flanked the palace. Only government officials and specially invited Duvalierists were permitted inside the palace gates.

Apart from his looking thinner and older – his hair was turning white – there were no visible signs that the heart attack had induced any mental or physical handicap in Papa Doc, as opponents later claimed. (They would later charge that Doc came out of his metabolic coma psychotic – in other words, crazy. But events proved that he was still the same Papa Doc – and still crazy like a fox.)

Late one June morning, a trustworthy *Haiti Sun* employee ushered two men into my office. They identified themselves as followers of exiled Daniel Fignolé. It soon became apparent that the two men had been caught up by the exhortations from exiles broadcasting from Havana and Venezuelan. The pair of visitors were leaders of a Fignolist "action cell," they explained. Moreover the taller, more intense of the two announced that they were going to "*craze* (destroy) Ti Barb" Morrison. Taken by surprise I asked, "Why?" From a servant at Ti Barb's house, they said, they had learned that he had guns. "We need his guns," the Fignolists added, "because the invasion is coming." They called Ti Barb a "degenerate" who "harmed" young Haitian girls and deserved to die. How serious or not they were, I cautioned them against any such action. And in any event, Ti Barb, though as arrogant as ever, did not turn up "craze."

It was not the last of many bizarre visitors to the *Haiti Sun*. The very next month, an oungan friend from the Cul de Sac paid a rare visit to my newspaper. A dignified gentleman, he said he knew that Secret Police Chief Barbot was giving me "problems." The *oungan* offered his services. I thanked the old man profusely, but replied that I was capable of taking care of my own problems – and I pointedly shook my fountain pen. Impressed by my gesture emphasizing the power of the press, the elderly *oungan* left, smiling.

CHAPTER 15

Algerian-Led Invasion

In Papa Doc's Haiti, unsettling news had a way of floating through the air like ether. Haitians had honed their senses to detect signs of trouble. To all but a select few, details of recurring clandestine intrigues were out of reach, but the "vibes" of the masses were usually trustworthy. Early on the morning of August 13, 1959, my own vibes directed me hastily to the airport.

The mood of excitement at the Bowen airfield was palpable. "*Yo debake*," ("They landed") whispered my old friend Mister Peedy, a Pan American Airways employee, who found it difficult to suppress his excitement. As to precisely who "they" were no one seemed to know. However, they were certain that the long-awaited invasion had finally happened. The signs were in full view from the Bowen Field airport.

All eyes were glued to the activity next door at the neighboring military air force headquarters. Regular flights of the C-47s of Cohata, Haiti's military-run airline, serving the provinces, had been cancelled. Troops from the Caserne Dessalines were being shepherded aboard the Cohata planes by their U.S. Marine advisors.

Mr. Peedy and others at Bowen Field confirmed that Col. Robert Heinl, commander of the U.S. Naval Mission, had taken off in the new orange-colored U.S. Naval Mission helicopter shortly after sun-up. His passengers had included the corpulent Haitian Army Col. Gerard Constant and Maj. Antonio Doublette. We learned that Secret

Police Chief Clément Barbot had flown by plane to Jérémie even before dawn. (Later that day, he hitched a ride back to Port-au-Prince with Colonel Heinl from Jérémie, the largest town on the coast nearest the landing.)

For me, alerting the Associated Press to the rumored invasion was the easy part. Getting the facts was something else. The usually resourceful Cuban ambassador, Antonio Rodríguez, was of no help. Shrugging his shoulders, he declared that he knew absolutely nothing about the putative landing. I did learn that he was concerned about his cousin, Luis Orlando Rodríguez, who had lately been dropped from the Cuban revolutionary cabinet as Interior Minister.

Colleagues based in Havana had alerted me to the fact that the Dominican invasion debacle of June 14 had dampened "liberation fever" among the Haitian exiles training in Cuba. News of Papa Doc's illness had even failed to galvanize them into action. They remained as politically divided as ever and some had already begun drifting off to their respective homes in exile. Officially, there had been two exile groups in Cuba: the Liberation Committee of Haiti and the Revolutionary Front. Senator Louis Déjoie headed the latter and considered himself the undisputed leader of Haitian exiles; he didn't look fondly on competition from fellow exiles. The inter-group squabbling among the Haitians had soured the Cubans who knew all about such divisions, having suffered much the same malady. Maj. Ernesto (Che) Guevara of the new Cuban Revolutionary Army had notified Déjoie in May that he would no longer receive any support from the Cuban government. That month Déjoie left Cuba for Venezuela.

In Port-au-Prince, the initial wave of anti-Duvalierist euphoria sparked by the reports of the new invasion was soon replaced by suspicion; it might all be a hoax. *Chapita*, as Dominican dictator Trujillo was known, could be up to his old tricks. Foreign ministers of the Organization of American States (OAS) were meeting in Santiago, Chile, to consider the deteriorating situation in the Caribbean. "How convenient" was the sarcastic quip of a Venezuelan diplomat in Port-au-Prince after meeting with his Latin American colleagues to discuss the rumored invasion in the south. The Latin envoys almost to a man believed that if in fact there had been a landing in Haiti — and they were skeptical — it could only be Trujillo trying to embarrass Castro before the OAS foreign ministers!

With such a shortage of facts it was difficult for a reporter to claim the high ground of truth and objectivity during that month of August 1959. If people's lives had not been involved, it would have been akin to covering a comedy show. There were plots, counter-plots and invasions real and purported, the latter complete with clandestine radios in the background endlessly intoning official disinformation.

*   *   *

Friendly U.S. Marine contacts, in off-the-record conversation, helped lift the fog of confusion that had initially enveloped the invasion reports. I wrote in my dispatch of August 15 to the *New York Times*:

> Port-au-Prince, August 15: Brig. Gen. Pierre Merceron, Chief of Staff of the Haitian Army, made an inspection trip today to the area in southwestern Haiti where invaders landed early last Thursday. The situation is apparently more serious than at first thought. Rumors circulating in the capital say that the invaders have recruited 200 Haitians and that they are equipped with heavy weapons. Army sources here said the invaders were distributing Haitian Army insignia among those they were recruiting. General Merceron flew to the Army's field headquarters at Jérémie in a transport plane of the United States Air Mission here [separate from the Marines' Naval Mission but under the overall command of Colonel Heinl] piloted by Col. Oscar Johnson, USAF. Clément Barbot, secretary to President François Duvalier, and members of the Haitian Army's general staff, accompanied Merceron.
>
> The group returned four hours and fifteen minutes later,

looking worried. General Merceron refused to answer any questions, but Mr. Barbot declared that 'everything is under control.'

Troops that were airlifted to the area yesterday have entered Les Irois, a village at the tip of Haiti's southwest peninsula near the invaders' landing site. The thirty men were said to have captured an Army outpost without firing a shot, but they evacuated the village yesterday morning.

It was made known unofficially that the invaders had headed toward Jérémie but took to the mountains when they were pursued by Army units.

No official statement has been made thus far. But the Government has promised to give some information tomorrow.

It was explained that since the Army has not yet made contact with the invading group, the invasion officially does not exist.

Mr. Barbot said the invaders were all Cubans, but other reports said the landing party consisted of eighteen Cubans, ten Haitians and two Venezuelans.

The invaders transferred at sea from a power-driven vessel to a small Haitian schooner that they seized at gunpoint, according to the owner, who escaped after the force landed.

According to a Government source, the boat owner said the men had long hair, spoke Spanish and gave him Cuban cigarettes.

Les Irois is a small fishing village of mud huts on a bay. It is thought that the invaders could hide in the mountains nearby and live off the land without difficulty.

It is rumored here that the invaders are commanded by a former Haitian Army captain, Maurepas Auguste. His second-in-command was said to be Louis Déjoie Jr., the son of President Duvalier's archenemy, a former senator now in exile in Venezuela. The south coast area where the

invaders landed is considered a stronghold of Déjoie supporters. (It later turned out that neither Capt.Maurepas
Auguste nor Louis Déjoie Jr was in the invasion force.)

The invaders also are reported to be operating a clandestine radio that began broadcasting at 6 a.m. today.
However, the Army denied that there was any such station.

Meanwhile, the Port-au-Prince airport bustled with
unusual activity this morning. Two United States Navy
planes and one Navy helicopter landed from Puerto Rico,
ostensibly refueling on a trip to the United States Naval
Base at Guantánamo, Cuba. All Haitian domestic flights
have been canceled.

It was frustrating work trying to assess with as much factual accu-
racy as possible the phantom invasion force, and much of my time
was taken up with weeding out hearsay and unfounded rumors.
Venezuela radio broadcasts monitored in Port-au-Prince appealed to
Haitians to aid the invaders. The broadcasts instructed Haitians to
provide food to the invaders, stating that they had money to pay for
supplies. The radio appeal called on youth, physicians and nurses to
join the rebels.

The Haitian government radio, for its part, declared that exiled
Louis Déjoie Sr. was behind the invasion, but that the invaders were
receiving no support from Haitians in the area. Haiti lodged a formal
complaint with the foreign ministers of the Organization of
American States, meeting in Santiago, Chile, accusing Cuba of being
behind the invasion. President Hector B. (Negro) Trujillo of the
Dominican Republic (Dictator Rafael Trujillo's younger brother) sent
a message to Duvalier offering any cooperation needed to repel the
reported assault on Haiti.

On August 18, a Haitian Army source reported that the invaders
had been trapped in the Caracasse Mountains behind the coastal
town of Tiburon. On the 19th army units finally caught up with the
invading band seven days after they landed. They were pinned down
by light machineguns and mortar fire. Twelve were killed on the spot

and the others fled into the mountains. (The total number of invaders ultimately killed was put at twenty-five.) No army casualties were reported. Haitian peasants who aided the invaders were said to have been killed along with the Cubans.

*   *   *

Scores of military officers, cabinet ministers and other government officials, and important Makouts waited in the shade of the small verandah of the Haitian Air Force flight office at Port-au-Prince's Bowen Field airport. It was hot and humid, and threatening rain.

Early on the morning of August 22, Haitian government vans toured the capital of Port-au-Prince blaring from megaphones the news that prisoners would be brought in from the south later in the day. The rendezvous was to be the airport, to celebrate the Duvalierist victory over the "invasion." By mid-afternoon, a crowd of some two thousand had gathered outside the small military sector at the Bowen Field airport.

The Duvalierist cheerleaders at the military airport were the usual chorus of bullies and braggarts who beat their chests and promised to annihilate Papa Doc's enemies. Only ten days earlier, the arrogant braggarts had been in a panic. Then they had feared the invasion might threaten their very existence. With victory over the invaders came the old false bravado. Thus the furniture maker was there, prepared again to dip his hands again into the corpse of a dead invader as he had done the year before with Pasquet's brains. Barbot, his Sten gun clasped at his side like an accessory to his dark suit coat, stared out from behind his ink-black glasses. Collectively, it was the kind of ominous image that is engraved on one's memory — the fraternity of Makouts and fellow Duvalier henchmen in a murderous mood prepared to lynch the prisoners upon arrival. Like wolves, they hungrily awaited their prey and congratulated each other on their victory.

The *New York Times*' Homer Bigart was with me. We stood apart. As the Duvalierists glared at me, Homer a well-seasoned reporter, commented, "they don't like you. That's good." He had arrived to cover the growing battle between Papa Doc and the Roman Catholic Church. My dispatches on Duvalier's fight with the church had made the *Times'* front page. In terms of long-term significance, it was a much more important news story than the invasion from Cuba. Working with Homer was always a learning experience. I watched as he used his stammer to an advantage in one interview after another.

When finally the line of four ragged, hapless prisoners finally came off the aircraft that had taxied up to the crowd, there was a curious quiet of disbelief. As they stood there barefoot and in tattered uniforms, the Makouts were caught off guard. There was general astonishment. One single cry said it all: "But they are only kids." They were not the bearded giants from the Sierra Maestra who had been expected to step off the C-47. The Makouts' lust for blood was momentarily frozen. They just gawked at the young prisoners as Haitian soldiers hustled them into a police wagon.

The following week, I was permitted to interview the five youthful Cubans—one Cuban straggler had been found in the south and brought to Port-au-Prince on August 29 to join the other four prisoners—as they sat together on a bench in the yard of the National Penitentiary. Among the prisoners were Lieut. Manuel Rodríguez, and Corporals Santiago Torres and Antonio Panseca.

Their expedition leader had been Maj. Henry Fuentes, alias Henri d'Anton. A *pied-noir*—French-Algerian—

Young Cuban invaders being held at the national penitentiary during an interview with the *Haiti Sun*. They were quietly released months later and returned to Cuba by ship.

Fuentes had lived in Haiti and married a cousin of Senator Déjoie. In 1958 he had gone off on a ship, landed in Cuba and ended up joining the *Segundo Frente Nacional del Escambray* fighting the Batista dictatorship.

When Fuentes-d'Anton climbed into the central Cuba Escambray hills and presented himself to Spanish-born Maj. Eloy Gutierrez Menoyo, commander of the Second Front, he had declared his ultimate intentions: "If I am lucky enough to survive this war, I will go on and liberate Haiti." *El Argelino* ("The Algerian"), as he became known in the Escambray, fought well but continued to declaim his end objective, "liberating Haiti from Duvalier." Time and again, he would voice his obsession to Major Gutierrez Menoyo whose force was fighting independently of Fidel Castro's 26th of July Movement against the Batista dictatorship.

With the triumph of the Cuban rebellion, Fuentes asked Gutierrez Menoyo, as a favor, to promote him to *comandante* (major) which he did. That was the last Gutierrez Menoyo recalls seeing of the Algerian with the luxuriant black beard. Fuentes, Gutierrez Menoyo told this author years later, was still consumed with his "magnificent obsession" to liberate Haiti.

Major Fuentes had first sought out Louis Déjoie in Havana in January 1959 with a plan of operations for the invasion of Haiti. But Déjoie rejected the Algerian's plan, telling him that he was not the appropriate person to lead the future invasion. Nor, Déjoie added, had the Haitians received the necessary training to engage in the guerrilla-type war that Fuentes proposed.

Undeterred, Fuentes had set up his own clandestine training camp at a sugar refinery near Holguin, Cuba. Two veterans of the rebellion against Batista, Captains Ringal Guerrero and Carlos Chidichimo, joined Fuentes, as did a Cuban journalist working for an Argentine publication. Campesinos, some under twenty years of age who had briefly served in Cuba's revolutionary army, and then mostly unemployed, were easily recruited around Holguín. They were told, according to the five survivors of the abortive Haitian invasion, that men were already fighting in Haiti, and that, once Fuentes' rebels landed, thousands were ready to rally to their cause. Déjoie had often bragged that the entire population of the southwestern peninsula was on his side. He had provided many of them with a livelihood growing the aromatic vetiver grass for his essential oil business. But, by August 1959, most known Dejoieists in the region had paid a heavy price for supporting Duvalier's opponent. Hounded by the Makouts, many had fled the area. Duvalierist repression had been particularly severe in that corner of Haiti.

Only ten days after he landed, Fuentes' destructive obsession was laid to rest in an unknown mountain cave along with twenty-four young, confused Cubans who knew only that they were fighting tyranny.

Once again, an invasion had benefited no one but strongman François Duvalier. As with the Pasquet expedition a year earlier, this incursion had ended in a Papa Doc victory. It proved to be the end of invasion threats by Haitian exiles from Cuba. It rid Duvalier of Cuban Ambassador Antonio Rodríguez who was declared *persona non grata,* and diplomatic ties with Havana were broken.

*   *   *

I considered myself extremely lucky to be working with a legendary newsman. Without doubt, Homer was one of the finest reporters of his generation, having covered major World War II stories ranging from flying on bombing runs over Germany to Pacific battles plus campaigns in Africa and Sicily. He described for me the scene aboard the battleship Missouri on September 2, 1945 when he covered the official signing of the documents of unconditional surrender by Japan. (I was at sea and our armed tanker was ordered to Singapore where we witnessed the surrender.) Homer covered the Greek Civil War, Korean War and was later in Hungary for the 1956 anti-Soviet revolt and also covered the Suez crisis.

He had started his reporting career as a copy boy in 1929 on New York's *Herald Tribune.* He talked glowingly of his years with the *Trib* from 1929 to 1955 when he moved from the financially troubled newspaper to the *New York Times*. His legendary one-liners were apt to be recalled whenever journalists gathered. He laughed at my cameras; a roleiflex still camera and a bolex movie camera strung around my neck, and confessed, "I can't take a darn picture."

Late one afternoon, sipping his rum punch, Homer Bigart gazed into the rainstorm. The story had been "put to bed"—completed and closed for the next morning's issue of the *Times*. We were seated on the verandah of the Grand Hotel Oloffson. Homer inhaled the pleasing fragrance from the garden and the earth dampened by the rain. Then he fell silent. Suddenly he spoke up, "These are the most beautiful and biggest rain drops I have every seen." He then broke into a dissertation about raindrops, their shapes and sizes. Coming from a man who had traveled the world and witnessed many a tropical downpour, Bigart's assessment that Haiti had the world's largest raindrops struck me as a distinct, if unexpected, compliment.

*   *   *

While the Cuban envoy was packing his bags, Clément Barbot quit the shadows and stepped into the public light, offering a press conference. Barbot did the talking. He didn't take questions. In my report to the *New York Times,* I noted: "Clément Barbot, Presidential Secretary and Government strongman, declared that secret papers discovered by the police had shown that that the Cuban ambassador was plotting against the Government of President François Duvalier. (He did not show the evidence to the press. They had to take his word.) Barbot told newsmen that the Cuban ambassador as having been a militant partisan of the late Clément Jumelle, a presidential candidate who had boycotted general elections charging that they had been rigged by the army in favor of President Duvalier." Barbot further declared that "the jeep of the Cuban military attaché had been sighted in mountains and on reconnaissance operations." He also said that Celestino Fernandez, onetime coordinator in the entire Caribbean area for the 26th of July Movement and now a Cuban official, had visited Les Cayes (Haiti) recently on a trip arranged by the Cuban ambassador.

In detailing a Cuban conspiracy, Barbot tied Catholic priests to activities with the Cuban military attaché, Capt. Armando Torres. Diagrams of bombs and grenades were found among papers linked to the Cubans, Barbot stated. Captain Torres and his assistant, Capt. Luis Perez, had returned to Havana in mid-July. While the Cuban ambassador refused to comment on Barbot's charges for publication, he told this author, "Everyone knows who Barbot is and now we know he has a vivid imagination. I am only surprised he didn't tie more enemies of the regime into his so-called plot."

As Barbot had gone public, *Time* magazine bought my idea of a story on this sten gun-toting rising star of the Duvalier regime. It was published on September 12, 1959 Hemisphere edition:

> To stay on top in Haiti, black President François Duvalier must do battle against invaders from Cuba, pressure from the Dominican Republic, his own weakened heart, and opposition at home from the mulatto elite. In the fight, Duvalier's strong arm is a wiry, sawed off (5 ft. 4 in.) silent man of many talents named Clément Barbot. Despite the fact that he has quietly and quickly made himself the most powerful man in Haiti after the President, few Haitians know Barbot. "The biggest trouble with Monsieur Barbot," sniped a longtime Barbot foe last week, "is that the only Haitians who have ever seen him are in jail."
>
> By title, Barbot is Duvalier's private secretary; in practice, he serves as head of a tough secret service. When a 30-man invasion force from Cuba invaded southwestern Haiti a month ago, it was Barbot who jauntily slapped on a side arm, clapped on a helmet, and rode an orange helicopter belonging to the U.S. naval mission to the invasion site for a personal look. When two French priests were expelled from Haiti three weeks ago for opposing Duvalier, it was Barbot who ordered them out and threatened to expel the archbishop as well (*Time* Aug. 31).

Major René Leon who led the troops that defeated the young disoriented Cuban invaders (led by an Algerian). One of the more bizarre invasions during Papa Doc's tenure.

Barbot's strength is his secret police, the Tonton Macoutes. Transparently camouflaged in snap-brimmed felt fedoras and dark harlequin sunglasses, the Tontons Macoutes swing into actions whenever they want to haul someone in, beat them up, or break up an opposition violently . . . Barbot himself is far from grand. Dressed in quiet khaki he shuns parties and pomp and protocol relishes by Duvalier intimates, such as Herbert Morrison, white press agent from Brooklyn (*Time* June 21). He prefers to sit in his tiny office in the presidential palace and keep an eye on things. The room is decorated with the tools of his trade, a Sten gun, an assortment of pistols and revolvers, a shotgun, machine pistol and a bulletproof vest.

Before he met Duvalier 15 years ago he worked as a rural schoolteacher and as an informal commission agent ready and able to sell a second-hand washing machine or a building lot.

About his fellow Haitians he is forcefully blunt. "We were born black, a Negro republic," he says, "and we are tired of those of our elite when they go to America or to Europe and say, 'I'm not a Negro. I am a Cuban or Indians'–or anything but a Haitian Negro." What about the short shift some times given democratic processes in Haiti? "We do not pretend," purrs Barbot, "to have anything like the degree of democracy achieved in the U.S."

As usual, the Port-au-Prince airport censor discovered the story in *Time* and it was instantly removed from all copies sent to La Caravelle, the capital's bookshop that then distributed the magazine. At least one copy of the article was dispatched to the palace for the president's eyes only. Police Capt. Jacques Laroche, who remained close to Duvalier, told me the following week that the president had been upset with a *Time* story. When I pressed Laroche as to which story had displeased Papa Doc, he smiled and said, "You know, the Barbot story."

President Duvalier personally pins the rank of colonel on Rene Leon in his palace office. Colonel Leon later fled Haiti and joined rebel attempts to overthrow Duvalier from the Dominican Republic.

In an August 19, 1959, congratulatory letter, Stanley M. Swinton, general news editor of the Associated Press World Service, wrote: "Nice going on your coverage of the 30–man 'invasion' (sic) force. Your coverage has been clear, thorough and superior to anything else sighted hereabouts. . . . When things settle down we would appreciate a political situationer. Since AP correspondent Tom Whitney is no longer available [to help in Haiti coverage], please be sure to answer all the questions in it. Also let me know whether you want it under a Port-au-Prince dateline or whether we should use your background material for a story prepared here. Specify which you want—we don't want to add to your difficulties. I was very sorry to hear about the *Haiti Sun* and do hope that permission to resume publication is given you soon."

*   *   *

The OAS foreign ministers meeting in Santiago, Chile, appeared to have degenerated into a shrill diplomatic brawl. Cuba's foreign minister, Raul Roa, charged that the Dominican regime had organized a revolutionary attempt against his government, which had been crushed. Trujillo's new foreign minister, Porfirio Herrera Baez, called the thin, bespectacled Roa a "squid" spouting "red ink." Tad Szulc, covering the conference for the *New York Times* wrote that Dr. Roa "shot back a salvo of derogatory adjectives, of which 'moron' was the mildest." The Cuban delegation even accused the Dominicans of threatening to kill Roa.

U.S. Secretary of State Christian A. Herter, referring to mini-invasions of various Latin American countries with the announced aim of spreading democracy by overthrowing tyrants, warned that "history has shown that attempts to impose democracy upon a country by force from without may easily result in the mere substitution of one form of tyranny for another." Therefore, any effort to promote democracy in a state through outside intervention was "self-defeating." Nonetheless, Herter declared the OAS meeting a success, saying it had strengthened the Inter-American Peace Committee's endeavors to ease tensions in the area.

CHAPTER 16

The Bizarre Morgan Plot

That summer of 1959, I received request after request from my foreign media editors for information about reports that something truly bizarre was happening in the Dominican Republic and Cuba. It turned out that the rumors had their basis in an incredible invasion scam that even a Hollywood scriptwriter would have found difficult to imagine. The staged event was the main topic of conversation at every Latin American embassy cocktail party in Port-au-Prince—an international sleight of hand that made Cubans laugh, and left Dominican dictator Trujillo ridiculed throughout the hemisphere.

The principal actors were Maj. William Morgan, an American in the Cuban rebel army, and Maj. Eloy Gutierriez Menoyo, his commander, on one side; and the notorious Dominican Spy Chief Johnny Abbes Garcia, and a mysterious pistol-packing Spanish priest, on the other. The two title roles were played by Generalissimo Rafael Trujillo, benefactor of the Dominican Republic, and Fidel Castro, Premier of the eight-month-old Cuban revolutionary government.

According to reports that were widely deemed authentic, the plot unfolded as follows: In February 1959, an American resident in Havana for more than eighteen years, Frank Nelson, returned from a trip to Ciudad Trujillo allegedly with a million-dollar contract offer for Maj. William Morgan. All Morgan had to do was launch a counter-revolution against Castro.

Trujillo's agents had decided to enlist the thirty-year-old Morgan, believing he was a mercenary — and mercenarys had their price. Morgan's past encouraged the agents. They knew he had had a troubled youth and had added to his clouded past with a dishonorable discharge from the U.S. Army. In Japan, he had gone AWOL to spend time with a Japanese girlfriend. Morgan had ended his military life serving jail time in a brig. Married with two children back in Ohio, he ended up in Havana in 1958. But Morgan had joined the Cuban revolution that turned his life around.

It was in the Sierra del Escambray, the mountain range in east-central Cuba near the city of Cienfuegos, that Morgan had made a name for himself. He had risen to the rank of major, fighting under Maj. Eloy Gutierrez Menoyo in the Second National Front of the Escambray.

With victory, both he and his commander had been incorporated into the Cuban Revolutionary Army with the rank of major. Following the rebel victory, the American adventurer had set up a frog farm in Las Villas province.

Morgan reported the Dominican bribe offer to Gutierrez Menoyo, and they informed Castro. Trujillo wanted not just Castro's assassination but also an overthrow of his rebel regime. Fidel ordered his two subalterns to string Trujillo along. Gutierrez Menoyo said he was placed in charge of Castro's sting operation, which was to be kept secret from Cuba's revolutionary G2 which was then handling security.

(Later, the Dominicans claimed that it was Morgan who had initiated the deal—and that he had written to Trujillo in a letter postmarked Miami in late February, 1959, a month after Batista fled, offering to help overthrow Castro. It was well known that the Second Front of the Sierra del Escambray was at odds with Castro's 26th of July Movement. The Dominican said it was the first of long series of letters from Morgan.)

Trujillo placed his spy chief, Johnny Abbes Garcia, in charge of the Dominican side of the plot. Two Dominican army radios—Abbes was a radio buff—belonging to his *Servicio Inteligencia Militar* (SIM) were smuggled into Cuba and handed over to Morgan. The American was instructed to cut Cuba's central highway, blow up bridges and seize the seaport town of Trinidad in south-central Cuba. With the island cut in half, a force of some 800 anti-Castro Cuban exile troops under Cuban General Pedraza would land, to be followed by 600 mercenaries of Trujillo's Anti-Communist Foreign Legion.

Meanwhile, a Spanish Catholic priest arrived in Havana, dressed in his religious robe with a pistol in his waistband, and introduced himself to Gutierrez Menoyo as Rev. Father Velasco, the emissary from Ciudad Trujillo to work out certain conditions of the deal. Gutierrez Menoyo says he told the Spanish priest, a man in his forties, that he, Menoyo, hadn't fought against Batista to exchange one tyrant for another. Gutierrez Menoyo and Morgan themselves would lead the "counter-revolution" on their own condition that when they triumphed, Trujillo would turn over some of the "unsavory" Batista exiles El Jefe had under his protection, including former Cuban police

This photograph taken in the summer of 1959 shows Maj. William Morgan talking with Fidel Castro. Maj. Camilo Cienfuegos with arms folded in a pensive mood. (From the collection of John Hlavacek)

chief, Capt. Esteban Ventura. Trujillo agreed to the "deal."

(El Jefe, Menoyo reported later stated he wanted the country home of Miguel Angel Quevedo, the publisher-editor of *Bohemia*. Angel Quevedo's popular Cuban magazine had made a habit of publishing uncomplimentary Trujillo stories. The exchange of prisoners as prizes of war appealed to El Jefe's sense of double-cross and Maj. Gutierrez Menoyo believe it helped seal the deal.)

On August 5, Morgan returned to Cuba from Miami with $170,000 in cash, given him by the Dominican consul, plus some weapons. Morgan turned the money over to Fidel Castro at the INRA (Agrarian Reform Institute) and before Maj. Ramiro Valdes, then in charge of Las Villas Province, telling him to use the money to build a cooperative in the Escambray. Moreover, according to Maj. Gutierrez Menoyo, arms were dropped by parachute and one of the largest yachts he had ever seen arrived with an impressive cargo of arms that included .30- and .50- caliber machine guns and bazookas.

On Wednesday, August 11, in Trinidad, a farming community and commercial center of 15,000 ringed by mountains 175 miles southeast of Havana, Major Morgan was photographed (the picture appeared on the front page of the *New York Times*) in a white T-shirt shouting into a microphone he held in his hand. Other officers present in the photograph were all smiles. Morgan yelled, "Hello 12SN, this is 6BF (The letter they later testified stood for "Six Ferocious Barbudos"). "We hold the town (Trinidad). Am fighting off government troops. We urgently need more arms and munitions." When Johnny Abbes relayed the message to Trujillo, El Jefe gave the order for the first plane to take off with arms. Members of his Anti-Communist Foreign Legion and Cuban exiles were ordered to stand by and be prepared to move on their target.

When the first plane arrived from the Dominican Republic at the Trinidad airport with arms, the five-member flight crew and the mysterious Father Velasco were treated to a fireworks display in the distance that would have done justice to Beethoven's *Ode to Joy*. They heard the heavy explosions of war and automatic fire of various types of machine guns as they left the plane to confer with Major Morgan.

Bearded men waved their weapons and shouted, * "*Viva Trujillo*" and "Down with Fidel." As Morgan talked to Padre Velasco, a barbudo rushed forward and grabbed the priests robe and begged, "Father, when this is over, when we are free will you baptize me. "Yes, yes, my son, " said the startled pistol-packing priest.

On August 11, Premier Castro himself had suddenly disappeared from public view. There was a news blackout on his activities. Exasperated by only rumors, the *Times of Havana*, a tri-weekly English-language newspaper, ran a headline: "Frankly, We Don't Know What's Going On Here."

There were disturbing reports that fighting was going on in Las Villas province, the territory over which the Second Front of the Escambray had fought during the revolution. Travelers from Las Villas province confirmed that all transportation between Cienfuegos and Trinidad and other coastal towns had been cut off. There had been no telephone communications with Havana for three days. The Cuban public, already conditioned to Castro's marathon five-hour speeches, was deeply perturbed by his silence. Finally, Maj. Raul Castro, commander of the armed forces, announced on a Thursday that his brother would probably talk on television on Saturday. Raul was carefully vague, blaming a "conspiracy" for the delay.

Meanwhile, a powerful clandestine Dominican radio broadcast, on a frequency close to that of the official Voz Dominicana, declared that Majors Gutierrez Menoyo and William Morgan were leading a counter-revolution in Las Villas. The broadcasts exhorted Cubans to rally to the counter-revolution and join the anti-Castro rebels on their march to Havana from Trinidad—"Join the revolt against Communist infiltration!"

What about Castro's thirty-third birthday on August 13? No official birthday party was planned. James Buchanan, a veteran *Miami Herald* reporter, wandered around Las Villas province in a jeep, seeking the fighting. "Castro Back in Hills to Defend His Own" was the *Herald*'s headline over Buchanan's story, suggesting there was fighting—but still unseen. Other reporters were duped by official disinformation into believing the stories of a counter-revolution, and those sounds of gunfire in Las Villas were real. Back in his palace in Ciudad Trujillo, El Jefe read the news reports out of Cuba which purported to confirm that fighting was underway in Las Villas province, specifically at the southern town of Trinidad. The reports helped convince Trujillo that his plot was working and that his money had been well spent. There was excited talk among newly arrived Cuban exiles in Miami, Florida, of the reported attack on Castro from the Dominican Republic.

Back in Ciudad Trujillo, El Jefe personally interrogated the priest and the flight crew. Trujillo was said to have been impressed with their reports of all the background noises of war. Those aboard were equally impressed with the cool of their counter-revolutionary fighters.

Back in Cuba Major Eloy Gutierrez Menoyo, adding concealed insult to injury, asked Johnny Abbes by radio to secure a gala uniform like one of those El Jefe wore on special occasions. Gutierrez stated he wanted the uniform when they triumphantly entered Santa Clara, their next objective. His request was taken seriously and suddenly Trujillo's own tailor was requesting measurements for the rush uniform order.

Alas it was only show business. The Associated Press dispatch, datelined Trinidad, reported that Castro had watched the Oscar-winning performance at Trinidad airport seated in the dark beneath a mango tree, 150 feet away from where the second plane came to a stop. Fidel decided that the sting was getting out of hand and ordered the craft seized. The pilot, exiled Cuban Lieut. Col. Antonio Soro, who had flown Batista into exile in Ciudad Trujillo in the same plane, realized too late that it was a trap and tried to make a last-minute take off. A gun battle ensued inside the plane between the crew and the barbudos. Pilot Soro was killed as was another exiled Cuban. On Castro's side, Lt. Ellopez Paz and a civilian, Frank Hidalgo Gato, were killed. Hidalgo Gato had just taken the photo used by the *New York Times* of Morgan talking into a radio microphone. Among the prisoners captured by the Castro forces were Luis Pozo Jiminez, a former Cuban senator and son of the former mayor of Havana during the Batista regime; a son of former National Police Col. Martin Perez; and a

Spaniard, Alfredo Maribran, an ex- member of Spanish dictator Francisco Franco's Blue Division and a member of Trujillo's Foreign Legion. Fidel Castro ordered them flown to Havana where they were exhibited on television.

Later that day (August 13), Castro spoke to a crowd from the balcony of the mayor's home in Cienfuegos, a city on the south coast near the Trinidad mountains, declaring that the "counter-revolution has been crushed." He declared the carnival could continue.

Then Fidel gave a five-hour TV-radio speech to his nation that ended at 3 a.m. on Saturday morning. He explained how they had sprung the trap on Trujillo. Major Morgan, Castro stated, had followed his orders and become the head of the Trujillo sting operation. Castro asserted that the Trujillo conspiracy included a priest, who reportedly came to Havana three times, on one occasion bringing ten bazookas for the counter-revolutionary plot.

The Dominicans professed their innocence, declaring that the Trujillo government had played no part in any attempted invasion of Cuba. Gen. Jose Garcia Trujillo, Dominican armed forces secretary, and El Jefe's brother charged that Castro himself had set up the alleged invasion of Cuba.

Nevertheless conversations between William Morgan and SIM Chief Johnny Abbes, plotting the expedition against Cuba, had been secretly recorded and were broadcast over Havana radio. They proved the fact of one of the most incredible geopolitical plot-counterplots in Caribbean history.

A popular song about the episode, which became an instant hit around the Caribbean and across Latin America, made fun of Trujillo. Composed by two Havana comics, it ridiculed Trujillo based on Eloy Gutierrez Menoyo's request for a gala uniform like Trujillo's to wear while entering victoriously into Santa Clara. The lyrics concluded:

"Listen to me, Trujillo! Today your medals are junk . . . ."

Postscript: William Morgan was a young rebel from Toledo, Ohio. He quit school and went off to sea at age fifteen, then enlisted in the U.S. Army's 82nd Airborne Division and saw duty in Japan. He spent time in an army stockade before receiving a dishonorable discharge. He had already left his wife and two children behind in Ohio when he disappeared from the U.S. at the end of 1957. It later developed that he climbed into the Escambray mountains after the death of a former army buddy at the hands of Batista's police, and joined the Second National Front under Maj. Eloy Gutierrez Menoyo. Then, in August 1959, the short, well-built thirty-one-year-old American became the hero of the hour in Cuba.

Later, in October 1960, Morgan took up arms once again, this time against Castro. He was caught moving arms into the Escambray Mountains for disenchanted veterans of the Second Front, his fighter friends. Found guilty of treason, the American adventurer was eventually executed in Havana's La Cabana fortress on March 11, 1961. A month later, the not-so-secret, ill-fated CIA's planned and executed Bay of Pigs (Playa Girón) invasion of Cuba took place. Trujillo was said to have gloated over Morgan's fate but El Jefe had only a brief time to live before he too was in effect executed. Two months after Morgan was shot by a Castro firing squad, Trujillo died in a hail of bullet fired by a group of patriots who had decided to commit tyrannicide. Morgan's Cuban wife fought successfully to have Morgan's U.S. citizenship restored.

Gutierrez Menoyo, born December 24, 1934 in Madrid, had participated with his brother Carlos in a 1957 attack on Batista's palace. Carlos, who had planned the attack with Jose Antonio Echevarria of the anti-Batista movement, *Directorio Revolucionario*, was killed in the assault. Another of Eloy Guterriez Menoyo's brothers had died at aged sixteen while fighting on the Republican side during the Spanish Civil War. Eloy, along with a group of Cuban rebel officers, had abandoned Cuba in 1961 for the United States; in 1965 he decided to return clandestinely to Cuba from the Dominican Republic and challenge Fidel, only to be caught and spend twenty years in prison before being freed in 1986 (after Spanish Prime Minister Felipe Gonzalez intervened for Eloy's release.) Eloy Gutierrez Menoyo became head of a Cuban advocacy group, *Cambio Cubano,* in Miami that called for peaceful change in Cuba, and he returned to Cuba to live in 2005.

CHAPTER 17

Catholic Church on It's Knees

S ome erstwhile supporters of Papa Doc believed that Duvalier's illness had fundamentally changed him for the worse, by inculcating him with certain madness. It was also their excuse for having supported him in the first place. They literally believed that the exercise of power in Haiti could make one delusional. While this theory was not without its persuasiveness, and while Doc indeed seemed to have changed, it was not in the way such new critics believed. Duvalier emerged from his physical ordeal, not crazy, but simply more power hungry. In spite of his weakened heart and chronic diabetes, which required daily doses of insulin to regulate his body's sugar metabolism, he was more determined than ever to take control. He had visited his mortality and knew his time was limited.

By mid-August 1959, he had decided to quicken his crackdown on old and new enemies, real and perceived, all in the name of his "mission sacrosainte." He was determined more than ever to target those forces that could be an obstacle to that "holy mission." He appeared either oblivious to, or not to care about, the fact that traditionally a deadly combination for any Western Hemisphere strongman was the combined opposition of the Roman Church, students, the business sector and the local U.S. embassy. However, by the summer of 1959, "the Embassy" had dropped out of the combination in Port-au-Prince, as Washington feared that only chaos would ensure if the Duvalier government collapsed. To be sure, while some Duvalierists were concerned principally with promoting their own enrichment and social status, others actually believed in Papa Doc's promise of a social revolution that would finally change Haiti, benefit the poor andthe middle class, and give equal rights, justice and freedom from misery. However, by late1959, the economy was stagnant. Coffee, the country's main export, had fallen because of drought from a record 1957–58 season of 565,000 bags (120 pounds each) to 250,000 bags. Tourism, which pre-Duvalier had begun to rival coffee as Haiti's major income-earner, was expected to generate only five million dollars, down from seven million in 1956. The National Bank of Haiti had imposed drastic controls on credit. Facing this situation, Duvalier expected the U.S. government to help bail him out. It did.

Of all the opposition forces, the Catholic Church and the students remained the most powerful. The pallid countenances of the prelates of Haiti's Church, mostly stern-looking Bretons, gazed down from the walls of the reception hall of the archiepiscopal palace in Port-au-Prince. The earliest portrait dated from 1860 when Haiti's concordat with Rome was signed. But no visage was sterner-looking than that of *Monseigneur* Francis Poirier, the fifty-two-year-old Brittany-born Archbishop of Haiti since 1955, when he had replaced the kindly old Msgr. Joseph Le Gouaze. Archbishop Poirier, a tough no-nonsense cleric, played by the church rules, which was enough for Duvalier to see Poirier as a threat.

Nevertheless, when Papa Doc did move against his country's Catholic hierarchy, it took most Haitians by surprised.

Duvalier's tensions with the Church had actually dated from his early political career when he had espoused the theme, popular among nationalistic Haitian intellectuals, that foreign priests—French citizens, who allegedly owed their secular allegiance to France, not Haiti—shouldn't control the most important educational institutions in the country. These intellectuals also accused the Church of favoring Haiti's wealthy mulatto elite to the detriment of the country's African-rooted culture, including Vodou, which the Vatican at the time vehemently opposed. During Duvalier's political campaign for the presidency, his advisers managed to have him steer clear of controversy and placate the Catholic clergy. Duvalier even appointed a Haitian priest, *Père* Jean-Baptiste Georges, as minister of education in the first Duvalier cabinet. Although Father Georges during his tenure was more concerned with education than politics, his successor as Education Minister, Father Hubert Papailler, turned out to be a Duvalierist ideologue.

When Duvalier finally moved against the Roman Catholic Church in Haiti in August 1959, it was actually only one step in his quest for total powers. The Haitianization of the Catholic clergy, a dream of many nationalists, proved secondary. In fact, Duvalier had already decided it was preferable politically to allow an influx of white Protestant missionaries from the southern United States who were even more violently opposed to Vodou than the Catholic Church, and whose own teaching and language skills left much to be desired. However, the Protestant missionaries lacked political clout in Haiti, were easily manipulated by the National Palace and in many cases were supportive of Duvalier's dictatorial tendencies, believing that the population was not ready for democracy and therefore that Haitians needed a firm and forceful leader.

On August 12 of that pivotal summer of 1959, a newly energized Duvalier fired the first salvo against the Catholic Church. He began by officially banning the *Union des Membres de L'Enseignement Secondaire* (UNMES), accusing the Union of Secondary School Teachers of being infiltrated by Communist ideology. A government communiqué further accused the UNMES of being responsible for a recent rash of bombings in Port-au-Prince. It was four days later that he had ordered the expulsion of the secretary of the union, the popular rector of Haiti's most prestigious boys' school, Petit Séminaire St. Martial. The rector was Alsatian-born Father Etienne Grienenberger, who had served in Haiti since 1942 and was also the superior of Haiti's Holy Ghost Order of priests. Under Grienenberger's rectorship, St. Martial's buildings had been reconstructed and from its new high-level classrooms the National Palace was in full view. Papa Doc, with his uncanny memory, especially for hostile acts, had not forgotten that Grienenberger had given Duvalier's political rival

Clément Jumelle, an alumnus of St. Martial, the last rites and had had the priestly audacity to broadcast Jumelle's political testament. Along with Father Grienenberger, the Catholic curate of the town of St. Marc, Joseph Marrec, was also ordered expelled. The rabid Duvalierist cleric, Father Hubert Papailler, who became Education Minister, had purportedly settled an old intramural grievance by putting Father Marrec on the expulsion list. Papailler was said to believe that Marrec had instigated Marrec's expulsion in 1948 from the parish of Petite Rivière de L'Artibonite, for want of discipline in the exercise of his ministry and refusing to obey his bishop.

Archbishop Poirier and French Ambassador Lucien Felix requested the specific grievances against the priests. The government refused to give any details.

Then things exploded. On Tuesday evening, August 18, hundreds of Haitians and some foreign and Haitian priests and nuns among them filed into the capital's Notre Dame Cathedral in a silent prayer protest against the expulsion of the two clerics. Witnesses described the ensuing scene as follows: The protest began peacefully. Then, suddenly, fearful piercing cries drowned out the murmur of prayers. Makouts, wielding the hardwood *kokomaks batons*, materialized everywhere, striking at mourners. Secret Police Chief Barbot appeared in battle dress, armed and dangerous, inside the cavernous sacred sanctuary along with steel-helmeted police.

When I arrived at the Cathedral to chronicle the prayer demonstration, I encountered a wild and frightening tableau. The street was littered with shoes lost and left behind by protesters as they fled in panic. Nuns and priests in their clerical robes had taken fearful refuge in the neighboring archdiocesan palace. Several men who had refused to flee were being severely beaten as they huddled in the Cathedral pews. Approximately forty persons were arrested and dragged off to police headquarters.

The following day, Port-au-Prince was in shock. Stories circulated, accusing Barbot of committing terrible acts in violating the "House of God."

Dr. Louis Mars, one of Haiti's first psychiatrists and Minister of

Foreign Affairs and Cults, in an interview a week later with Homer Bigart of the *New York Times* and myself defended the government's action, charging that the Cathedral assembly was not spontaneous but a well-conceived anti-government protest. "Jesus Christ himself once took the whip to drive people from the temple," Mars said softly. Bigart jokingly wondered whether the minister had suddenly elevated Barbot to rank with Jesus Christ, as in this case Barbot had wielded the whip.

The event was too much for Archbishop Msgr. François Poirier. He issued a pastoral letter to priests throughout the country, a copy of which was published the next day (Wednesday, August 19) in Haiti's Catholic newspaper, *La Phalange*. The angry archbishop denounced the government's order to expel the two French priests, noting that no reason had been given and stating that church authorities had not been consulted. The action, the prelate declared, was "contrary to the spirit of the 1860 church-state convention." In the pastoral letter sent to all Catholic churches in Haiti, the archbishop asked for prayers for the "two worthy and deserving priests" who had been unjustly ordered expelled. He also asked prayers for priests who remained in Haiti but could no longer rely on government protection.

On reading the pastoral letter in *La Phalange* that Wednesday morning, according to palace sources, it was Duvalier's turn to react angrily. He instructed Information Minister Paul Blanchet to reply. The two priests had been ordered out of the country, Blanchet stated, "for giving moral and material support to the enemies of the government." The government had acted, Blanchet, a onetime leftist not known for his piety, said, "to preserve the spiritual unity of the nation," adding that the two priests were working for the "social disintegration" of the country. The official government gazette, *Le Moniteur,* which published the expulsion order, making it binding, gave as the reason for the expulsion not only to "maintain the safety of the state" but also "the peace of the continent."

Papa Doc then ordered Port-au-Prince District Attorney Max C. Duplessy to issue a warrant calling for the Archbishop Poirier to appear before the district attorney at his office to answer charges of violating a section of the Haitian penal code prohibiting a minister of religion from censuring or criticizing public acts.

When the churchman failed to appear, Duvalier promptly ordered Duplessy to change the warrant to an arrest order. Police officers arrived at the archdiocesan palace with orders to arrest the archbishop for "crimes against the state." Confronted by the forces of justice, Poirier told the officers he could not and would not comply with the order as he had to first consult the local Vatican envoy, the apostolic charge d'affaires.

Momentarily discombobulated by the prelate's obstinate manner, the police departed. However, they returned later in the day and were met by the Vatican envoy. He told the officers that the papal nunciature had refused to allow the archbishop to answer the summons. A priest who was present added that only the government ministers of justice and interior had the right to summon the archbishop. The archdiocesan palace was then placed under police "guard."

That same day, Clement Barbot knocked on the rector's door at St. Martial College, and under heavy police escort, the two priests, who had been ordered expelled, were taken to the airport and placed on a Pan American airliner. (On arrival in New York City, Father Grienenbeger protested at a news conference, "How could a Catholic priest who has seen the awfulness of war be involved in bombings?" — a reference to his experiences in World War II. Two days later, both of the expelled priests were treated to lunch with Francis Cardinal Spellman, Archbishop of New York.)

Back in Port-au-Prince, the pending arrest of Archbishop Poirier brought instant reaction from Rome and provided me a series of page-one stories abroad. Foreign news editors wanted all the details. Perhaps for the first time Duvalier had gotten the world's attention, no matter how controversially.

Appended to my dispatch published in the August 21, 1959, *New York Times* was a warning to Duvalier datelined Vatican City. In a thirteen-line notice appearing at the top of Page One of the Vatican newspaper *L'Osservatore Romano*, the Church had put Papa Doc on notice, cautioning, "it would be superfluous in any case to recall the penalties '*Latae Sententias*' with which the code of Canon Law safe-guards the sacred character and freedom of bishops." The Vatican made it clear that if Msgr. Poirier was arrested, everyone associated with such action would be automatically excommunicated.

At *Le Nouvelliste* that day, several colleagues and I sat around in editor Max Chauvet's little office speculating as to just who would be excommunicated besides Papa Doc.

However, the following day, on August 22, I had another front-page story in the *New York Times*, which was headlined: "Prelates' Arrest Is Stayed in Haiti.—Warrant Is Suspended as Vatican Issues Warning of Excommunication from Haiti's State Religion."

President Duvalier was reported to have issued the order to sus-pend the arrest warrant. The suspension was said to have followed an appeal to District Attorney Max. C. Duplessy by three Haitians priests. The report, in the newspaper *Le Nouvelliste,* quoted Information Minister Paul Blanchet as stating that "by suspending the warrant President Duvalier was demonstrating his desire to col-laborate with the clergy."

However, the Archbishop considered himself a virtual prisoner in his palace as long as the government did not rescind the order for his arrest, which the government had only "suspended."

In an editorial the following day, Sunday, the *New York Times* commented that "President Duvalier was wise not to follow through. The dictators of Argentina, Colombia, Venezuela and Cuba all found in recent years that it does not pay to get embroiled with the church...."

Closer to home, a *Miami Herald* editorial took note of Papa Doc's fight with the Roman Catholic Church and assessed the Duvalier regime as being on the point of collapse. The *Herald* went on to list Haiti's ills. It saw the country approaching the brink, observing that a "tense and uneasy watchfulness prevails. This alone would be a matter of serious concern. But it is only one of the manifold troubles that is pushing this Negro republic of 3,400,000 souls towards cata-strophe . . . ."

"The nation is slipping towards bankruptcy," the *Herald* added,

"Always dwelling in poverty, this most densely populated nation in the hemisphere depends on the market for coffee, which is in a state of acute depression."

The *Herald* ended its editorial with: "It is a dreary prospect for the nation, which has always had such close ties with the U.S. To be economically and politically sick has been its lot for a long time. The spiritual illness that now threatens it could be fatal to the Duvalier regime."

The church story proved important enough for the *New York Times* to send one of their best reporters to take over coverage. Homer Bigart arrived on Saturday, August 22, and we set to work together. It turned out to be a week of non-stop reporting, moving from one interview to another. When Homer sat down at his old portable (typewriter) it was front-page copy he was typing. He insisted on going with me to the RCA cable office to file his story. He elevated me from legman, driver and translator to fellow correspondent.

Competitive newsman though he was, he assisted me in filing my own dispatches to the Associated Press and *Time* magazine, encouraging me to use material from our joint interviews.

Daily, he won front-page "play" in the *Times*.

In a lengthy dispatch published on Monday, August 24, under the headline, "Brutality Protested by Haiti's Prelates," Bigart reported: "The protest today by four Bishops of the Catholic hierarchy in Haiti—including the Haitian-born auxiliary Bishop of Port-au-Prince—is reported to have accused the regime of promoting disorder, creating fear and violating human dignity. The incident, which is reminiscent of clashes between state and church in Iron Curtain countries, perplexed United States officials who have defended the Duvalier regime as tolerably democratic and in any case preferable to opposition groups."

His story continued: "Church sources confirmed that the root of the tension was the nagging resentment of the regime against the preponderance of French-born clergy of the French-speaking Negro republic, and the fact that three of the four Bishops are French."

"But these sources pointed out that the number of Haitian priests

CATHOLIC CHURCH TO ITS KNEES

has risen to 110, compared with 180 Frenchmen. In addition, there are forty Oblate fathers from Canada and the United States and twenty Belgian priests recently expelled from Communist China. Their presence has served to dilute the resentment against the French priests.

"Moreover, sixty Haitians are in seminaries—the largest such class to receive training for the priesthood. Nine have been ordained this year. . . ."

The following day, Bigart's *Times* story, "Haiti Will Demand Removal of Prelate," reported that Haiti would demand that the Vatican recall Archbishop Poirier for allegedly criticizing the Duvalier government. Our source was Clément Barbot. The secret police chief was in his element, having elevated himself to the lofty post of Presidential Secretary, and he spoke on the record in the interview. He declared that the government was collecting evidence that the archbishop had been plotting against the regime. He said that the evidence would be submitted to Vatican authorities by the Gen. Antonio Kébreau, Haiti's ambassador to the Holy See, with the request that Pope John XXIII remove the prelate. When Bigart asked Barbot whether Duvalier would insist to the Vatican that Poirier's replacement be a Haitian, Barbot replied, "No, no, we will not ask for a Haitian archbishop. We will leave the choice up to the Pope."

Barbot went on to charge that Archbishop Poirier had "created an impossible situation" by publishing his pastoral letter criticizing the government for ordering the expulsion of the two French priests. By publishing the missive, Barbot said the archbishop had deliberately tried to foment anti-government sentiment. The government, Barbot added, had advised Archbishop Poirier that it wanted to expel the priests secretly "so they could leave without scandal."

It was a lengthy interview and Barbot, obviously enjoying himself, went to great lengths to paint both the archbishop and two expelled priests as dangerous anti-Duvalierists. Nevertheless, contrary to rumors, he said the government had no intention of terminating Haiti's 1860 concordat with the Vatican. "There is no conflict whatsoever between the government and the Church," he maintained.

Either Barbot thought erroneously that he was making policy—the President's domain—or else it was all a propaganda ploy because the very next day Bigart and I were visited by a high government source—Dr. Elmer Loughlin, the American, at the time the adviser closest to Duvalier—and told that the government had no intention of demanding that the Vatican recall the archbishop for "sedition" against the state. However, according to Loughlin, President Duvalier expected Poirier to issue a statement that the prelate's pastoral letter denouncing the government for the expulsion of the two French priests had been "misinterpreted" as an attempt to overthrow the regime. The archbishop did not comply with Duvalier's wishes.

Correspondent Bigart treated the Haiti story with the same thoroughness reflected in all his other famous datelines that included most of the world's hotspot for the proceeding past quarter of a century. After a reporting visit to the U.S. embassy in Port-au-Prince, he included some incisive paragraphs assessing U.S. policy, noting, "United States circles, still convinced that the Duvalier regime is preferable to any of the opposition groups, are fearful that the strife will result in the overthrow of Duvalier. Believing that the collapse of the Government would plunge Haiti into chaos, these United States circles are eager for a prompt settlement of the quarrel with the church."

Buttressing this interpretation, Bigart reported in a follow-up story that, "a United States operations mission [in Haiti] has been expanded. Haiti will also receive about ten million dollars in economic aid from the United States this year. American experts are being brought in to advise the government on finances, budgetary reforms, taxes and customs."

In spite of the hectic news-reporting atmosphere, there was time for some tension-breaking interludes. During dinner, one evening at the Grand Hotel Oloffson, Bigart, famous for his one-liners asked whether I had attended a journalism school. When I told him that I had not, his instant response was: "That's good!" Explaining how he himself had quit the New York University School of Journalism because he thought the professors knew next to nothing about journalism, he said he learnt more about the craft as a copy boy in 1929 with the old *New York Herald Tribune*. Homer talked nostalgically of the *Trib*. He had only moved to the *Times* four years earlier and confessed that he had left his heart at the *Trib*.

Shaking hands with me as he boarded his plane to depart Haiti, Bigart stammered, "The story is all yours now, good luck" He felt "my" story was just beginning. The order expelling Archbishop Poirier hung over the country like a descending pendulum that would eventually reach its nadir.

*   *   *

No sooner had Homer Bigart left than the church-state story exploded again. Five priests accused the government publicly of resorting to "totalitarianism" in its campaign to oust prelate Poirier. The government, the priests charged, was trying to force the Church to pledge "absolute obedience" to President Duvalier. "No creature on earth is due absolute obedience," they declared. Their views were published on the front page of the Catholic daily *La Phalange,* Haiti's largest-circulation newspaper. The edition quickly sold out.

The Church, the five clerics wrote, refused to accept government charges that "certain priests," including Archbishop Poirier, were involved in anti-government activities. Two of the priests, both Haitians, Fathers Ernest Verdieu and Antoine Adrien, appealed to the government to exercise "good sense" in dealing with the respective rights of church and state. "Abusive interpretations" of Haiti's penal code, they warned, was rendering a disservice to peace and tranquillity in the country. Moreover, they said, the government's attack on the Roman Catholic Church was hurting Haiti's world prestige.

The declarations of the defiance by the five priests garnered me more news space in the *New York Times* and my other media outlets.

*   *   *

As if his battle with the Church was not enough, Papa Doc then proceeded to launch a war against his own congress. On September 19, 1959, Duvalier asked the congress for full powers for a period of a month. While the motion passed, six senators had the audacity to abstain from voting. For Papa Doc, this was treason. Already enraged by the fact that the same six congressmen had spoken out the year before against granting him special powers, Doc—exercising his new dictatorial prerogatives—ordered the six impeached and their senatorial immunity lifted. Coming after his crisis with the Church, Duvalier's action against the six senators sent shock waves throughout the capital. Incredulous Haitian asked each other: Were there congressmen brave enough to face down Duvalier?

The short answer was no. While the lower House of Deputies announced diplomatically, so as not to arouse Duvalier's ire, that they felt the new decree giving the president full powers was unnecessary, the deputies had no other response. The Haitian Senate for its part remained silent.

In a special edition of *Le Moniteur*, the official government gazette, the six dissident senators were formally charged with plotting against the state in league with communists. In the Senate, all six had been impeached. These were all men who had campaigned for Francois Duvalier. Two immediately fled the country and three, including Senator Jean Belizaire, sought and received political asylum in the Mexican embassy. The sixth senator, Episcopal Father Yvon Moreau, refused to flee the country and went into hiding or into an embassy, declaring, "They had to invent a story to dispense with me. I am a believer in democracy and I thought I was doing my job when I criticized what should be criticized to protect the welfare of the people and the country. . . . I have never been involved in any subversive activities and I don't intend to be used now by any group of politicians. Despite the action against me, I will continue a normal life."

But life was far from normal in Haiti. Moreau was a marked man.

Duvalier scheduled elections, the following month, November 1959, for six replacement senators. As absurd as the accusations were of the ousted priests-senators plotting to set up a "Communist regime," such charges worked time and again for Duvalier since Cold

War ideology was the main concern of the day in Washington. In branding his enemies Communists, Duvalier was reassuring Washington of his ideological reliability.

CHAPTER 18

Return of the Sun

I t verged on the ridiculous if not surreal. When I arrived with cash
at the Tax Office to pay off the last payment of money the Tax
Office had demanded of the *Haiti Sun*, the officials on duty were
genuinely puzzled. There appeared to be no record of any government debt owed by the *Haiti Sun*. The demand, I explained, had also
been a mystery to me. However, with generous smiles the Tax office
functionaries happily accepted the money. As I departed I noted the
two officials grinning at each other. The impression they gave was,
"How can we split it?"

Freelancing for foreign media had been particularly rewarding, and
by October 1959 it was possible not only to settle the Tax Office bill
but also to arrange for the purchase of a second-hand printing press
in Florida.

The magnificent New York linotype machine and a fine collection
of hand setting type for headlines made it possible to compose the
pages of the Sun in our own print shop behind the *Haiti Sun's* editorial office. The showpiece of the Sun's print shop was a huge, ancient
two-ton "guillotine" (paper cutter) we had been able to purchase from
La Phalange. Robert Deschamps, then running his family printing
business, had contributed a small proof press. A stock of newsprint
left over from when the Sun had been closed was a reminder of just
how far the newspaper had come since those days in 1950 when we
often had to search grocery stores for white wrapping paper on which

to print. Meanwhile, the Haiti Sun's small but loyal staff had been waiting impatiently to resume publication and was elated that we were back in business.

A new director at L'Imprimerie de *L'Etat* (the Government Printing Office) greeted us warmly. He was happy for the business of printing the Sun temporarily even though we expected to receive our own printing press within three months, when we would be completely self-sufficient and independent printing-wise. The scuttlebutt around *L'Imprimerie de L'Etat* was that Papa Doc's pet Brooklyn mischief–maker, *Ti Barb* Morrision, was abroad, was in arrears with his printing payments for publishing his English weekly, and had begun to loose interest in it. In spite of his having been discredited among U.S. officials, he had nevertheless been accepted as a member of the Inter-American Press Association, to which the *Haiti Sun* and I belonged. When I learned that *Ti Barb* had also been accepted for membership in the IAPA, I resigned from the organization, which was ostensibly dedicated to freedom of the press in the Americas. Unfortunately, in those days, the IAPA with a couple of exceptions was considered little more than an association of wealthy Latin American oligarch-publishers.

Publishing a newspaper in a restrictive environment such as Haiti had become under Papa Doc was not so much an ethical challenge as a practical one. The *Haiti Sun* was not about to become musique palais ("the palace tune" or propaganda). However to exist and resist it was necessary to be a realist and understand the limits of journalistic syntax. Thus one had to learn that it was often a case of how one reported the news, rather than distorting or ignoring events in order not to offend the authorities. So we employed a certain "code" nomenclature, which we counted on our knowledgeable readers to interpret. In fact, that the *Sun* was an English-language paper in a predominantly French and Kreyòl speaking country also helped. However, all of the foregoing is not to say that some self-censorship was unavoidable.

Our French-language sister publications, Le Nouvelliste, Haiti Journal and Le Matin, had managed to survive knowing how to adapt to dictatorships. They also knew how to enjoy the rare moments of press freedom that usually came between the downfall of one regime and the rise of a new would-be Papa. The exception to the pattern of prudently circumspect reporting of events was La Phalange. As the official Catholic Church daily, it had no choice except to publish the church's interpretation of local news position regarding same which by the end of 1959 was heading for a confrontation with Duvalier.

The Sun's small staff also felt we owed a debt to our own faithful readers in Haiti as well as abroad (we had just over 2,000 subscribers as far away as Detroit and Tahiti) and these were thrilled with the prospect of publishing the *Sun* again. In the streets of downtown Port-au-Prince, I answered to the simple name of "Haiti Sun." As for my foreign media outlets, they were of course keen on my reporting the Haiti story to the best of my ability, but all were sensitive to the dangers involved and solicitous of my well being.

To the Eisenhower Administration in Washington, Papa Doc by the winter of 1959 had become an improbable Caribbean ally. Castro was suspect—he was moving too far left—and his anti-U.S. rants increasingly concerned the administration. The Dominican Republic's Trujillo, on the other side of the political spectrum, was growing more irascible and unpredictable by the day. He was an embarrassment in spite of his extreme anti-Communist views. Consequently, Duvalier, in spite of his idiosyncrasies and anti-democratic methods, looked like the only viable alternative in the interests of Caribbean stability, and so the United States decided to shore him up.

At times, it appeared that Washington was in charge in Port-au-Prince and that the Cold War was the real motivator. It was a green light of sorts for Haiti as amber was turning to red in Cuba. Along with Washington's new interest in Haiti, there was a feeling that thanks to or in spite of Papa Doc, the country was at last moving into a development phase.

There was cautious hope that at last things just might change for the better. Development projects seemed to be blossoming all over. Harry Warner Yoe headed the U.S. aid mission, the largest in the

Western Hemisphere, with a staff of experts that reached nearly 100 by the end of the year. In addition to the American staff, some 3,000 Haitian technicians, office workers and manual laborers were employed by the U.S. aid mission which, if it continued to grow, was destined to rival the Haitian government in size. The U.S. government had even built its own new air-conditioned offices off Port-au-Prince's Harry Truman Blvd. next to the American Union School and facing the Bois Chêne canal. To Duvalier's chagrin, at the opening, Archbishop Poirier had been invited to bless the building. Mission Director Yoe explained that the aid mission sought to "bring about conditions for private enterprise to develop [in Haiti], both Haitian and foreign." To this end, the mission had been advising the Duvalier government on developing and strengthening national institutions such as key ministries and schools, and on specific projects to assist poor farmers.

Duvalier, whose acting ability was nothing to be laughed at, made his own pitch as favoring democracy when one day he walked into the Caserne from the palace back door dressed in ordinary military khaki pants, open-collar shirt and olive-green campaign cap. Members of his family and officers of the Presidential Guard accompanied the president. His words echoed by a sound truck, Duvalier gave the assembled soldiers a pep talk. Several of the U.S. Marine advisors present believed the performance was staged for their benefit. Capt. Charles Williamson, the Marine advisor to the Presidential Guard, took notes. Papa Doc's main statement was that Haiti's new army would be "dedicated to the youth of the country." He instructed the soldiers to work hard, to learn and to listen. "In Haiti we are striving to achieve democracy . . . . The only way to achieve democracy is to combine the power of the government and army with the power of the people."

The country itself possessed the remarkable ability of adopting an air of normalcy even when the occasional bombs were exploding and Tontons Makouts were rapping on doors. This facade of peace was helpful as the country's tourist industry was seeking to benefit from the winter season. *Time* felt that the Caribbean was the "in" place and we reported on island tourism. Illustrating one article was a photograph I had taken of the Grand Hotel Oloffson's nightclub, which then lease-owner Roger Coster had literally carved out of the adjacent mountainside. *The New York Times* also requested a tourist feature, which I illustrated with a picture of a colorful coastal sailboat gaily, painted up with flowers like one of Port-au-Prince's colorful "tap-tap" jitney buses.

Finally on November 8, 1959, after a four-month eclipse, the Haiti Sun *was back on the streets and at ten cents a copy it quickly sold out.*

Our editorial, entitled, "The Tenth Year," once again set out the paper's policy. We told it as we wished it to be:

The Sun returns to publication after a short interruption, coinciding with the anniversary of its founding in 1950. We do not, on this occasion, intend to list the trials and tribulations. The Sun returns to publication after a short interruption, coinciding involved in publishing a newspaper nor to detail what caused the Sun to disappear for the last four months.

But we do want the people of Port-au-Prince and the Republic of Haiti to know once and again that the Sun has only one cardinal aim: That is to encourage, help and publish the news of the march of the Haitian People towards a better, more prosperous and happy life.

The Sun has been—and always will be—a newspaper reflecting the interests of the Haitian community. It never has –and never will—serve the interests of any power- seeking clique. Every Haitian has a rightful place in The Sun.

Our guidepost is the motto of the American press: 'To give the news impartially, without fear or favor, regardless of any party, sect, or interest involved.'

There will, of course, always be some who will accuse us of veering from that clearly defined road. The answer to these is that the news columns of The Sun, which cannot be bought, are open to those who choose to disagree. The

Sun never has, and never will, accept subsidies or money from the government of Haiti or any other State, organization, group, or individual. It is the newspaper of the Haitian people. It will never fear honest competition, for that is a condition that fosters private initiative and enterprise, and enhances the sacred trust the people should always have in their press. The Sun will vigorously fight against any publication that violates this trust.

The Sun has an unshakable faith in the future of Haiti and its people. It hopes eventually to publish a pictorial edition in Creole. For the nine years that have passed and the tenth and the other years ahead. The Sun gratefully acknowledges the support of its advertisers and readers. It pledges itself to strive in every way to be a bigger and better newspaper. Nothing could please The Sun more than to have nothing to publish but 'good news'. But there always must be the bad along with the good. Whichever category into which the news falls, it belongs to the people of Haiti.They will always find it in the columns of this newspaper. They will always find, too, that The Sun, as in the past, will whole-heartedly support every move designed to strengthen the bloodstream of the nation's economy.

That includes everything from boosting Haiti's tourist attractions, the products she wants to sell to the rest of the world, to obtaining substantial loans—particularly from the United States—aimed at achieving financial and economic stability which in turn strengthens the government and the nation's administrative machinery.

This is your newspaper. Every community gets the newspaper it deserves. The Sun confidently believes that you— the people of Haiti—want it to be the best newspaper.

It is here to serve you. It will never falter in that duty.

The Sun will always publish—knowing that a happy and prosperous future is assured in the hands of an enlightened people.

"New Taxes and Trim Budget to Show Haiti Can Help Self," was the *Haiti Sun* headline of an interview with President Duvalier which Peter Kihss of the *New York Times* and I had shared. In his palace office Duvalier, sporting a Trumanesque bowtie, showed no outward sign of the heart attack that had incapacitated him for nearly two months. He insisted on speaking in English instead of French or Krèyol, and when we left his high-ceilinged National palace office, we both realized Papa Doc had afforded us an hour and a half. At times, he was lost for a word in English and his syntax poor. Nevertheless, he managed to make an articulate political sales pitch.

Political conditions, he said, had improved, and it was the Congress' job to lift the continuing state of siege, in effect since May 2, 1958, suspending constitutional guarantees on search, arrest, freedom of speech and trial by civilian courts. "We don't need it," he declared. Duvalier also maintained that he had never sought reinstatement of the dictatorial power by which he had ruled by decree for six months ending the previous January 30. It was, he said, a misunderstanding when the Senate voted him decree powers for one month on September 19, and he noted that the Chamber of Deputies had decided he did not need such powers, and they had never become effective.

Painstakingly, Duvalier, who was notorious for having scant knowledge of economics, listed a dozen new taxes in the works. (They would be only temporary, he contended, and would include a one-cent increase in postage stamps for domestic mail and two cents for foreign. The stamp tax increase would go to the campaign against illiteracy, he explained.)

His government hoped to raise an estimated $1,000,000 to $1,500,000 to be able to balance the budget for which he would propose $27,800,000 in expenditures. Spending for the fiscal year ending on September 30 was $33,600.000, he said. It was balanced with a $6,000.000 United States budget grant. The President noted that it had been a "very bad year" because of drought and a smaller coffee crop than usual. The International Monetary Fund, he said, had been dissatisfied, as Haiti had had to draw $5,400.000 in foreign exchange and in return impose government austerity. His government, he said, would depend more on income taxes that provided only seven percent of the government's revenue. He promised to do away with nuisance taxes that hurt mostly the poor.

Overall, Haiti's array of taxes would be streamlined and made more equitable, Papa Doc vowed, and he expected to balance the budget without having to ask the U.S. again for fiscal support. Any money left over would go into development projects such as his "long-term" priorities: roads, irrigation, anti-erosion measures and industries that processed Haitian raw materials, including cotton, textiles, vegetable oils and soap.

Sitting across from us, Duvalier appeared the most caring person in the world. In his marked nasal tone, he explained his austerity measures as if they hurt him personally. The cuts included reducing the salaries of 27,000 state employees by ten to twenty percent. Identity cards required for each citizen—but few had them—would be necessary for cashing checks, he said.

His face hardened slightly, in what up until then had been a genial report on tax collection, when Duvalier stated that notices had gone starting with the Department of Health, warning that "the inefficient, irregular and undisciplined who entrench themselves behind their Duvalierism will be fired without mercy" if they don't do the work for which they are paid.

On the political front, Papa Doc charged that "there is a Communist infiltration in Haiti." He had been "obliged to remove from our educational system some very active elements." This was a reference to the dissolution the preceding summer of a secondary school teachers association, and the firing of teachers who were members of the executive committee of the primary school teacher's union.

He denounced "terrorist bombings." Some terrorists, he asserted, had gotten asylum in the Cuban and Venezuelan embassies. Bomb terrorism, he said, seemed to be "a new system in the Western Hemisphere in several countries." (That month, a *machine infernale,* as the explosive was termed in French, had wounded a law student when it exploded in front of the law school where the director of the Regie Du Tabac, Frederic Desvarieux, parked his car. Another had exploded near the U.S. Marine headquarters before the Paramount cinema where the movie *Le Mysterieux Dr. Satan* was playing.)

Miniature flags of the Organization of American States member countries sat on the top of the bookshelf behind Papa Doc's desk along with sketches of new projects including Texas entrepreneur Clinton T. Murchison's meatpacking plant at Damiens that would finally replace the turn-of-the-century abattoir on the bay side of the open-air La Saline market. As noted in *Sun* editorials over the years, the old abattoir was a shocking, unsanitary monstrous eyesore, offensive to all the human senses, to say nothing about the cruel manner in which cattle driven along roads for miles from the south and north were slaughtered in the most primitive manner. Also on display in the president's office was the first set of maps of Haiti that had been presented to him by the U.S. Army Inter-American Geodetic Survey which was working with the department of *eodesie et Cartographie* to complete a new mapping of Haiti, a project that was expected to be completed by mid-1961. A hopeful sign was that no firearms were visible in the president's office.

Duvalier went on to deny the rumor that there might be as many as forty persons incarcerated on political grounds. He confirmed however that he had recently ordered the release of a number of such individuals, but declined to discuss reports that the United States had interceded on their behalf. (Haiti's ambassador to Washington, Ernest Bonhomme, had had to relay to Duvalier a list of U.S. State Department complaints about beatings, jailing and political murders. Yet it was only after the U.S. Embassy in Port-au-Prince handed the government a list of twenty political prisoners and inquired about their fate that Duvalier had freed them all at once. And it was the last time he would accommodate a U.S. request regarding political prisoners.)

Duvalier stated in our interview that it was always "my habit to take out of jail, to release people, since I took office. Some people [however] can get crazy, they are not responsible, and I am a doctor."

He said he knew of only two current political prisoners—Jean Brierre, a poet and former Haitian ambassador to Argentina, and Gustave Borno, a reporter for *La Matin*. Duvalier called Brierre "an old friend" whom he wanted to release, but declared, "The police department asked me to wait." (Not long after the presidential interview in a December issue of the *Haiti Sun*, we published a poem by Jean Brierre, noting that he was still in prison. He and ten others benefited from a presidential clemency. Nevertheless, Haiti lost one of its finest poets when Brierre was ultimately forced into exile and spent the rest of the Duvalier years first in Jamaica and later in Africa.)

The president asserted that there was "no conflict" with the Roman Catholic Church despite the ouster the preceding August of the two priests, who the president said had been "involved in political matters." Papa Doc pointed out that his was the first Haitian government ever to name a priest as Minister of Education, and to turn over to Roman Catholic nuns a girl's teacher college.

He acknowledged that he was asking for United States military aid to re-equip his entire army.

*   *   *

Elections, we noted in the *Haiti Sun*, for the seats of the six senators who had been ousted by presidential decree on charges of plotting to set up "a Communist regime," were scheduled for Sunday, November 15. The elections evinced little interest as Haitians viewed them as a pre-selection of Duvalier loyalists to give his parliament the right rubber-stamps bounce.

Meanwhile, photos the *Haiti Sun's* front page showed a rotund Rollin Atwood, the director of the U.S. Point IV assistance program for Latin America down from Washington, D.C., pausing during a tour of a *Polé Colé* cacao nursery near Grand Riviere du Nord. During the visit, he exulted over "the tremendous progress" that had been made in Haiti in only one year. *Poté Colé*, Krèyol for "Pull Together," was a comprehensive, well-planned, development project, and a joint U.S.-Haitian effort to boost agricultural production and rural education. The project encompassed 300 square miles in Haiti's north and potentially affected the well-being of more than half a million poor farmers.

Another photograph displayed on the *Sun*'s front page during this period of 1959 portrayed the five young Cuban captives from the August 13 invasion seated on chairs in their uniforms, barefoot in the National Penitentiary. On another topic, in a brief paragraph, we quoted the Catholic daily *La Phalange* as reporting that the August 29 arrest warrant against archbishop Msgr. François Poirier had been annulled. However, for Haitian taxi and taptap drivers there was bad news. Parliament had authorized a new tax on fuel bringing the price of gasoline to forty-five cents a gallon. This could only expand a custom then for taxi and tap-tap drivers to keep switching on and off the engines of their vehicles in the belief it would save gasoline, when in fact restarting the vehicle used more fuel. The driver drove with one hand on the ignition key switching it on and off to let his vehicle coast. It was a metaphor for how the Duvalier government operated by switching on and off development projects depending on the politics of the moment.

Taxes were also hiked that same week on alcoholic beverages, including Haiti's favorite rum as well as cigarettes. The people had no choice but to accept the new taxes without even a murmur.

The *Sun* carried a long review of Alfred Metraux's new book on Voodoo (he used this spelling of Vodou), an English translation of which had gone on sale at La Caravelle bookshop for twenty-five gourdes (five dollars). There was no dearth of social and visitor news for the Ti-Joseph column. *Time* magazine had opened a new Caribbean bureau in Havana headed by Dwight Martin, who had closed the Vienna bureau. The Caribbean had become an important domestic story in the United States, mainly because of Cuba's leftward tilt. Thirty-eight-year-old Martin spoke Mandarin, having spent most of his career in the Far East. *Time*'s Bruce Henderson, based in Panama, was expected to continue to visit Haiti occasionally while covering the rest of his wide-ranging beat in Central and South America.

A tireless academic researcher, Professor Sydney W. Mintz of Yale University's department of anthropology, provided the *Haiti Sun* with details of his landmark study of "The Place of the Internal Market System in the Haitian Economy," part of his vast research work in Haiti. My lengthy interview with Georges Liautaud, 59, the renowned metal sculptor of Croix des Bouquet, recounting his fascinating rise from blacksmith to leader of a whole new school of art, took up an illustrated full page in the *Sun*. Businessman Fortune Bogat had come late to the *Sun* as a columnist specializing in a subject in which he was well versed: The Macho Male. "The male who makes tourism spin," was his new contribution that noted how women were attracted to an island not only by the beauty of the beaches but that of the handsome male. Bogat had a well-earned reputation with the ladies. Marc Petit, our oldest staff member, provided the Cric Crac column featuring Bouqui and Malice, two antagonistic folklore characters. "Bouqui inherits a kingdom" was the title of his latest endeavor.

Among our many photo features was one of members of the U.S. submarine squadron based in Key West, Florida, who donated food and clothing for a famine in Haiti's Northwest and had delivered it by subchaser. Sailors from the aircraft carrier *USS Boxer* enjoyed a festive liberty in Port-au-Prince. Only one bomb exploded that same week but it panicked some 5,000 fans watching wrestlers Marcos Brando of Jamaica and "El Chileno" of Chile flail away at each other in a *lutte libre* (free for all) at Silvio Cator stadium. A Haitian soldier suffered a broken leg in the panic to exit the stadium.

There had been another Brando in town. And the other Brando was a scoop that we had lost during the *Sun*'s eclipse. Nonetheless it was a tantalizing story, and on the principle that better late than never, we published it on Page Seventeen following the *Sun*'s resurrection. Our headline: "Idyllic Two Weeks in Haiti for Stars [Marlon] Brando and France Nguyen." The story reported:

One quiet afternoon in September, a shapely young brunette and a muscular (flat stomach) companion flew in from Miami and brought Haiti worldwide recognition as an island of romance.

Not since James (From Here to Eternity) Jones wed at the Grand Hotel Oloffson nor French actress Martine Carol danced at the Ibo Lele Hotel has the republic received such a chunk of publicity.

The curvaceous, French-speaking Timy Van Nga [her alias] in a clinging cotton dress won the scene from her cleverly disguised dentist [Brando], garbed in the tradition of a rascal from a silent movie spy-thriller.

Adjusting his Pancho Villa mustache, dark glasses and beatnik cap, Miles Graham of Omaha, Nebraska, was filling out his landing card in the Bowen Field waiting room when official Tourist Board greeter Aubelin Jolicoeur, a man not easily fooled, popped up with a hail of "Hello Mr.

Marlon Brando, using the alias Miles Graham of Omaha, a Nebraska dentist, and his pretty young actress companion, France Nguyen, posing as Timy Van Nga, arrived for a secret vacation. They were surprised by Aublin Jolicoeur, who immediately recognized the movie stars, much to their chagrin.

Marlon Brando . . . welcome to Haiti." "Oh, no, no, no,"
cried the Omaha dentist. "Please, please do me a favor, get
me on the first plane out of here . . . I'll come back tomorrow or the next day—incognito. If people know I'm here
my vacation will be ruined," the tourist pleaded. Assured of
heavenly peace, privacy and no publicity the vacation was
on again.

Like wartime U-Boats in the North Atlantic, Timy and
Brando were only sighted fleetingly during their two-week
vacation. They were glimpsed presiding over gregarious
meals at the Picardie, dancing at the Bacoulou, Montana,
swimming at La Mer Frappe, Kyona and tooling around
the countryside in a rented Volkswagen beetle.

Except for a short blurb in Time magazine which un-
masked Timy as France Nguyen of the Broadway play,
"The World of Suzie Wong," they were given complete
peace of mind.

With their Haitian vacation over, the peace ended.
Returning to Miami a highly trained squad of veteran photographers was lying in ambush. The result brought Haiti
before millions of readers of magazines and newspapers,
and TV and radio audiences as a romantic isle.

The Brando story was illustrated by Aubelin Jolicoeur who
snapped photos of the couple's arriving on the Panam clipper at
Bowen Field—Marlon carrying a gift flight bag (and Colonel Hienl,
who coincidentally enough arrived from Miami on the same plane,
striding by in the picture). The photo that we did not get was of the
two celebrity visitors in the nude. I learned of this missed opportunity when the old Haitian farmer who rented me a slice of beach at La
Mer Frappee a few miles south of the capital came to the office to col-
lect the rent. He reported that we had had two intruders. They had
driven up in their rental car and taken over the little isolated beach.
The old man thought that I had sent them. He had withdrawn from
the beach but did observe, he said—when he learned that they were

not my guests—that they had taken off their clothes and were bathing in the nude! Being a gentleman, he declined to give me further details of their sojourn at the beach.

Everyone in Port-au-Prince involved in tourism was making an effort to dress more elegantly in order to encourage more tourists. And homegrown styles often proved inviting to visitors. French actress Martine Carol dumped her Parisian wedding dress in favor of a Haitian creation. The *Sun*'s "cheesecake" included a photo of a blonde German beauty bathing at the Hotel Choucounne pool.

*   *   *

Returning to Haiti, Peter Kihss as usual complained that he didn't know why the *New York Times* kept sending him on foreign assignment when he was really a metropolitan reporter. Nevertheless, as always he set to work in incongruous coat and tie immediately. As a hard-working correspondent who spoke both French and Spanish and like his *Times* colleague Homer Bigart, had a slight stammer, Kihss was a demanding taskmaster. Yet he had a compassionate streak totally unlike many tough-edged foreign correspondents.

If our interview with Colonel Heinl had been published in their entirety it is doubtful that the Marine Mission commander would have survived as long as he did in Haiti. His provocative description of the Haitian army was that of a gonorrhea-infected bunch more interested in feeding their fighting cocks than in cleaning their rusty old rifles. He did however succeed in sending the Haitian army's high command into a fit of deep nationalist anger. However, as Heinl had *carte blanche* from Duvalier to re-equip and train his army, the officers knew that the American colonel was untouchable. Heinl, whose father interestingly enough had also worked for the *New York Times*, understood the media very well and sold the story over and over again on the need for arms for Duvalier's army.

Nor was Heinl without controversy in the Marine Corps. Because of his candor in once having revealed and documented for the first time certain inter-service intrigues after World War II, which nearly resulted in the abolition of the U.S. Marine Corps as a fighting force, the Defense Department would not clear Heinl's book, *Soldiers of the Sea,* for publication for almost a year. Even during the colonels' Haiti mission, the Marine Corps commandant was said to have kept a personal check on Heinl. There was even concern that Heinl's ancillary interest in Haiti's environment, specifically in reforesting the country, could result in a personal injury case. That was because the colonel made a habit of dropping golf-ball size mahogany seeds from the Marine mission's helicopter, hoping that somehow they would sprout and grow into fine trees.

In November 1959, I shared an interview with Colonel Heinl with *Time* magazine's Bruce Henderson. It was what *Time* and the *Haiti Sun* published following that interview that finally evoked a newsworthy reaction story from Haitian army headquarters.

As a seasoned Marine and spit-and-polish officer, Heinl couldn't stand the sight of soldiers that were not properly equipped. I knew his pitch almost by heart. Begging for a modern rifle for the Haitian army, he invoked the excuse that its troops were still armed in part with Krag rifles from the Spanish-American War. (The U.S. had indeed sold Haiti a thousand Krags in 1915 at the beginning of the American Occupation for use of the *Garde d'Haiti,* the Haitian army's original title.) The colonel would go on to paint a picture of an army that resembled more a Keystone Cop comedy, with the famous U.S.-made Springfield rifles from 1903, three kinds of Belgium Mausers, British Enfield rifles and a few hundred U.S. M-Is from World War II.

In one of his stories, Kihss had reported that the Haitian army wanted "a single modern rifle instead of seven types now used by the 4300 soldiers...." Its additional needs included communications equipment and even Jeeps. Colonel Heinl, in outlining the principal purpose of his mission, said, "What we are interested in is developing Haitian forces that are suited to the real requirements of the country—primarily an internal security force that can maintain Haitian peace and order and protect the integrity of Haiti's frontier and coastal waters against anything short of a serious invasion which would require action by the Organization of American States."

As *Time* needed a picture of Heinl for their story, with the troops he was training, he escorted Henderson and me to the Casernes Dessalines and ordered a Haitian officer to call out the troops for inspection—or rather a photograph. When the Caserne's officer on duty, Col. René Leon, who had routed the Cuban invaders, heard that Colonel Heinl had taken it upon himself to have his (Leon's) troops ordered to parade, the young Haitian officer stormed out of the barracks and onto the parade ground. Ignoring Heinl, he snapped out the order: "No photographs! This is a Haitian military establishment! No photographs." Henderson and I lowered our cameras. He had his picture (which was published in the November 9, 1959 issue of *Time*): Heinl standing at attention posing with swagger stick and pith helmet, giving his profile to the Haitian troops who were still endeavoring to assemble in something resembling disciplined military fashion. The picture that was precluded was that of a Marine colonel whose face suddenly turned crimson with indignation. As Heinl stomped off in the direction of the palace presumably to report the Caserne's colonel to Duvalier, a young Haitian officer said angrily: *"Maleduquee"*—meaning Heinl was badly educated and in fact rude.

That evening, the president's American friend, Dr. Elmer Loughlin, came to the Oloffson Hotel to apologize to Henderson, declaring that Colonel Leon had been out of order. We were startled because, under the broadest interpretation of international protocol, it was clearly Heinl who was out of order.

When Henderson's picture of Heinl's posing before the troops in the Casernes appeared in *Time,* there were serious repercussions in both the Haitian army top command and the National Palace. Actually, when the issue of the magazine arrived in Port-au-Prince only two paragraphs were devoted completely to the U.S. Marine presence. The paragraphs read:

> **Out of the Past**. Twenty-five years ago, the U.S. proudly ended a 19-year Marine occupation in Haiti; the return of the Marines is ironical but seemingly vital. Colonel Heinl

(Pearl Harbor, Iwo Jima, Korea), Yaleman ('37) and
Marine historian arrived last January with red mustache,
pith helmet and fluent French to find the Haitian army in
horrifying shape.

He discovered rusted rifles of every conceivable make,
bullets so old that only half of them would fire. Among the
debris in one corner of the armory, he even found a long-
forgotten coffin containing the body of the daughter of
President Alexandre Pétion (1808–18). But he also found
old blue ceremonial uniforms in the army warehouses and
soon fielded a band that gives rousing renditions of the
Marines' Hymn, as well as a passable version of the
Haitian anthem, the Dessalinienne. More important,
Heinl's 40-man team taught the troops how to get from
bunks to battle stations all over town in 30 minutes flat.

The tomb proved not to be a "coffin" but an empty marble sarcophagus. Moreover, in moving it the Marines suffered their first mission casualty when the sarcophagus' lid slipped and took off the tip
of one officer's left finger.

The *Time* article continued: "The U.S. had hoped that a greater
sense of security would lead Duvalier, a cold-eyed autocrat, back to
more democratic ways. . . ."

Pouring a little salt into the Haitian high command's wounded
pride—perhaps innocently—was the mission's celebration of the U.S.
Marine Corps 184th birthday. The inimitable Colonel Heinl hired
Cabane Choucoune, the spectacular Pétionville nightclub, in
Pétionville, a favorite with Haiti's wealthy class. Under Choucoune's
African-style peaked thatched roof, the U.S. Marine birthday ritual
was enacted down to the smallest detail. For the unsuspecting Haitian
army and high-level civilian government officials and their wives, present owing to protocol, this formal birthday party for a foreign military contingent was pure shock. One had only to recall that during
the unhappy American occupation of Haiti from 1915 to 1934 when
the Marines had been barred from the capital's elite Bellevue Club.

And until recently Marine guards at the U.S. embassy had worn civilian clothes in order not to upset the sensibilities of Haitians. At the birthday bash Colonel Heinl led the ceremonies and called on the Minister of Interior and National Defense, Jean Magloire, to stand beside him in the center of the circular dance floor along with Army Chief of Staff, Gen. Pierre Merceron, and U.S. charge d'affaires Philip Williams. I was also present and as the ceremonies dragged on, I could see that the Haitians standing under the dance-floor spotlight were perspiring and obviously uncomfortable in their roles as stage props for the Marines. The Haitian band on instructions played both the American national anthem and the Marine Corps hymn but astoundingly not the Haitian national anthem. Even though this was primarily a U.S. Marine party, the lack of such a basic courtesy to the host country—especially by someone as sensitive to protocol as Heinl—was inconceivable.

Finally, lights were switched off and six Marine officers carried a mountainous birthday cake, adorned with 184 candles, forward. The problem was when all the candles were lighted the heat began literally to fry the icing as the band played *Auld Lang Syne*. Once the cake fire was finally brought under control by the hard blowing of a dozen Marines, Colonel Heinl read the prescribed birthday section of the *Marine Corps Manual*, a short history of the Corps, and a message from the commandant of the Marine Corps. Heinl produced a sword, which he explained to the Marines and their guests, had been carried by Col. Louis McCarty Little with distinction during the Boxer Rebellion in China and then on to Haiti. (In Haiti, Colonel Little had been commander of the First Marine Brigade during the Occupation.) As if the mention of Little and his sword were not enough to insult the sensibilities of the Haitians present, Heinl served the first piece of cake not to any Haitian official guest, but to Marine gunner Perry Davis, the oldest member of the Marine mission (with over 20 years of service). Then the youngest Marine present received a piece of the cake. Lt. William J. Bonthron got the next piece because it was his birthday. General Merceron, I noticed, had lost his appetite for cake and it remained on his plate.

Publishing our shared interviews with Heinl in that first edition of the reopened *Haiti Sun* plunged us into immediate controversy. The Haitian army struck back in the guise of a joint interview with *Le Matin* by General Merceron and Colonel Paul Laraque.

Faithfully, we translated every word of the general's reply to Heinl and illustrated our rendition with a picture of Duvalier standing in a Jeep along with General Merceron inspecting the "new army." The occasion was November 18, known as Army Day, commemorating the last decisive battle at Vertières against the French in 1803. It was celebrated by a ceremonial parade before the old tribune on the Champ de Mars.

The president also that day inaugurated a new building on the west side of the palace to house his Presidential Guard.

Though wounded by Heinl's assertions the army was careful to throw the blame on the messenger, *Time* magazine and the *Haiti Sun*. *Le Matin* stated, "Alarmed by the allegations contained in an article published by the American magazine *Time* of November 9 and which was reproduced with more details by the *Haiti Sun,* and to dissipate somewhat the apprehension of a ticklish public opinion with regard to national dignity, we delegated our editor, Dumayric Charlier, to interview Brig. Gen Pierre Merceron, chief of staff of the armed forces." According to the article, General Merceron and Col. Paul Laraque of the general staff received Charlier at army headquarters. An officer friend in army headquarters told me privately that the interview, which was published in a question-and-answer format text, had been prepared by the general staff, mainly Colonel Laraque, in advance and cleared personally by President Duvalier for publication.

Regarding Heinl's statements that he had found the army in a "lamentable state," the two officers—mulatto brothers-in-laws—answered: "It would be a gross error to consider here the American standard as a basis of comparison or criterion of appreciation. First of all it is advisable to note that before the arrival here of the American Naval Mission, the armed forces of Haiti, in spite of the errors and the blunders committed, had attained, under the Haitian command, a status distinctly superior to the organization which was

left here by the Marines on their departure from the country, particularly from the viewpoint of technical preparation of the cadets. For
years, many Haitian officers, graduates of our military academy, have
benefited from scholarships to study abroad, in the United States as
well as in Latin America or in Europe. Several among them were outstanding and were laureates of their classes. They know, besides, better than anybody, the problems of their organization and of their
country."

The officers did concede that, "It is true that since the fall of
Magloire, the vicissitudes of politics have caused us to lose competent
technicians (in mechanized transportation) but that is another story."
However, Merceron and Laraque credited the army leadership
(meaning themselves) with creating plans, operations and training as
well as organizing tactical units in Port-au-Prince and the provinces.
They asserted that their initiative had "brought fruit at the time of the
recent [Cuban] invasion of our territory, which was settled by the
crushing of the foreign invaders, without loss of life for our troops."

Listing the armed forces fundamental missions as interior security
(police) and exterior security (army), they noted that these two distinct corps have been fused into one. "It is the model handed down by
the U.S. Marine Corps." They saw no possibility "in the immediate
future of separating the police from the army, as it should be, normally. We therefore had to constitute, in the cadre of our present
structure and according to our limited means, these tactical units
which are like the embryo of our future National Army."

Answering Heinl's pet argument that the army needed to get rid of
its antiquated guns such as the Krag rifles, General Merceron and
Colonel Laraque pointed out that Haiti had no arms or munition
manufacturing facilities of its own and thus had to purchase arms
where they found them abroad. They agreed it was true that "we have
arms and munitions of American and European manufacture," but
protested that "the facts are misrepresented and caricatured. Thus,
everyone knows in Haiti that our soldiers do not use Krag guns. Only
certain rural police agents still have a few of these."

"But the article in the *Haiti Sun* [quoting Heinl] declares that it was thanks to these Krag guns that the invasion was crushed. Aside from the burlesque aspect of the affair, what should be remembered is that this information, false in its presentation—either due to a poor comprehension impelled by a taste for the sensational or by the spirit of disparagement, or finally for any other reason—can cause us much harm because it can easily be utilized for any kind of purpose by any eventual enemy of the country!"

The fourth question asked was whether the chief of the [U.S.Marine] mission was authorized to discuss such questions with journalists.

"Absolutely not!" was the shortest answer of the "interview." "They are military questions of a secret nature. The agreement relative to the American Naval Mission in Haiti stipulates that in matters of this kind, the members of the said mission are equally bound to secrecy."

The officers were then invited to clarify the purpose of the American Naval Mission in Haiti. "The object of this Mission such as it is defined in the above- mentioned agreement," they replied, "is to collaborate with us with a view towards increasing the efficiency of the different services of the Army and of the Coast Guard. There already is an independent mission for the Aviation wing of the army."

The two officers added that the "power of decision" in this collaboration was theirs "by right and fact ...the [mission's] advisers are attached to certain organizations of the armed forces of Haiti. As their title indicates, they give advice and this advice is not obligatory; they make suggestions and recommendations that the army staff may appreciate and study for their value. But they have no authority to demand anything whatsoever. The command is exclusively under the army chief of staff and his collaborators, the officers of the armed forces under the high directives of His Excellency the president of the republic."

"As for the *Time* magazine article illustrated by a photo of Colonel Heinl with Haitian soldiers, the interview question was: "Is the training of troops done under his personal direction and what of his American collaborators?"

"Absolutely not," was again the unequivocal answer. "Contrary to what was stated by *Time* and the *Haiti Sun*, the training of troops is not done under the direction of the Mission for it does not have any command. This training is done under direct orders of Haitian officers, with the help of the American military advisers. The photo in question may have been taken as a scheme to illustrate the thesis to the contrary or to create ambiguity but cold facts are hardheaded. You will note that the photo shows only part of the troops and not the soldiers in complete formation. The Haitian officer who is commanding these soldiers and who does not appear in the photo normally is to be found in the center of the formation. It amounts to a sort of trick photo."

*   *   *

To assist Haiti in setting its house in order, the U.S. aid program arranged for the services of a number of specialists to work in a variety of Haitian government agencies. Nolle Smith, a seventy-year-old American black, tax specialist had worked in Hawaii and served as adviser to the Virgin Islands administration and government of Ecuador before being assigned to Haiti. There he worked in the finance ministry a few doors away from Finance Minister Andre Theard. Three other U.S. aid specialists were working in the finance ministry. A former Washington State police chief was assisting on Port-au-Prince's growing traffic problems. Consultants from a Boston firm were surveying ways to improve the capital's water system. Other experts were advising the agriculture and health departments.

Peter Kihss and I visited the ODVA (French initials for the Artibonite Valley Development Organization) in the Artibonite. The lead paragraph of Kihss' article in the *New York Times,* dateline: Borel, read:

Bare-legged Haitian peasants wade at work today in paddies of green rice plants where only three years ago there were increasingly salty deserts specked with cactus and

mesquite. This is the dramatic change that has come over
the Artibonite Valley

. . . The Artibonite Project—denounced by all sides in
the 1957 presidential campaign as a multi-million dollar
fizzle and conduit for graft—is throbbing with new life and
is paying returns to Haiti. The overall power and irrigation
project, once envisioned as Haiti's Tennessee Valley
Authority, has never gotten any electricity originally
planned from its 120-foot-high Peligre Dam.

This is despite Haitian spending of $30,000,000 so far,
mostly through United States loans, as against an original
estimate of $14,000,000 in 1951. There are three idle
32,000-kilowatt generators on hand but Haitians estimate
it would cost an unavailable $7,000,000 more to finish the
electricity phase. Irrigation and drainage canals, however,
have given an upsurge to the entire area in which 102,000
inhabitants dwell on 200 square miles.

Both Kihss and I were impressed with Garvey Laurent, the thirty-
five-year old Haitian administrator of the government's Artibonite
Valley Development Organization. Laurent told us that he had been
given a free hand by President Duvalier to work for efficiency, instead
of politics. On the job at ODVA headquarters since October 1958, he
said he had slashed the staff from 1,200 to a low of 600. It was now
back to 800, with the start of construction under a new U. S. loan to
finish the irrigation work.

Laurent had returned to Haiti with a master's degree in agricultural economics from the University of California at Berkeley, and an
American wife whom he had met at the university. The OVDA was
Haiti's most impressive advancement in agriculture with 35,000
hectares of desert; its salt now washed out giving new life to the land.
Rice yield had jumped to 4,000 pounds a hectare (2.75 acres). With a
rice-processing mill operating and plans to build a vegetable canning
plant, Laurent shared the local farmers' enthusiasm for a better
future. Working with Laurent were five United States International

Cooperation Administration (the new name for Point IV) experts headed by Norman Ward, an old Haiti hand.

Yet not everything was rosy on the development or fiscal front. Papa Doc clearly needed to put his administration house in order. A sixty-three-page report by the Chicago-based private firm known as Public Administration Service warned that the Haitian government was "on the brink of insolvency."

Commissioned by the U.S. government, the PAS survey found that among the Duvalier administration's many shortcomings was its failure to utilize "its talent and natural endowments consistently and systematically to its advantage." The report also stated: "It is true that personal considerations, as contrasted with concerns for public welfare, encroach inordinately in the conduct of Haiti's public affairs [and] that Haiti's administration is sometimes lethargic and unresponsive. . . ."

Yet Papa Doc's regime became more and more cloaked in secrecy. Duvalier had long since given up the pretense of cabinet meetings. Single-handedly, he ran the country from his little office, often taking money from his desk drawer to pay a citizen with a sob story, a spy for his information, or to reward someone for performing a special task.

What no American expert could see into was the government's gigantic piggy bank from which Duvalier could draw funds without having to record the transaction. Papa Doc could draw monies he needed from the Regie du Tabac, a monopoly in cigarettes, matches, soap and cooking oil. Launched in 1948 by President Estime, this state monopoly had become the palace's slush fund. And Duvalier was already in the process of extending the state monopoly to include numerous other import items. Tax receipts had quadrupled. But it was common knowledge among foreign economists that good financial administration was impossible until the government fiscalized the Regie, which the palace was not about to do. In the words of Jules Blanchet, head of the Government Accounting Office, "Papa Doc knows how to squeeze the gravy out of Uncle Sausage."

*   *   *

Looking over the *Haiti Sun*'s subscribers' list illustrated the poly-
glot nature of the business world of Haiti. Apart from the hundreds
of expatriate Americans, there were Arabs (known as Syrians) and
Jews in retail and import businesses; Italian moneylenders; Germans
who had survived World War II; Poles; Austrians (Kurt Fisher, an
anthropologist, gift shop owner and loyal advertiser); Danes;
Russians; British and Jamaicans. Haiti had always-close ties with
English-speaking Jamaica as it had with Cuba. It was to Kingston
that ousted Haitian politicians often sought refuge and some
Haitians of the upper class studied at business schools there. Santiago
de Cuba, with excellent medical facilities, sometimes attracted
wealthy patients from Haiti. (There was little traffic to Miami because
it was an inhospitable racial turf.) By the 1950s, there were daily
flights linking Kingston and Port-au-Prince. Besides Pan American
Airways, KLM, the Dutch airline, also served the two cities.

A number of Jamaicans had migrated to Haiti and by the 1950s
they were important cogs in the service sector as well as the most
devoted *Sun* readers. Frank Wilson had built a new modern store and
automobile showroom on Rue des Caserne. As well as being the agent
for Hudson automobile and the REO trucks, Wilson had the Sears
Roebuck agency; Cyril Powell owned a large furniture shop and
garage and his two sons helped run the business which expanded into
producing oxygen and $Co2$ gasses. Allan Bryan worked for the
Haitian-American Sugar Company (Hasco) and among his six children was Thelma, who along with her sister Rosa, eventually bought
out the Don Mohr gift shop. There were other Jamaicans who were
employed by the British consulate and American Electric Light
Company. Jamaican Jocelyn McCalla promoted sports, mainly soccer
matches between the two countries; Oswald J. Brandt, who had come
to Haiti from Jamaica as a bank clerk, had built up a business empire
and by the 1950s was the richest man in Haiti. Another successful
Jamaican was Ernest Burkett who with Haitian partner Charles
Fabius took over The West Indies Garage on Rue du Centre when its
owner Arnold Braun, a German, retired. During one period, the
Haiti Sun ran a column by Jamaican newsman Frank Hill, datelined

Kingston. Yvon Blake of *Spotlight* magazine wrote enthusiastic columns on the Magloire regime. Guyanese and other Caribbean students, especially those studying French at the University of the West Indies campus in Kingston, visited Haiti often and two spent time as interns at the *Haiti Sun*. There were two African-Americans: Pilot Jimmy Plinton, the dry-cleaning pioneer, and a big African-American named Cleveland who was the fingerprint expert at the police department.

*　　　*　　　*

The departure of Clément Barbot to Europe should have been a banner headline, but we handled it as a brief news item at the bottom of Page One to which we consigned news we could hardly dramatize: "Presidential Private Secretary M. Clément Barbot left suddenly for Hamburg Thursday afternoon (Nov. 12) upon receiving word from his wife, who flew to Germany Sunday, that their son Herve had taken ill. Mr. and Mrs. Barbot had been concerned over the health of their son who was studying medicine in Hamburg. Mr. Barbot accompanied by an aide, Lt. Armand St-Remy, and friend, Mr. Edmond Khouri, clippered to San Juan and New York and jetted to Germany. President François Duvalier and members of his immediate family were at Bowen Field airport to see him off. The other Barbot children are studying in Europe."

Barbot, a strong family man in spite of his often-harsh political duties, had not traveled overseas before, and his absence raised questions about the future of his power base next to the president. The subject was discussed one day at *Le Nouvelliste*. A group of us were sitting in publisher Max Chauvet's little office trading gossip. Barbot became the topic and whether he could survive politically, having left town. Many Duvalierists were jealous of his power. When Barbot did return on December 1, Papa Doc was not at the airport to receive him. Some Haitians saw that as a bad sign. Yet Barbot not only survived but had elevated himself to Duvalier's "private secretary" and no longer needed to accompany the president as bodyguard. That chore had been given to a big, burly, former enlisted army man, Colonel Gracia Jacques, who with pistol in hand offered Papa Doc a much larger shield than Barbot did.

*   *   *

Rollin Atwood, the director of Point IV for Latin America, visited Haiti in October 1959. "Judging from one year ago, I would say that have made tremendous progress," declared Atwood after a visit to U.S. aid projects in Aux Cayes and Cap Haitien.

By now, the weather was turning cold in Washington and several U.S. senators found a decidedly warm and hospitable climate on Hispaniola. The Dominican Republic's Trujillo reportedly spent millions attempting to curry favor in the U.S. Congress, especially for a larger sugar quota. As for Haiti Senator Homer E. Capehart, a Republican from Indiana, on a visit, declared he supported loans for Haiti, and Kansas Senator Frank Carlson, a member of the Foreign Relations Committee, promised Duvalier that he backed a bigger sugar quota for the country. Antoine Marthod, president of the Haitian Senate, assured Capehart: "The Republic of Haiti, whose destiny lies in the hands of our venerable chief of state, Dr. François Duvalier, is a democracy, sailing courageously toward its goal!"

And Senator Arthur Bonhomme, president of the foreign relations commission in the Haitian Senate, told a meeting of the Society of Evangelists in Chicago that Duvalier was inviting the United States to establish a naval base in Haiti if the Americans were forced to abandon their Guantánamo base in Cuba. That was too much even for Deputy Alphonse Lahens, a rabid Duvalierist, who protested loudly only to be reminded that Bonhomme was speaking for Papa Doc.

Such solemn affairs of state were leavened somewhat by the 1959 Miss Haiti beauty contest, which gave the *Sun* a chance to adorn our font page with some of the most attractive young ladies in the country. The winner was startlingly beautiful Claudinette Fouchard, a daughter of an old elite family. On a rather more urgent topic, La Belle Creole department store in downtown Port-au-Prince announced that they now had a toilet especially for tourists, which was a merciful amenity in a city of 200,000 without a public pissoir. Episcopal Bishop Alfred Voegeli returned from a trip to the United States in time to say Thanksgiving service at St. Trinity Cathedral. A scowling President Duvalier was photographed as he arrived, standing next to Ambassador Drew. The American envoy had returned that week from two months' home leave. He read President Eisenhower's Thanksgiving message. Meanwhile, controversial Roman Catholic Archbishop Poirier was interned in the Saint François de Sales hospital, suffering high blood pressure and fatigue. After a brief rest in hospital, he was released.

There were both encouraging and discouraging signs regarding private investment. An American, David Scharf, had invested $300,000 in a chocolate factory at Bizoton, two miles south of the capital, and which would use locally grown cacao. He expected to process 36,000 pounds of cacao a day. And Haitian businessman Clément Joseph Charles bought a full page in the *Haiti Sun* to advertise the opening of a new bank, whose inauguration was presided over by Papa Doc. The stated aim of the bank, backed by Florida investors, was to create employment and better housing, not for the rich but those who "really need it."

A small item on our front page, worded in our carefully coded style, told of a different private endeavor: "Well-known *homme d'affaires* Eric Tippenhauser and friend Gerard Dufanal were reported this week as guests of the Mexican embassy on Morne Noire. The *Sun* was unable to clarify their position, and the reason for the change of address."

Haitian businessman Eric Tippenhauser, who had been a silent business partner of past presidents and police chiefs, had literally been taken for a ride in true Chicago gangster-style. Fortunately, he had escaped with his life. A high-ranking officer of the Presidential Guard had sought to go into the lucrative cigarette-making business and Tippenhauser happened to have an unused cigarette factory. The officer wanted it and with several of his men, took Tippenhauser "for a ride." He had managed to break loose, escaping into the home of a

missionary on the Delmas Road linking Port-au-Prince with
Petionville. From there, Tippenhauser sought political asylum in the
embassy of Mexico. After a week, he was able to return home. The
cigarette factory changed hands. (Eric Tippenhauser was seized in
April 1963 and executed along with two of his sons.)

Andre Apaid and a fellow entrepreneur launched Tele-Haiti, the
country's first television station promising during its evening hours (6
p.m. to 9.05 p.m.) to offer *The Frankie Lane Show* among others. The
others included *Flash Gordon, Captain Grief,* cartoons, Haitian music
and five minutes of news.

One of the more interesting writer-researchers in town was Francis
Huxley, the young British anthropologist. We noted in our columns
that he was studying normality and abnormality in Haiti's peasantry.
(Our politicians would have been another apt subject.) Francis was a
son of writer-philosopher-biologist and former head of UNESCO
Julian Huxley; a nephew of Aldous Huxley, the famous novelist; and
grandson of Thomas Henry Huxley, the famed scientist on man's
evolution. Francis Huxley produced six years later his book, *The
Invisibles,* an excellent study of the gods of Vodou. "He recounted his
experiences in Haiti with warmth and directness and humor and
without an ounce of condescension," the *Sun* quoted a review of the
book. Huxley did say that he found that Haitians only half-believed
in the entire phantasmagoria of Vodou deities they loved to talk
about.

Another social item: Married: President Hector (Negro) Trujillo,
51, to Alma McLaughlin, 38, after a 22-year courtship. The bride is
the daughter of a Marine Sergeant Charles McLaughlin who stayed
on after the 1916–24 U.S. Occupation to become a colonel in
Trujillo's army and president of the Dominican airline. Hector's elder
brother, El Jefe had finally relented and allowed them to marry as
their mother, first lady Dona Julia Moline de Trujillo was getting old
(93) and the second first lady, Maria, El Jefe's wife, had no objection.

There was a disconcerting postscript to *Time's* story on the U.S.
Marines in Haiti. Dr. Elmer Loughlin, on returning from a trip to
New York, paid me a visit. "You are very lucky," he said, "I saw the

Time file in New York of that story that has upset so many people (Duvalier as well as the Haitian Army) and it didn't have your name on it!" How he could have gotten hold of a *Time* magazine original story file was beyond me, but it was a lesson and from then on whenever I filed to *Time* I signed telexes "George Bernard" and much later simply, "Marlene."

Our linotypist, Theodore Auguste, returned crestfallen from celebrating the return of the *Sun,* at Houses of Flowers, to inform us in disgust that both the Paradise Bar and La Paloma Blanca, two famous bar-brothels, had been turned into elementary schools. His report of the demise of the two celebrated recreational institutions became a news item.

CHAPTER 19

To the Sacred Waters

In those early years in Haiti, I joined pilgrims whenever possible for the July fête. I published stories about the holy occasion in the *Sun*. It was more than just a story; it was a time of personal renewal that brought the pilgrims closer to their gods. Faith in their *lwas* as well as the Catholic saints brought them joy and happiness, physically washing away their sins, sadness or sickness, sacrificing the little they had to reach the waterfall of miracles.

It was usually on July 15, three days before my own birthday, when I journeyed to Ville-Bonheur on the eve of the feast of Our lady of Carmel. The road out of Port-au-Prince across the Cul-de-Sac plain and up to the summit of Morne á Cabrit was dangerous as trucks and buses filled with pilgrims were always overcrowded and accident-prone on the narrow winding gravel road.

Upon reaching the summit of the harshly arid mountain fit only for goats, the traveler is treated to a spectacular view, a panorama of a luxuriant green world with trees heavy with fruit—a vision of the garden of Eden.

The dirt road from the town of Mirablais to Ville-Bonheur was always a struggle even in a jeep. Muddy and narrow, the road becomes choked with pedestrians; oungans, mambos, *oun'sis* (their assistants and choir members) patriarchs and matriarchs with their flock and families in their wake. Catholic and Vodou penitents, some dressed in sack clothing, sing amid a profusion of colorful Vodou flags to drums, trumpets and vaccines. There are always trucks or buses stuck in the mud and abandoned by their passengers.

The little town of Ville-Bonheur sits on a narrow mountain ridge in Central Haiti that becomes so packed with pilgrims that moving along the narrow main street is like trying to swim against strong ocean currents. Side streets are crammed with vendors and gamblers seated at little tables, squeezed among local food stands and beverage *tonnelles.*

The major luxury of the small, single-room, and basic peasant-style hut rental is its roof. But few pilgrims bother about sleep. At night, the town has a carnival atmosphere with dancing to bands for the youthful urban visitors more interested in a having a party. The entire night can be spent following the sound of the drums to one Vodou service after another.

In the refreshing cool morning, the pilgrims awake to the aroma of coffee and set out for the climb to the waterfall singing, waving their Vodou flags and beating on their drums, like thousands of human magnets being drawn by mystical forces to this place of miracles. More than anything else, the lwas demand songs, and the pilgrims must sing their songs over and over.

The human flow is constant. We ford the shallow Rivière Tombé that originates in a spring in adjacent bald Doscale mountain. Some pilgrims become possessed as they enter the water. A large woman, staggered, jumped and threw herself into the muddy river. She had suddenly become possessed. The small, slow-moving muddy stream next to the potato field, hardly worthy of the percussive title, "Rivière Tombé," disappeared among the profusion of creepers, between two trumpet trees, then reappeared below as sheets of sparkling, crystal-clear water in a magnificent waterfall. The damp humid earth in the hollow leading into the waterfall by mid-morning was churned into mud by the wet feet of thousands of bathers completing their ritual.

It is a scene from another world. Dark and cavernous, mysterious and mystic. Nymph-like naked figures frolicked far below. Some with arms outstretched amid the tumbling water and the rising spray stood as statuettes of young Aphrodite in erotic ecstasy. The sunlight had not yet penetrated the falls when we peered down through the creepers on the edge of a field freshly planted in sweet potatoes. It could have been a panorama conjured up by Jules Verne's *Into the Center of the Earth.*

The tide of pilgrims quickly swallowed the splashing woman from view. Mounted pilgrims, mostly urbanites, trot along while their guides running beside hired horses shouted, "*bête, bête,*" ("animal, animal") to make a passage amongst the throng of pilgrims. This trip is not for people suffering from claustrophobia.

The access to the waterfall is not easy. The descent is down a steep trail to the hollow that serves as a platform into the waterfall. Sure-footed peasants trot down the incline while urbanites hold onto protruding tree roots and carefully slide down to the rocks and water.

A woman, her eyelids heavy, carried a large framed chromolithograph of the Virgin and the Child Jesus, as she swayed gently to the music of her small group from Grand Bois in the Cul de Sac plain. In her group, a *Guede*-like character, with dark glasses and a pipe, wore a long white smock that reached the ground, not unlike that worn by a Catholic priest.

A wizened old mambo and members of her society led a docile young black and white bull in tow. They had walked for a day and a night from Petit Rivière d'Artibonite to reach Ville-Bonheur. The bull was being taken to the waterfall to prepare it for sacrifice. A red and white mantle had been placed on its back. During the evening, the mambo, small and gray-headed, had danced like a woman half her age. A rich ceremony was held in the small red house that the Vodou priestess and her society had rented at the main intersection on the edge of town where the farmers gathered with their horses to rent for the ride up the hill to the waterfall. The drums spoke until the break of dawn.

At the waterfall, the mambo bathed and anointed the bull and washed it with herbs in preparation for sacrifice to *Lwa Simbi.* The mambo had the bull taste the water. (When we returned from the waterfall in the afternoon only the bull's head and horns remained in a large pot. The mambo and her oun'sis at the sacred grove, Nan Pal St. John Baptiste, were preparing the meat according to ritual and feeding the *sevitès*.)

By midmorning, the hollow before the waterfall looked like a public dressing room as well as prayer center with pilgrims shedding their clothes and moving into the waters. Returning from the bath, some carrying bunches of medicinal leaves they have dunked into the sacred waters to improve their magical strength, they appeared energized, their bodies glistened and some had spiritually rapt expressions.

Vendors sit patiently before their stacks of candles, medicinal leaves, bottles filled with roots marinated in *tafia* (raw rum) complaining that business is off this fete. Pilgrims standing before their lighted candles imploring their lwas above all to be "understanding." Some came alone while others came in groups in their best peasant garb, dressed like Zaka, the peasant god and agriculturalist, having walked for hours and days, waving their flags and singing.

There were vodouisants and Christians in search of help, a miracle, and there were those who simply came to "change their luck," or get rid of their hangover from too much *bamboching* (partying). There are city dwellers and poor peasants, all sharing the water. Most of the women bathed bare-breasted and some throw off their old under-garments and allowed the water to sweep them away. If not for the prayers, which were laments of the poverty and misery, it was a joyous scene where for a brief few minutes they were in communion with their gods, and forgotten was their despair. Hope bubbled briefly to the surface again. They were in search of magical solutions. Many carried away bottled jars and gourdes of the water to be used later in their homes or *ounfôrs* (temples).

The tumbling water amplified the noise-level of the shrieking bathers and those who appeal loudly to their gods with arms outstretched for help in this enchanting setting, which gave them back, even momentarily the beautiful continuity of hope. The water glowed as it fell with promise.

This is the domain of Damballah and his wife Aida-wedo, the rainbow. The water-falls resemble a giant cathedral, walled in on three sides and shaded by trees. There is a wondrous moment during the day when the sun manages to penetrate the rising mist, causing a rainbow to arch over the falls, which brings forth a cry, "Damballah-Wedo." There is also sadness here. It is a sharp reminder of how Haiti was once a land of hardwood forests and filled with fine waterfalls. No more. The land is parched and depleted and can no longer feed its ever-growing population.

Rare, mysterious and rewarding as these falls are today, it may not be long before they too disappear. The gods will then be truly angry. No place in Haiti does water cascades down out of the sky like millions of liquid diamonds as at Saut d'eau. In the middle of a searing hot summer's day, it is cool and refreshing.

A well-dressed young girl climbing out of the falls suddenly sprang forward and then collapsed onto the mud. She slithered around, her body one minute rigid and the next twisting and turning. Her face pressed into the mud. Only her companions took note that she had been "mounted" by the snake-god *Damballah* and sought professional help from an oungan. With rage she tore at her plaited hair and she rolled back and forth. "This *chwal* (horse) riding her sometimes burns the hair among the candles," explained a knowledgeable young Vodou sevitè from Port-au-Prince, who paused to watch the rigid girl being lifted like a log to her feet. With extraordinary strength, she suddenly lashed out and pushed backwards the two men trying to help her. They came close to falling over the edge of the hollow that fell sharply away to a pond below. A dangerous fall. Possession is not a spectator sport here. Everyone is busy with their own mission and ignore those possessed. On the eve of the feast day of Our Lady of Mount Carmel, the sacred Vodou waterfall at Saut d'eau, pronounced "Sodo," was rich in possessions.

"Yes, Damballah inhabits here," said the old man patting the huge trunk of the tree lovingly. He identified the giant tree as a white fig. It stood on the promontory overlooking the entrance to Saut d'eau. Here resided the most venerable of ancient lwa, in the Vodou cosmogony, the heavenly serpent, Damballah. The old man took his job as guardian of the white fig tree seriously. Leaning back against the tree, its age, he said, was many times his own, the old man described his own lwa as the aquatic deity Simbi, also a guardian of the source of fresh water. Haiti is a land of guardians. Even after death, ancestors join the lwas as guardians and with such large numbers unemployed someone is always prepared to be a guardian. Simbi, the old man explained, is not vindictive like some lwas and among her attributes are wealth and happiness. In some very special cases, he said

Simbi can bestow the gift of clairvoyance. Had Simbi given him such a gift! His face broke into a wrinkled smile. A pilgrim placed a few coins in the enamel plate at the old man's feet and lit a small white candle she attached to a porous rock besides the root that had become an alter of candles. The only word distinguishable in her pray was *lamizè* (misery). A man poured a libation of *kleren* (raw rum) in three droplets before the ancient tree and began his worship to his gods. On the opposite side of the tree, a peasant woman tended two half gourdes of water and medicinal herbs. Pilgrims occasionally bathed their hands in the gourdes before they prayed and left offerings.

Besides the pool, technically the end of the falls, the water is muddy once again. Next to the pool, a pilgrim slapped a royal palm tree's smooth trunk as he ended his prayers.

A young man was carried out of the falls by two men, their arms interlocked under him making him appear like a bird on a perch. He just sat there rigid, his neck extended but it was his eyes that drew my attention. They had popped almost out of their sockets, dark pupils surrounded by the white sclera unblinking and hypnotic even at a distance. I forgot my camera and just gazed at him wondering, who is this? Damballah? Loko, Zaka, Guede? As I drew closer, he suddenly collapsed and fell to the ground and lay there hidden by the human flow of pilgrims. They were not snake eyes. They were eyes of a fish. It was Simbi.

Another old man sat on a log across a damp and dark grotto on the side of the hill; a plate next to candles contained a few centimes. Staring into the dark green foliage, pilgrims prayed before the log. This guardian of the grotto offered them a word or two, like a blessing. At first he identified himself as a *bòkò* (witchdoctor) but when pressed for information, he changed his profession to that of a *doctè-fèy* (herbalist); then his son, who sat next to him and was his apprentice said his father was a *Pèr-savan* (bush priest), who helped the pilgrims recite their prayers. He was probable all those things. Times were tough, he said, "There hasn't been enough rain," adding, "Many have not served their lwas. Their ancestors are not happy."

A young bare-foot peasant stood alone nearby before a single candle he had planted in the damp earth. He earnestly recited a litany of problems with which he needed his lwa's help. His appeal over, he strode off and disappeared into the crowd.

The pilgrims usually believe that there are two basic causes for their misfortune; their lwas were not served properly or someone is doing ill to them and they must take counter measures. Hearing snatches of their pleas, it is easy to understand what this pilgrimage means to them. These are bad and difficult times in Haiti and so many of their problems are now born from despair.

The most fervent prayers overheard those last three days of the pilgrimage were mostly laments for help, support for relatives and friends. Because of their poverty, many made their long overdue offerings to their particular lwas as best they could, but their offering according to one guardian of the faith, was meager indeed.

The number of pilgrims reflects the state of the nation. On my last visit to the waterfalls before being exiled in 1963, Makouts had begun to claim the place as their own. Papa Doc's nasty henchmen were establishing themselves, building elaborate houses and living like feudal lords. Makout chieftain Tijé Woolly had established his residence. There seemed to be a decrease in the number of professional beggars attending the fete, they too were obviously fearful of the Makouts. Some local oungans had moved away. A guide whispered that the Makouts were not like the other pilgrims — they were not generous; in fact, he said, they didn't even pay for services. They had brought economic depression to Ville-Bonheur. Even the holy place of miracles had become politically dangerous. The Makouts, the new money-eyed malevolent class, we were told by town's people, had their own *bòkòs*, specialists in *magie noire.*

*   *   *

Nowhere in Haiti is there such a striking example of religious syncretism between Haiti's folk religion, Vodou and its official religion, Catholicism, as during the fete. A vodouisant has no trouble lighting a candle to Damballah at the foot of the cascade's giant white fig tree or any other trees for that matter which are the *reposoirs* of the lwas, and the very next day light a candle to the Our Lady of Mount Carmel in the Roman Catholic Church, the major structure in Ville-Bonheur.

The Catholic faithful in Ville-Bonheur refer to Our Lady of Mount Carmel as Our Lady of Miracles, while the *serviteurs* of Vodou see the Virgin Mary as Ĕzili, the *lwa* of love; specifically they see her as Ĕzili Freda-Dahomey or Ĕzili Danto two of the various personaes of Ĕzili.

The family of Ĕzilis are hardly up to the Catholic image of the Virgin Mary, symbol of womanhood, as each Ĕzili has her own characteristics like Danto, who likes to sleeps around, has many children, shares the life-making process, is a symbol of fecundity and identifies with sex.

Yet whether the prayers were to lwas or Catholic saints, they appeared to be the samethey say at the sacred waterfall, at the sacred grove where the apparition of Our Lady of Carmel is claimed to have happened more than a hundred years ago, or at the Catholic Church dedicated to Our Lady of Mount Carmel. They sounded mostly like personal pleas for help, for divine or magical intervention to lift them out of their misery.

*   *   *

Back in the village at night, hundreds sleep in little clusters. Most of them wear white, the color favored by *oun'sis,* the helpers in the *Vodou peristyle* (the ceremonial part of the temple). Despite the rain, scores of little lighted candles remain lit. Vodou services continue as some sleep. The groves are set aside for pilgrims.

It was at one grove on the edge of town that the story of Saut d'eau and Ville-Bonheur began. Yet even its oral history is confusing. Each visit provides more details.

Near the bottom of the grove which is still high above the plain, sèvitès light candles before a remarkably tall royal palm, the only remaining palm in the grove; its trunk a few feet above the ground is black from being burned by years of flickering votive candles. Nearby, the huge roots of an old mango trees runs like boa constrictors in all directions. A blue cross had been painted on the enormous trunk of the mango tree.

It is strictly a Vodou zone. It is there that the bòkòs set up shop, giving advice for a price. There oungans read cards. A young man wearing dark glasses was smoking two filtered tip cigarettes, one in each nostril. Many came up to shake hands with this possessed man. He twisted their hands with an iron grip. A small ceremony was in process in one corner of the grove. This was once the battleground between the old Catholic Church and old Vodou.

The scene at 6 a.m. mass on Thursday the sixteenth, celebrating the feast of Our Lady of Mount Carmel, was not unlike service at the waterfall, only in the Ville-Bonheur Catholic Church the worshippers planted their little candles on the floor and prayed before them. All night, the church yard and entrance were crowded with the devoted.

High Mass was standing room only. The public address system had to be rewired quickly and mass began a half an hour late. It was sweltering in the church. The entire congregation sang, their eyes on the little statue of Our Lady in her niche high above the altar. Towards the end of the nearly two-hour mass, the words of one Krèyol song harked back to the old days of the anti-superstition campaign when the catechisms used in the countryside singled out the oungan as the "slave of Satan." In that rural catechism, oungans were painted as evildoers who like Satan were liars. Some priests in the past described the lwas as wicked angels.

The congregation sang in Krèyol:

On Menm Mari,
O manman Bondye ba nou
kote w paret satan disparet,
n ape konbat vin pran devan nou manma,
leve talon w kraze tet dyab la.

Basically the prayer calls for action against the devil, and the devil in this case is none other than Damballah.

Oh Mother Mary
That God gave us
where ever you appear Satan disappears
We are fighting, come and lead us mother
Lift your heel and smash the head of the devil!

Except perhaps for a minority of liberal priests, the Catholic Church and especially its conservative Haitian hierarchy, is still very much opposed to Vodou. Yet many Haitians, and it was obvious at Saut d'eau and Ville-Bonheur, have no problem in relating their Vodou beliefs with those taught by the Catholic Church.

The Catholic Church is however not as extreme today as the Protestant sects are towards Vodou. Most Protestant sects don't have any saints and are on a continual war-footing against Vodou, specifically Satan and the *Dyab* (Devil). Ironically, there were Protestant churches of various denominations in and around Ville-Bonheur, although their church doors were closed during the feast days and the pastors kept a very low profile.

One night, an old man wandered into Boss Veve's lakou where we were staying on our last trip. Some men were playing checkers down Rue St. Gérard. (Boss Veve had rented us two little rooms at an exorbitant price for two nights.) Sharing a tot of kleren, he said he had heard that many "miracles" had happened in the old times in the sacred grove. There had been various apparitions there too, he said. There had been a lot of trouble, his father had told him, with the French priests, not one but several. One priest had offended, *Gran-mèt la* (God) by chopping down the royal palm tree on which Our Lady, or Ezili, had appeared. When people continued to worship the stump of the palm tree, the parish priest got the local army commander to guard the place and shoot anyone who appeared, even the Virgin Mary if there was another apparition. That had angered Ĕzili Ge-rouge and she reacted violently. The priest returned to find his little presbytery burned down, later the chapel was destroyed by fire and then he lost both legs in an accident and then he became completely paralyzed and died. The army commander who had cooperated with the Abbé became *fou* (crazy) and appeared like a zombie, completely naked in the grove. When did this all happened? One old man said he had heard it was before the U.S. Occupation. Another old man chimed in and said it happened during the 1915–34 U.S. Marine Occupation of Haiti when Vodou was "persecuted." Another, more savvy old man of the town, theorized that it had been during the last big Church-led anti-superstition campaign that began in 1939 and was sanctioned and aided by President Elie Lescot. "It was a time when the old Breton priests forced the chopping down of a lot of trees because they were after the lwas."

The church, at that time, insisted upon an anti-superstition oath of so-called rejection of the religion of their ancestors. Vodou sanctuaries were looted of all their sacred objects and burned together in auto-da-fe. Drums disappeared in flames and there was silence. Without drums, the lwas couldn't be summoned for a ritual. No catacomb was possible except within a person. He kept his faith while rejecting it officially. Because the church decided members of the upper class also should take the anti-superstition oath, they were shocked, indignant and angry to be included in a religion they disdained as primitive and beneath them, as it was the belief system of "ignorant" peasants. The government in early 1942 saw fit to curb the Catholic Church's ferocious fight against "satan."

It was not until the coming of President Dumarsais Estimé (1946–50) that Vodou emerged once again from near-clandestinity. (It remained outlawed on the books until the post-Duvalier constitution of 1987 recognized Vodou as a cult.) Some oungans sought to make it the country's national religion in place of Catholicism.

In his ground-breaking, historic book, *Ainsi Parla L'Oncle*, published in 1928, the remarkable Haitian intellectual, Dr. Jean Price-Mars, set out to restore the value of Haitian folklore in the eyes of the people, and did just that, disrobing the Haitian of his pretences and spooking the elite. Dr. Price-Mars wrote that, "Nothing makes more of Catholic imprint on the evolution of the old cult than the solemnization of some parish festival where the faithful, hovering between both beliefs, mix with equal fervor." In his opinion, there were two parishes in Haiti that contend for the favor of the populace and one was Ville Bonheur which he visited during the July1926 fête. Except for the fact that a large church has replaced the little chapel, the flavor of the pilgrimage he described so eloquently is almost unchanged today. He wrote:

The crowd, as heterogeneous as one could wish, swarms in the street that leads to the chapel and to the Saut. It huddles and presses together in a constant, eager, seething mass. It is singularly composite and yet very much the same in the psychological and miracular unity. One might compare it to foaming waves in which the bright sunlight catches the glint of many-colored grains of sand. Pilgrims, the curious, gallivants, the pious, peddlers, peasants in their Sunday best, superstitious bourgeois, they are all there jostling, pushing, impatient with each other, but resolved to advance towards whatever is on the other side of the street—completely to the other end of the path—the chapel or the falls. And there they all are with the awe-inspiring gregarious instinct which forms the crowd. See there the pitiful sick, emaciated with suffering, out of breath from the clutches of syphilis or tuberculosis, there the professional beggars, haggard from misery, infected by the rags they wear and their skin ulcerated by vermin. Here come a group of prostitutes, unbecoming for their age, worn out by greedy, moneyed debauchery, then the peasants gripped by devotion in motley colored blouses—in sandals of penitence—every one a pilgrim of woe on the point of redemption. A little farther there are some peasant women in votive robes of blue, white, or gray cotton, small cords crosswise over the shoulders. Some, dressed in flowing garments made of many pieces of various colors fitted one to the other with a subtle and singular artfulness, resembling nuns escaped from some outlandish convent. But notice how, challenging attention above everyone in the tumult and disorder, the young people stand out conspicuously: occasional defectors from Port-au-Princien dance halls that debauched dissolute living transfers into the patronage of cheap public dances, revelers whose sunken eyes express the senseless effects of sleepless nights, young fellows experimenting with venal passion and who find in this unique day of the 16th of July the long-awaited occasion to sow their wild oats in exhaustive and lascivious extravagance. And how shall we describe the distress of the very young, the bawling of small children perched on their mother's shoulders amidst the vast surge of people, carried there in homage of gratitude towards the divinity who was compassionate towards the prayers of sterile couples cries of the human crowd?

Dr. Price Mars also notes that, "The mystical mentality became master of the senseless act and gave it the interpretation of affective logic. And the notion of miracle became further ingrained as the credulous crowd longed for the marvelous."

"We are very certain that mysterious apparitions may be a product of the collective imagination determined by crowd psychosis . . . but we are also entirely certain that in this mystical milieu of Ville-Bonheur that the sick who had given up hope recovered their health, particularly those with nervous ailments whose cause was unknown to them."

The Rivière Tombé, choked with discarded undergarments, becomes a river and eventually flows by the town of Mirablais and into the majestic Artibonite River.

CHAPTER 20

May I Borrow Your Saints?

The Vatican may have cast adrift some Catholic saints, dropping them from the liturgical calendar because their historical authenticity was questioned or some discrepancies were found and the church sought any way to limit the number of feast days. But the saints are secure forever in the Vodou pantheon in Haiti and very much alive today. During the old days, the rural catechisms taught by the old Breton clergy that painted the oungan as the agent of Satan asked the following question: Why do oungans give Satan the names of angels and saints? Their answer? —"oungans call Satan after saints, angels and even the dead in order to deceive us more easily."

Inside the large yard of the church to Our Lady of Mount Carmel in Ville-Bonheur, vendors sell chromolithographs of the Catholic saints, holy medals and plaited colored votive cords as well as candles. Outside the yard, on the steps, a twenty-three-year-old sat shuffling the chromolithographs after selling St. James, wearing armor on horseback, to an old man who put it carefully away in his woven *Makout* bag hanging from his shoulder. Discussing the day's sales as only moderately good, the young vendor offered iconographic details of each of the saints and their identity in the Vodou pantheon. Most of his customers, he said, were "oungans and mambos." His position was next to a *borlette* bank (lottery based on numbers and New York and Dominican lottery winners). His mother looked on proudly as he picked up the chromolithographs from a big weaved flat basket used to clean rice and ideal for a vendor to display his or her wares upon at the market. Two laundry lines stretched behind him on which hung t-shirts of various colors with *"bonne fête, Vierge miracle,"* the imprint of Our Lady of Mount Carmel. She was pictured standing on the sea with the child Jesus on one arm and ships in the background as well as little cupid angels. "Made in Mexico," the chromolithograph which is reprinted on the T-shirt announces the Virgin of Carmen (not Carmel) as patron of the navy.

The young vendor with a small wooden cross hanging from his neck said he purchases the chromolithographs in Port-au-Prince and resells them at the various religious fêtes throughout the country, mostly in the north of Haiti. "Our Lady of Mount Carmel, he identifies, as Ēzili Freda Dantor, the wife of St. Jacques. St. Patrick, patron saint of Ireland who is always pictured standing on a promontory with his snakes slithering around at his feet. St. Patrick is Damballah, the oldest and most celebrated of lwas," he said. He offered a woven votive plaited cord with light and dark green, yellow and silver colors which, he said, matched St. Patrick's robe, and he produced the chromolithograph of St. Patrick and pointed to the colors of his robe. All the votive cords could be identified by color with the lwas. The busy salesman rattled off the lwas and their wives. He showed the difference between St. George slaying the dragon, St. Jacques in a warlike stance and St. James the elder in his heavy armor. Even in Vodou there are those who may have different identities for different saints. A merchant in Port-au-Prince, who imports them from Mexico, doesn't know much about their significance, explained the young vendor but, he says, they are good selling items and the merchant in Port-au-Prince is prosperous. This was not a good business year, he said, people don't have much money.

The seller of holy pictures showed off the black Polish Virgin, Our Lady of Czestochowa. "St. Jac the major did this," he said, pointing to the two parallel marks on her right cheek. He identified the black Virgin as Ēzili Ge-rouge, the terrible red-eyed Ēzili. (In the 90s, an order of Polish priests built a very large shrine to Our Lady of Czestochowa in Doylestown, Pennsylvania, and reported that every year more and more Haitians living in the U.S. are turning up in Doylestown to venerate her.)

"I serve Ězuli Dantor," explained the vendor, adding, "She is not easy to please either."

The young man said his next stop is on July 24 at the Fête St. Jacques in Plaine du Nord, not far from Cap Haïtian. He rattled off his summer schedule: fête St. Anne August 2 at Limonade; St. Claire at Marchand Dessalines; St. Rose at Pilat; fête Philomes at the sea front of Limonade near Cap Haitien; Fête Notre Dame de Activity in Verette in the Artibonite and St. Jerome in Petit Rivière de l'Artibonite.

*   *   *

Strong men lifted the small but heavy statue of Our Lady of Mount Carmel onto the top of the big truck away from the maddening crowd and in the quiet safety of the presbyter yard. Some years, the priest refuses to allow the statue to be paraded through the town because vodouisants co-opt the Catholic procession. All the white and blue bunting hid the big passenger camion, with its riotous red color. As they secured the statue with ropes, the priest took up his battle station on the running board of the truck, hanging on to the driver's cab. It also allowed him to control the procession through Ville-Bonheur's crowded streets, giving the driver directions and orders when to stop and when to proceed.

When the bus finally lurched into the packed street, the thunderous cries echoed over the mountains. "Manman chérie," they screamed, hailing the passage of the statue of Our Lady of Carmel. There were only hushed cries of "Ězili," as the vodouisants knew the priest was listening and would halt the parade if their cries of worship drowned out those of the good Catholics. But both vodouisants and Catholic saluted with tremendous joy the sight of Our Lady-Ězili as the statue passed. They prayed imploring her intervention, her help and like at the waterfall, many of the prayers and requests were personal and exposed the tragedy of the people. A neatly dressed lady in prim white blouse and pleated white and blue shirt with a large hat marched at the head of the procession. She turned her gold-rimmed glasses towards me. This is probably one of the Catholic ladies who helped put together the fête this year, I thought. Then I recognized the well-dressed lady. It was handsome Lolotte, a mambo as dignified as royalty. Two ladies dressed in white, her ounsis, accompanied Lolotte.

Later in the day, the procession was over; Vodou groups drumming and singing danced in the streets, waving their Vodou flags. As they came abreast of the big Catholic church, each dancer made the sign of the cross. Haiti was indeed a Nation of many Gods.

CHAPTER 21

Love in the Time of Papa Doc

Ayiti chéri,
Pi bon péyi pasé ou nan pwen,
Fòk mwen té kité-w
Pou mwen te kapab konprann valè-w...

From "*Souvenir d'Haïti*" by Othello Bayard
(Haiti Chérie, sweeter land than yours does not exist,
I had to leave you to understand your worth...)

The post-invasion midnight curfew had ended and the "search and detain" roadblocks had been removed. Under the guise of our *Haiti Sun*'s "*Sans Blagues*"[32] column, I had written about the "latest fad in Port-au-Prince": the "halting and searching of motorists." But it had been no joke, and a *Time* magazine Caribbean correspondent experienced this firsthand; at one such roadblock in Port-au-Prince, Bruce Henderson had recently faced the barrel of a rifle held by a nervous soldier, whose finger could be seen twitching around the trigger. Henderson had credited my Kreyòl with saving his life.

The Catholic Church solicited help for victims of hurricane Ella, which on September 1, 1958 had swiped Haiti's southern peninsula, forcing the population to face food shortages. The call went unanswered.

225

One afternoon in early September 1958, I had gone to the Hotel Splendid to meet with hotelier Maurice de Young, whom had formerly leased and operated the Oloffson in Port-au-Prince. Maurice was returning to Haiti to produce microfilm copies of Haitian newspapers for the University of Florida. I carried to him several volumes of the *Haiti Sun*, to be given to the university's Gainesville library.

The Splendid had once been Port-au-Prince's top hotel, but time had passed it by. Madame Maria Frankel and her administrator Alberti had grown old along with their inn. Having just checked in, a young woman, obviously a tourist, was standing there amidst the Splendid's brilliant bougainvillea. She wore sandals, a gypsy-type flowing skirt and a white blouse. As I passed her, she smiled and asked me the names of some of the profuse tropical plants. I loved the way she impishly screwed up her pretty face in interrogation. I then heard myself offering this young lady: "Would you like me to show you *my* Haiti?"

It could only have happened in Haiti. She had just arrived from New York by ship and sailed right into my life. In Vodou terms, credit goes to *Papa Legba*[33] for having had my path cross with that of this interesting young lady from Manhattan. Èzili would have then taken over; we fell under her spell.

Her name didn't mean a thing to me. It was only as we began enjoying our time together that we began sharing our little histories. I learned she was a twenty-seven-year-old actress newly divorced and at a crossroads in her life, similar to the one I had faced in December 1949 upon arriving in Haiti by accident. She was full of doubt about her career, even though she said the two-character play she was appearing in on Broadway was a success. The more I got to know Anne, the more she talked wistfully of the things missing in her life because of her demanding career.

She made me forget the past and even the present. We made the best of the week we had together. Each day ended with an enchanted evening.

One morning, we drove out to Plaine du Cul-de-Sac to welcome Doc Reser back from a two-and-a-half-year stay in Miami. This old

Actress Anne Bancroft on her first vacation in Haiti, enjoying Kyrona beach resort with the author.

American friend, an initiated oungan, was happily ensconced in an attractive new wooden house that replaced his old *kay pi* (little peasant house) on the highway next to the Pont Beudet insane asylum, twenty miles from Port-au-Prince. Gwo Roche and other oungans of the region had celebrated his return with a special Vodou service.

Anne was a good sport and didn't mind sharing Page One of the *Sun* with Papa Doc on September 21, 1958. The president was to celebrate his first year in power on the following day. A photograph showed Anne standing at the gate with Doc Reser before his new house. The caption read: "(...) attractive Anne Bancroft, a top screen and stage actress currently the star of the Broadway play, *Two for the Seesaw*, visiting Haiti." Also in the picture were Reser's longtime friend, sugar planter Rodolphe Dontfraid, who had built the house for Doc, and Stanley Mills Haggart, a leading TV art director who had escorted Ms. Bancroft to Haiti.

The following Monday, message after message arrived at the office of the *Haiti Sun*. Wally and Dave Talamas, who advertised their

Canapé Vert tourist emporium in the *Sun*, needed to speak to me urgently. They revealed that they were stargazers, perhaps the only ones of their type in Haiti at the time, and were quick to spot the front-page photo of Anne Bancroft. They were ecstatic with meeting Anne. The following week, the *Sun* featured photographs of Anne visiting their Grand-Rue store.

"These two young enterprising businessmen have their ear to the ground, and if a star should fall on Haiti, even for a quiet vacation, they are quick to register their footsteps.... Wally and Dave, who knew about the entire career of Anne Bancroft, laid a carved wooden head at the feet of the star in tribute," stated the Haiti Sun report. Unlike the Talamas boys, I was completely ignorant of Broadway and of who was playing there. The following week, French heartthrob Martine Carol glamorized the *Sun*'s front page. The two actresses couldn't have been more different from each other. Ms. Bancroft preferred the old elegance of Hotel Splendid, while Ms. Carol was a guest at the ritzy El Rancho. To the delight of her Haitian fans, Carol became the toast of Port-au-Prince, posing for photographers and public alike. Haiti's touristic viability was well proven by Carol's stay; the country was still on glamorous tourists' maps.

Anne was a funny, great, adorable comedienne, and a born mimic. She was like a tidal wave washing Papa Doc out of our minds. I was impressed with her knowledge of French and of Italian. Her real name, she said, was Maria Anna Italiano. Anne talked of her Italian-American upbringing, starting from the times when she would sing on a neighborhood corner near her home in the Bronx, as a child. Then she sang wonderfully, to the delight of my ears, and said that perhaps with the aid of a few singing lessons, she hoped to be able to play in a musical one day.

Bancroft was her stage surname. In the field of acting, her heritage brought with it a downside; a touch of bitterness would creep into her voice when she'd describe how critics sought to typecast her. It really riled her so that some, she said, insinuated that she was just playing herself in *Two for the Seesaw*, as Gittel Mosca, a bohemian gal from the Bronx. For me, Anne's words were educational, as I ascertained

Vacationing Anne Bancroft posing at the Port-au-Prince Cananpé Vert tourist emporium of Wally and Dave Talamas.

the trials, tribulations and pitfalls of a young actress. But in reverse, as we got to know each other, I think I took the place of her Freudian analyst, as I listened to her questioning her career. She had played in so many Hollywood films that few people had ever heard of. She was already such a great figure and thespian, but at times appeared very frail. Anne was truly a loving person, still filled with self doubt and seemingly in search of a fuller family life. As I got to know her, I did my best to reassure her that she could make it.

Her leading man in *Two for the Seesaw* had been Henry Fonda. She had liked to play with him much more than with Dana Andrews, who had taken over the role after Fonda had moved on. Fonda, she said, had always been so stable and secure, and he had given the play great dignity and stature, whereas Dana did not. But thinking it over, she granted that Dana did give warmth and tenderness to the part.

We had great fun at Pierre d'Adesky and his wife Future's Kyona Beach resort. I teased her time and again, warning her about Èzili, the lwa of love that can stir hearts in magical Haiti. Our time together proved more than just a romantic interlude in both our lives.

Our parting was not unlike that in the film *Casablanca*, but Anne didn't disappear into the night on a plane; she took off on a ship, agreeing for us to see each other again soon. A tourist couple we had befriended at Kyona Beach sailed off for New York with Anne, aboard the Panama liner *SS Cristobal*. Hardly was she over the horizon than a telegram arrived:

> Sept 25., 1958 at 8.02 p.m.
> Bernard Diederich, Press, Port-au-Prince, Haiti.
>
> I knew you were somewhere nearby, love.
> Anne.

Shirley Gumpley, of *Life en Español*, and her husband Len Gumpley, of CBS, were company for Anne on her return to New York. Shirley wrote me, describing their trip:

> "Oct. 13., 1958
> Dear Bernard—
> (...) How we loved Haiti (...) short as the visit was, and we really hated to have to wave to you as we sailed off into the sunset. And what a dramatic, romantic sunset it was! I imagine Anne has written to you about it—but may I repeat (...) it was quite an experience. Port-au-Prince looked like a white shimmering jewel at the foot of the mountains, the sunset was lovely with the light it cast, and the dark glowing clouds with the streaks of heat lightening only accented the drama—which was made more of a drama itself because we knew of the emotional experience it was for Anne. It certainly was tough on her (...) and I must admit, after seeing you people together, Len and I, watching you wade into the picture, standing on the edge of the dock in the dimming light and disappearing finally in

the distance, couldn't help but share your and Anne's good-bye vicariously! I almost felt like crying along with Anne!

The trip back was, I guess, quite pleasant. Certainly we couldn't complain about the weather, and the enforced rest was good (...) as well as helping to make the transition back to NY a little easier. But the other passengers were most uninspiring, and certainly contributed nothing to the pleasure of the trip itself. In fact, if it hadn't been for Anne, I think we probably would not have talked to anybody for the whole trip, outside the necessary formalities. As it was, I think Anne shared our feeling, and we ended up being a fairly anti-social trio (...) except for the last night out when we finally ended up with the other drunken guests in the bar, and really had quite a bit of fun (...) Anne being "on" and entertaining us beautifully! She was really funny!

The only one upsetting thing in the whole vacation was the discovery on shipboard that Len's color film had not caught—or slipped, and we didn't have a single damn picture of Kyona Beach and environs, Len's water skiing, picture of you and Anne, or of Anne on the boat! We thought we'd send you some of the latter, too (...) And then when we saw all the other pictures of Haiti and Jamaica we had taken—Len was fit to be tied! They had all turned out well—they truly are impressive—that we know the ones of the beach, the sunset, etc. that we lost would have been just as good, and since that day with you had been so, so pleas-ant, we were exasperated to have no record of it! Damn again! I get riled up just thinking of it! But (...) well, what can one do.

We were amused to see the enclosed item (...) hurry to assure you that we are not responsible. But I was interest-ed, because for the first time I was able to read an item like that and know for once it was not a press agent's idea of a good publicity gag, or else not true at all!

Enclosed was "It Happened Last Night," an October 9, 1958 piece by Earl Wilson of the *New York Post*: "Anne (*Two for the Seesaw*) Bancroft's new beau is a New Zealand reporter she met in Haiti."

Then, a Walter Winchell piece stated in the October 18 column: "Anne Bancroft of *Two for the Seesaw*, getting two dozen roses (no card) nightly in her dressing room. She met him last month during her vacation in Haiti." Anne didn't mention them, so I guessed they were the usual PR man's work.

On September 26, I received the first of a dozen letters from her. I no longer recall what I wrote, but I found the small bundle of Anne's letters tucked away amidst recovered *Haiti Sun* files. Addressed simply to "*Haiti Sun*, Port-au-Prince," this mail proved that the post office had remained efficient, in spite of censorship.

I had become Anne's *potomitan,* the strongest post in the center of the ounfò temple, onto which she could firmly hang. Her letters were caring, very personal, filled with self-doubt, the *Seesaw*, her life and much love.

On October 23, 1958, I finally got to fly to New York. I had a busy schedule but longed to see Anne. I was there to arrange the purchase of printing machinery for the *Haiti Sun* andmeet with my brother Brian, who was on a yearlong world trip; he was coming down from Canada to see me. I had not seen him since he'd served in the New Zealand army in Japan, and later had run several successful business-es in Australia. I really had a lot on my plate.

The night of my arrival, I picked Anne up after her habitual hour-long session with her analyst. We were gaily walking hand-in-hand, window-shopping on Lexington Avenue, when suddenly, out of the early evening, my Haitian life caught up with me. Hurrying to the subway from her part-time job at the United Nations' post office was my most precious young Haitian friend. She was working her way through her college studies at NYU.

It was for me one of the most embarrassing encounters ever. I had known Ginette Dreyfuss' family since she was twelve years old. She and her family were going through a particularly difficult time; back in Haiti, her pregnant eldest sister Ghislaine had been imprisoned along with her brother-in-law, Jean Desquiron, Ghislaine's husband. They had provided funds for the building of a bomb, in a plot to blow up Papa Doc.

As I overcame my surprise, Ginette spoke up: "When did you arrive? How come you haven't come to see us?" When I finally found my tongue, I tried to explain in Kreyòl, but Ginette swiftly cut me off: "I speak English, so don't embarrass your friend." I mumbled that I had just arrived and had intended to call. Papa Legba was at it again. He had made our paths cross. Èzili had quickly deserted me. I had lost not one love, but two.

As Ginette bid goodbye and hurried off to catch the subway, Anne watched her disappear and then turned to me with an understanding smile. "What a beautiful young woman; is she your girlfriend?" she asked. Anne was incredibly perceptive and had noticed the disappointment in Ginette's voice. I blustered out that I was one of the closest friends of her family. Later on, Ginette was told by an American and his Haitian wife that Anne and I were to be married. It gradually became a truly miserable weekend....

I saw the *Seesaw*, in which I witnessed a great actress at work. Subsequently, I met Brian but had too short a time to talk with him; we had a Chinese lunch together, and then I had to rush off and pick Anne up. I had promised to drive her to the Berkshires in a borrowed auto. The car had bald tires and on wet road, it was a danger to us both. It was nerve-racking. We spent the weekend there with Arthur Penn, the director of *Two for the Seesaw*. Anne and Dana Andrews put on the play locally as a campaign favor for a female Democratic congressional candidate, whose name I forget; I do remember that she lost. Besides Penn, another interesting visitor was historian James MacGregor Burns. I admired him for his book *Roosevelt: The Lion and the Fox*, which had won him the Pulitzer Prize two years earlier.

Everyone was talking about Vladimir Nabokov's novel *Lolita* – the book had just come out. *Lolita* was about a preteen love; it made me wonder if Anne believed that the young Haitian girl was my Lolita....

If you were not a New Yorker and thus hadn't kept up with the fads and books prevailing at the moment, you knew you were an outsider and didn't belong; such was the perception I had of myself, in the group. At the time, McGregor Burns was working on a profile of John F. Kennedy. If I felt a bit out of the loop with my new friends, at least I knew I was among Democrats.

Upon our return to the city, Ed Morrow was going to visit Anne's West 12th Street brownstone house in Manhattan for his TV program. To help her decorate her home for the interview, I sent her the best (Jacques-Enguerrand) Gourgue painting of my collection; it depicted a Vodou service celebrated outdoors in the tropical night.

But it was already the end of our affair. I like to think that perhaps I helped Anne a little, at that crucial time in her life. Undoubtedly though, I indeed recognized her as a great actress and encouraged her vehemently.

On December 21, 1959, Anne appeared on the cover of *Time* magazine. The story was pegged to Anne's tremendous success in the Broadway play, *The Miracle Worker*, another one of William Gibson's productions; Anne was on her way: "Beginning of an era. Even for the vast and vocal audience that recognized the Bancroft talent two years ago in Gibson's *Two for the Seesaw*, this season's Bancroft is a stunning spectacle. As Gittel Mosca, the heartbroken Bronx-to-Bohemia hoyden of *Seesaw*, the young star still had an uncertain luster. There was a feeling that perhaps the back-stocking beatnik was only playing herself. What would happen if she really had to act?"

Well, Ms. Bancroft gave them her answer. It was definitely the beginning of an era for her. There no longer was any doubt about Anne's acting skills. *Time* had asked for my input and when the cover appeared, I received the following cable on December 13, 1959: "Thanks for succinct penetrating guidance on Anne Bancroft, which was not specifically used in cover but most helpful in editors' evaluation of her."

Anne did return to Haiti. Lodged at the Hotel Oloffson this time, she was accompanied by fellow actress Hilda Brawner. I played guide for a second time, but as an "old friend," *nada más*. Again, Anne received front-page treatment in the *Haiti Sun*, in its Sunday, May 15, 1960 edition. This time, I concocted a story about the photographs of Anne and her friend plastering their faces with what was actually ... mud. The spontaneously discovered facial cosmetics product had once been top soil from the mountains, before being driven by rains and erosion into the sea. Under the headline "Actress discovers threat to cold cream industry," I wrote:

Geologists and metallurgists have made extensive studies and conducted research work in Haiti over the years but it took a hard working stage actress on a week's vacation here to discover a face cream from under the sea.

Anne Bancroft, star of the Broadway hit '*The Miracle Worker*', on her second Haitian vacation in 15 months, discovered bluish tinted sand under coarse white coral [matter], off the beach at Cacique island resort (...)

With a decidedly sulphurous odor, the sand has essentially the same properties contained properties so beneficial to the human skin that the cold cream industry could well be threatened.

It was also uncovered at Kyona beach, a few miles up the coast. The first export shipment of the 'wonderful cream' left Haiti on Tuesday in two medication jars from Miss Bancroft's luggage, and without doubt if they're inspected by U.S. customs, they will be classified as mud by those astute gentlemen.

Miss Bancroft, who has monopolized the trophy winning for the past three years on the Big White Way for her outstanding performances in '*Two for the Seesaw*' and '*The Miracle Worker*', was holidaying in Haiti with fellow stage and television actress Hilda Brawner—herself now thoroughly addicted to the Haitian beauty cream which removes dead skin and gives tautness and youthful glow.

If Anne had arrived two weeks later, she would once again have met up with my friend Ginette Dreyfuss, whom I expected to welcome home upon the summer holidays from NYU. The circumstances for both of us were very different in 1960. Two years later, Èzili saw to it that Ginette and I marry. We've been for forty-five years and have had three wonderful children.

I was among those saddened by Anne's death in 2006, at age 73. She was survived by her husband, director and comedian Mel Brooks, and also by a son. Anne always wanted a family and I was happy for her that she'd had one. I'm glad that my life was touched by this great human being, whom the movie world will perhaps best remember as Mrs. Robinson from the movie, *The Graduate*.

Notes

1. "Bearded ones," in Spanish.
2. *Rebelde*: rebel.
3. White Bear.
4. Acronym for the 26th of July Movement.
5. *Servicio de Intelligencia Militar* (Military Intelligence Service)
6. As a swarthy man, he added it for the whitening effect.
5. Party hangover.
6. More than three years later, after Trujillo's assassination, a well-preserved copy of that same issue of the *Haiti Sun* turned up in the Dominican palace archives, with each person in the photograph from the Cuban embassy takeover identified by name and marked down as pro-Castro. Separately, I was also identified in Trujillo's files as a Castroite.
7. Newsman.
8. Women's platoon.
9. Free pass.
10. "Liberty or Death."
11. Four months later, they were married.
12. White brats.
13. Countryside Cuban.
14. These old Haitian saying translate as "Mind your own business. I'll give you some advice. The business of a goat is not the business of a sheep. Beat a dog and wait for its owner. Watch out for the consequences of your acts"; this is a quote by Antoine Lan Gommier who was an ancient soothsayer.
15. Long, handcrafted, and single-toned tin trumpets.
16. "Go away! Go the h*** away!"
17. "What a fairy tale!"
18. "Off with their heads! And burn down their houses!"
19. Justice Section.
20. Blanquismo.
21. A distinguished college professor Galíndez disappeared after being kidnapped by Trujillo agents in New York.
22. Sorcerer who doesn't abstain from using his pharmacological knowledge to harm others.
23. I shall henceforth use the term figuratively.
24. Literally "zombie cucumber."

25. See short stories by René Depestre.
26. Malicious person, evil doer, etc.
27. Palm fiber.
28. Present-day Benin.
29. Dorsinville had been a close advisor and speechwriter to Duvalier during the electoral campaign of 1957; following the victory, he was very quickly shunned away from the president-elect.
30. Haitian Interior Revolution.
31. By the unsuccessful attack on the Moncada barracks.
32. "No Kidding."
32. Papa Legba, the initiator, opens the gates and is the communicator with the divine. There are a number of Èzili lwas (spiritual entities, gods) but the principal Èzili, whom I appreciated, was the goddess of love. She is known to setup erotic liaisons and doesn't believe in rationing love.